We Hold These Truths and More:

FURTHER CATHOLIC REFLECTIONS ON THE AMERICAN PROPOSITION

THE THOUGHT OF FR. JOHN COURTNEY MURRAY, S.J.
AND ITS RELEVANCE TODAY

EDITED BY
DONALD J. D'ELIA & STEPHEN M. KRASON

FRANCISCAN UNIVERSITY PRESS
FRANCISCAN UNIVERSITY OF STEUBENVILLE
STEUBENVILLE, OH 43952

Cover Design: Daniel Gallio
Cover Photograph: "Declaration of Independence" by John Trumbull.
Used with permission of Yale Gallery.

Copyright © 1993 by Stephen M. Krason. All rights reserved.

Published by:
Franciscan University Press
Franciscan University of Steubenville
Steubenville, OH 43952

We hold these truths, and more: further Catholic reflections on the American proposition : the thought of Father John Courtney Murray, S.J. and its relevance today / edited by Donald J. D'Elia and Stephen M. Krason.
      p.   cm.
  Includes bibliographical references and index.
  ISBN 0-940535-48-3 (pbk.)
  1. Church and state—United States. 2. Catholic Church—United States. 3. Murray, John Courtney—Contributions in philosophy of political science. 4. Political science—Philosophy. 5. United States—Religious aspects—Christianity. I. D'Elia, Donald J. II. Krason, Stephen M.
BR516.W39   1993   92-40082
261.7'08'822—dc20   CIP

Printed in the United States of America
ISBN: 0-940535-48-3

Contents

PREFACE, by Donald J. D'Elia and Stephen M. Krason vii

THE BACKGROUND OF THE MURRAY THESIS 1
1. John Courtney Murray Before Vatican II: Challenge and Response, by James Hitchcock 2

CRITICISM OF THE MURRAY THESIS 19
2. John Courtney Murray: The Optimism of the 1950's, by Frederick D. Wilhelmsen 20
3. John Courtney Murray: Defender of the Myth, by John A. Gueguen 33
4. John Courtney Murray and Christopher Dawson: The Pluralist Society or Jerusalem and Babylon? by John J. Mulloy 46
5. We Hold These Truths and More: Further Catholic Reflections on the American Proposition, by Donald J. D'Elia. 62

DEFENSE OF MURRAY AND THE MURRAY THESIS 77
6. The Truths They Held: The Christian and Natural Law Background to the American Constitution, by Robert R. Reilly 78
7. Murray's Transformation of the American Proposition, by Peter Augustine Lawler 93
8. Personal Recollections of John Courtney Murray, S.J. and Some Reflections, by Msgr. George A. Kelly 109

MURRAY AND RELIGIOUS FREEDOM 119
9. John Courtney Murray and the Privatization of
    American Religion, by Gerard V. Bradley 120
10. John Courtney Murray: A Reliable Interpreter of
    Dignitatis Humanae? by Father Brian W. Harrison, O.S .. 134
11. Religious Liberty and Political Morality,
    by Robert P. George 166

**MURRAY'S THOUGHT IN LIGHT OF
RECENT DEVELOPMENTS** 183
12. Murray and the Soviet Union, by John J. Carrigg 184
13. The Murray Thesis, Abortion, and the American
    Political Order, by Stephen M. Krason 195

**AMERICA, CATHOLICS, AND THE MURRAY THESIS:
THE FUTURE** 215
14. The Catholic Interpretive Tradition, Deconstruction,
    and the Murray Project, by Dominic A. Aquila 216
15. The Confessional State and John Courtney Murray,
    by Regis Martin 225
16. The Politics of Mysticism, by L. Brent Bozell 237

CONTRIBUTORS 242

**THE MARIAN INSTITUTE FOR
ADVANCED STUDIES** 248

INDEX 251

Preface

Father John Courtney Murray, S.J. stands with Orestes Brownson as the only two Catholics in American history that one might be prompted to categorize as genuine "political philosophers." Murray's *We Hold These Truths: Catholic Reflections on the American Proposition* is surely one of the seminal books written by an American Catholic in the twentieth century. In this book, published in 1960, the Jesuit scholar advanced what might be called the Murray thesis: that, in essence, the principles undergirding the American Founding were not only compatible with Catholicism—a proposition many had doubted and even attacked for much of our history—but it might soon be that only Catholics were going to be willing to uphold them. This is because, he said, these principles had their roots in the philosophical tradition most fully developed in the Catholic Middle Ages in Europe. The political tenets of our Founding, Murray held, were drawn from the truths of human nature and natural law jealously guarded by this great tradition.

The Murray thesis was, to say the least, controversial. It has continued to be the subject of debate in certain scholarly and Catholic journals and books and has attracted renewed attention in the last few years. This has been stimulated by the writing of such figures as Richard John Neuhaus, George Weigel, and Robert W. McElroy. In the background of this in recent years in American politics has been the spectacle of a substantial number of Catholic politicians who have announced that the Church's teaching on such matters as abortion will not be allowed to influence their public posture or decisions. They have thus made it seem, contrary to the Murray thesis, that Catholic teaching and the natural law are completely out of the picture as far as American politics is concerned and that, instead of seeing Catholicism as providing the front line of defense for the American Proposition, many Catholic politicians are scurrying to distance themselves from the teachings of their

Faith that challenge the secular agenda and are looking to that same agenda to shape their decision-making. American Catholics generally make decisions about political matters without much attention to the teachings of the Church. This is obviously a different situation from the one extant when Murray wrote his book, which was perhaps the time of Catholicism's greatest respectability in American history and one in which there might have been some reason for optimism that a Catholic population, stoutly embracing the teachings of their Faith, might have a serious leavening effect for truth in American life.

With the situation so drastically changed today, certain questions must be asked. Was the Murray thesis correct in the first place? Did Murray's analysis of our historical and philosophical background justify his conclusions? Was the thesis something that was merely a reflection of the attitudes prevalent about Catholicism at Murray's time, an exercise in empty optimism? How have developments in the thirty years since *We Hold These Truths*—which have been sweeping and corrosive of our national well-being—altered its plausibility? Have they, in any way, altered the American Proposition, the fundamental principles our political order stands for?

It was to examine questions such as these and, generally, to reconsider the Murray thesis in a scholarly, dispassionate, but fully Catholic, manner that various Catholic scholars connected with The Marian Institute for Advanced Studies believed that a major conference was needed. This book represents primarily the papers that were presented at that conference which bore the same title as this book ("We Hold These Truths and More: Further Catholic Reflections on the American Proposition"), held Nov. 8-11, 1990 at Franciscan University of Steubenville, Steubenville, Ohio.

This book is divided into six sections: "The Background of the Murray Thesis"; "Criticism of the Murray Thesis"; "Defense of Murray and the Murray Thesis"; "Murray and Religious Freedom"; "Murray's Thought in Light of Recent Developments"; and "America, Catholics, and the Murray Thesis: The Future." A brief overview of the essays in each section follows.

James Hitchcock examines "John Courtney Murray Before Vatican II" and argues that, despite the American hierarchy's ostensible conservatism at the time, only one bishop took public issue with his views articulated in *We Hold These Truths* and other writings. Cardinal Francis Spellman and Bishop John J. Wright, for example, threw their support to Murray; and the opposition of Cardinal Alfredo Ottaviani and others notwithstanding, Murray was invited to serve as a peritus to the Archbishop of New York at the Second Vatican Council.

Hitchcock makes a strong case for Murray's historicism, a theme running through several of these papers, and suggests the irony of the American Jesuit and Thomist attempting to justify the modern minimalist, pluralist, democratic state as a creative, dynamic, and unique adaptation to actual historical conditions.

"The American version of church-state separation, leaving the Church completely free to exist within society," Murray held, "is of a wholly different kind, a new phenomenon requiring new theological understanding."

Hitchcock evokes the times in which Murray wrote and leaves the reader with a heightened sense of the urgent questions Murray sought to resolve as an American and a Catholic.

The Thomist philosopher, **Frederick Wilhelmsen**, whose most recent book is *Christianity and Political Philosophy*, addresses himself to the question of whether Murray was right in his thesis. After a sympathetic discussion of Murray's "moment in history," the post-war period noted above of Catholicism's considerable respectability, Wilhelmsen turns to the Jesuit theologian's crucial and typically American failure to distinguish between power and authority (*confusio*, in the technical Thomistic sense), and to recognize that the Catholic Church is the authoritative interpreter of natural law.

"The American political experience," Wilhelmsen argues, "has wavered between an older order admitting the independent authority of God and His Law and the newer ethos of liberal democracy that identifies all authority with political power."

Murray's speculations are not free of a certain parallelism. "On the one hand, he glories in the development of natural law under Catholic auspices," Wilhelmsen concludes. "On the other hand, he would cut that development away from Catholic tutelage in the United States where the Church is simply one among several creeds competing for the ultimate allegiance of our citizenry."

John A. Gueguen argues that Murray's project of demonstrating the compatibility of Catholicism with the American experience is really a skillful attempt at myth-making, such as is not unknown in the history of political philosophy. He says that in his eagerness to accomplish this—and to make possible a common civil culture for Catholics and non-Catholics in the U.S.—Murray glosses over the significant differences between classical and modern thought, the Church being identified more with the former and America with the latter. Murray did a service by stressing the Church's natural law teaching as the basis for a new American public philosophy, but his unwillingness to confront the fundamental errors of modernity doomed this project to failure.

In his comparison of the Jesuit theologian and the British convert and historian, Christopher Dawson, **John J. Mulloy** notes that Murray, like so many of his countrymen, was victimized by that American messianism which is so much a part of our history.

Unlike Dawson, Murray failed to see beyond this naive optimism that the real life-and-death struggle in the 1950's was not among the four conspiracies of Protestant, Catholic, Jew, and secularist, as he called them in *We Hold These Truths*. Even then, the Judaeo-Christian tradition and secularism were battling for the "soul of America." Dawson saw this clearly. Perhaps the American's Jesuit background, with its alleged tendency to minimize Original Sin, Mulloy speculates, was a factor in his messianism.

Christopher Dawson remains the better guide. His historically mature awareness of the importance of "irrational and non-rational elements in human society" as well as civilized, public philosophy, and their "strength of influence," are in the best tradition of Catholic realism.

When Alexis de Tocqueville wrote in 1835 that the Christian religion was "the foremost of the political institutions of the United States," **Donald J. D'Elia** argues, the French Catholic author of *Democracy in America* was closer to the truth about the American Founding than are most historians who interpret the event in the Enlightenment liberal tradition.

D'Elia contrasts the thought of the American *philosophe* Thomas Jefferson and the Protestant Christian founder Dr. Benjamin Rush, both signers of the Declaration of Independence and leading Revolutionary patriots, and shows that the neglected Rush's political theology of the American Founding was much more representative of the American people at the time, a people still very much in the Calvinist tradition.

Murray, writing in the 1950's, accepted the secular historiography of the American Founding and overemphasized the rationalism of the Jeffersonian minority while failing to take sufficient account of the historical significance of late eighteenth century America as a Chris-

Preface

tian culture in the Dawsonian sense.

More recent scholarship, to which Perry Miller, Alan Heimert, and D'Elia himself have contributed, is helping us to see the American Founding in its historical context. **Robert R. Reilly's** essay is a forceful and thoughtful defense of the position that the Constitution embodies—and is only comprehensible in light of—Christian and (pre-modern) natural law assumptions. While Enlightenment ideas influenced our Founding, they were by no means predominant. As Reilly puts it, our Founding principles were shaped primarily by the heritage of the ancient Jews, Greeks, and Romans, and of Christianity. In the final analysis, the most central parts of this heritage for us are the belief in the Judeo-Christian God and the acceptance of the proper role of reason, which enables man to distinguish good from evil. It is this background which made possible our commitment to both limited government and respect for human dignity, because it de-divinized politics and made man realize that it "is not the salvific engine for the transformation of mankind and the elimination of evil." Reilly illustrates his point about the considerably greater influence of the above heritage than the Enlightenment on our Founders in the following ways: he explains how the Constitution recognized flawed human nature in its provisions; he tells us how one of our most Enlightenment-inclined Founders, John Adams, rejected important aspects of the thought of leading Enlightenment figures; and he discusses how a large number of the references in the Founder's writings were to the Bible or the classics. Father Murray, Reilly concludes, was correct about the roots of the American Proposition. It was *later* developments, after our Founding, which promoted such ideas as cultural relativism and attacked the highest tradition of reason. Nowhere was this more apparent than in the U.S. Supreme Court's *Roe v. Wade* abortion decision which purported to hold, against what reason clearly tells us, that "we do not know what a human being is." Its challenge to our tradition of high respect for human dignity is obvious.

Peter Augustine Lawler's thinking about Murray stands in contrast to Gueguen's. He agrees with Gueguen that Murray sought to modify the American Proposition, but not by way of erecting a myth that has no basis in fact but, in the manner of Lincoln, by *expanding* it. That is, he sought to moderate the Enlightenment-based individualism of our Founding Fathers and place their thinking about liberty, the nature of man, and political community on the more stable foundation of the medieval natural law tradition. He thus *transformed* the American Proposition, just as Lincoln did by holding it to be more firmly and conclusively dedicated to equality than our Founding Fathers probably really intended it to be. Lawler offers this starkly different interpretation of Murray from Gueguen's because, unlike the latter, he believes that Murray was fully aware of the flaws of modern political philosophy and of the need to address them. Lawler also understands Murray's view of pluralism differently from Gerard V. Bradley below, saying that it was something that Murray criticized rather than embraced.

Msgr. George A. Kelly, basically, is another defender of Murray. His essay consists largely of his personal reflections on Murray, whom he knew well. He paints a portrait of Murray as loyal to the Church and her doctrine, although there were some disturbing indications that he wavered on important teachings near the end of his life. Kelly argues that Murray's thinking on religious freedom, which seemed to diverge from traditional thinking in the Church, really did not involve dissent from the Church on a matter of theological doctrine. What's more, he says, Murray was always very careful to make it clear that doctrinal positions, contrary to prudential accommodations such as those relating to church-state relations, do not depend on historical circumstance. Neomodernist theologians and commentators after Murray may have tried to claim this, relying on his church-state analysis, but Murray never did.

The next three essays deal with the subject of Murray and religious freedom. This is something that he was very closely identified with in his life, of course. **Gerard V. Bradley** points to a paradox in Murray's thought: while making it clear that he opposes treating religion as a matter to be consigned just to the private realm of people's lives, his ideas about both religious freedom and the First Amendment provide no basis to back this up. That is, Murray's unwillingness to have any religious view acknowledged by government unfortunately puts truth and freedom in opposition, and directly results in privatization—i.e., the isolating of religion from American public life. There must be "articles of peace," Murray said, to avoid religious conflict; others have used this as the rationale to erect a rigid "wall of separation" between politics and religion which has little historical justification, and has led to our "naked public square." Bradley seems to suggest that simply endorsing "pluralism" for our public life, as Murray did, is inadequate; rather some attention must be given to the validity of the teachings of

Preface

the various perspectives—religious and secular—which are injected into our public square.

Father Brian W. Harrison, O.S.'s paper takes to task Murray's reliability as an interpreter of the Vatican II document, *Dignitatis Humanae* (the *Declaration on Religious Liberty*), which he undoubtedly had a considerable influence on. Harrison argues that while earlier drafts of the document reflected some of Murray's more questionable theses on the subject—his views on this have been a continuing source of controversy about Murray, of course—the final draft, which was the one promulgated by the Council, did not and was firmly based on traditional Catholic teaching. Murray favored a position on church-state relations which would essentially have had the Church endorse the reigning American model of state neutrality toward religious sects, Harrison argues. Actually, he says, the Council specifically upheld the obligation of all societies, including the state, to acknowledge the true religion. The post-Conciliar confusion about this point, Harrison contends, was due in no small part to Murray's somewhat misleading comments about the document in his copious footnotes to it in the widely-disseminated Abbott translation of the Vatican II documents.

Robert P. George's essay is an unusual one in the collection because it does not mention John Courtney Murray. What it does, however, is to provide, through philosophical reasoning, the rationale for why a political community should promote religion and religious liberty—the great concern of Murray—in its midst. He demonstrates why religion is a crucial part of the common good and thus within the scope of what a political community appropriately ought to seek to promote. George argues that the reasons a well-ordered political community should promote religious liberty are set forth very well in the first part of *Dignitatis Humanae*, perhaps due in no small measure to Murray. It rightfully holds that religion must be seen as a social phenomenon, it cannot be a strictly private matter ("privatized," in Bradley's term). As indicated, the obligation of government toward religion has both negative and positive dimensions: to not interfere with the religious freedom of its citizens *and* to encourage and promote their spiritual and religious well-being.

John J. Carrigg in his "Murray and the Soviet Union" reminds us that the author of *We Hold These Truths* warned Americans against the dangers of a Rousseauian "idolization of democracy" and a misguided national foreign policy based on anti-communism alone.

Yet Murray was second to none in his opposition to communism; and the Jesuit cautioned against unilateral nuclear disarmament at a time when it was becoming popular.

How would Murray have reacted to *perestroika* and *glasnost*? Skeptically. For in Murray's own words, "The basic Soviet structure is an indivisible and interlocking whole. It cannot permit itself to be tampered with at any point save on peril of destruction."

Whatever happens, Murray believed, the West remains in crisis, denying her own tradition, weakened by "internal contradiction." The United States, and the West itself, must go beyond mere anti-communism and stop "the most demonic threat to human values that the world has ever known." And this can only be done on the spiritual plane.

Finally, Carrigg discusses Murray's views on Just War theory as they apply to the War in the Persian Gulf.

Stephen M. Krason's essay considers how the Murray thesis might be evaluated in light of one of the most—if not *the* most—dramatic and tragic developments in American life in the generation since Murray's book appeared: the legalization of abortion. It shows that the English legal tradition from which America emerged as well as our earlier law condemned abortion and protected the unborn child. While it acknowledges that the distant roots of the pro-abortion mentality may be in the Hobbesian-Lockean thought which influenced the American Founding, the essay argues that pro-abortionism can be traced primarily to a number of strains of thought having their origins later in American history. Thus, Krason contends (in agreement with Reilly), that it is not essentially the content of the American Proposition itself (which was Murray's concern) which gave rise to pro-abortionism, but rather later developments which were at odds with the Proposition. Krason basically holds that Murray was correct about the natural law background of the Constitution and the current triumph of pro-abortionism illustrates how far we have deviated from that—much farther than in Murray's time.

In his commentary on Peter Augustine Lawler's paper, **Dominic A. Aquila** offers a new perspective in which to see Murray's interpretation of America's Founding principles.

Employing Theodore Lowi's thesis that there have been not one but four American republics, Aquila seeks to locate *We Hold These Truths* in the period of the fourth and present republic, beginning around 1937 with the rise of the Hegelian state, the abolition of the citizen in favor of the client, and the end of that civil discourse which is basic to the Aristotelian-Thomistic tradition of the American Founding and Murray's argument. Pluralism, a necessary evil in the Madisonian sense, now becomes a positive good. Along with citizenship, it undergoes radical transformation. The "common good" of the Fathers, of both the Church and the American Republic, becomes nothing more than competing interest groups.

Aquila notes the effects of Fourth Republic interest group pluralism, wrongly thought to be justified by Murray's work, upon the Catholic Action of the 1960's. He identifies today's deconstructionists as the "Brooks Brothers barbarians" that the American theologian forewarned us about. And he concludes, drawing upon the arguments of Hans Georg Gadamer, David L. Schindler, and others that the Catholic interpretive tradition, Luther and the deconstructionists notwithstanding, can provide us with authoritative interpretations of texts like the Declaration of Independence and the First Amendment.

Regis Martin's essay, as with all of the final three in this volume, proposes an alternative way for Catholics to approach American political life and society. As with all three, he says it cannot be primarily an immersion in political activity or movements. Martin says, rather, that it must be a spiritual undertaking. America, like any political order, must be remade for Christ, something, he believes, that the pluralism of Murray did not stress. Martin says that we would do well to use Jean Cardinal Danielou's thought as the standard for Christians to follow in thinking about political life and the civil order: the civil order and the Church simply *cannot* exist in separate worlds. If such separation were the norm, society could not shape itself properly. This is because the civil order has a role in helping the individual to find holiness; most men could not find God when the world—in secular areas, as well as ecclesiastical ones—is not organized to help them do it. Thus, God must be the foundation of any state. The confessional model of the state has been the model preferred by Catholicism for these reasons; it is not a mere juridical model. The reason, he contends, that Americans do not think about making their culture Christian is because our history has been characterized by the elimination of religion from our public and institutional life.

In his "The Politics of Mysticism," **L. Brent Bozell** addresses himself to the nature of that Catholic politics which inspired him to found *Triumph* magazine, the Catholic Rendezvous (with Mr. and Mrs. William C. Koneazny), and Mission Guadalupe.

The world of politics, he would remind us and the author of *We Hold These Truths*, "is, or can be—for this is the point—influenced by the world of mysticism...." And here, as elsewhere, St. John of the Cross should be our guide. The key to true Catholic politics is the Mystical Body of Christ, our recognition of the other as the Christ whom we are commanded by the Father to love with our whole heart, soul, strength, and mind.

"But it is hard to make love to our neighbor unless we remember that he is, in a mystical but fully true sense, God. So, when we don't make love to our neighbor, we make, whether intentionally or not, war. The whole impact of the politics which we Americans participate in and embrace is war against Christ and His things."

The only way that secular politics can be influenced by mysticism, can be redeemed—Bozell invokes the teachings of Vatican II—is by our conversion, our total love of Christ and the other in the Mystical Body.

We wish to thank the following for their financial assistance in making the conference on " We Hold These Truths and More: Further Catholic Reflections on the American Proposition" and the production of this book possible: Franciscan University of Steubenville; the Earhart, Homeland, St. Gerard, and Wilbur Foundations; the Intercollegiate Studies Institute; and the numerous individual benefactors of The Marian Institute for Advanced Studies. We thank Dr. John J. Mulloy and the Society for Christian Culture for publicity assistance. Special thanks are due to Rev. Michael Scanlan, T.O.R., President of Franciscan University and Messrs. Nicholas J. Healy, Jr. and John A. Madigan, Vice Presidents for University and Community Relations, respectively, of Franciscan University; Dr. Michael Healy, Dean of the Faculty of Franciscan University; Mr. Sterling Spears, Director of Franciscan University Press; and Professor Jack R. Boyde, former Chairman of the Department of History, Political Science, and Sociology at Franciscan University. We are grateful to Mrs. Lynn Cadman, Miss Stephanie Lester, and Miss Tammy Weiss for their typing assistance. Besides the paper-presenters at the conference—whose productions appear herein—we wish to thank those who took part as commentators or session chairmen: Dr. Sandor Balogh, Dr. John Crosby, Dr. Thomas A. Droleskey, Mr. Stuart Gudowitz, Dr. Andrew Tadie, and Dr. Raphael T. Waters. Also, thanks are due to the following for their helpful advice and assistance: Msgr. George A. Kelly, Dr. John Rao, Dr. Peter V. Sampo, Dr. and Mrs. William R. Updegraff, and the late Rev. Victor R. Yanitelli, S.J. Finally, we thank our wives, Margaret D'Elia and Therese C. Krason for their constant support and love.

It is our hope that this volume will help to provide deeper insights into both the strengths and weaknesses of Fr. Murray's thought and to shed some new light into the relevance and place of his thought in the America since his time. We also hope it will contribute positively to the on-going discussion about the proper relationship of Catholicism and American public life and the rightful role Catholicism should play in helping America to be redirected to the things of God.

Donald J. D'Elia
New Paltz, New York
Stephen M. Krason
Steubenville, Ohio
April 1993

"It is…necessary that Christians…conform their behavior in economic and social affairs to the teachings of the Church."

—Pope John XXIII

The Background of the Murray Thesis

1

John Courtney Murray Before Vatican II: Challenge and Response

by James Hitchcock

𝓔cumenical initiatives in Europe, which culminated at the Second Vatican Council, were given their principal impetus by the kinds of inter-religious cooperation made necessary by World War II, and in the United States as well the theological explorations of John Courtney Murray began near the start of the war, whether or not they were inspired by it.

As with many intellectual revolutions, Murray's differences with his traditionalist Catholic opponents at first seemed more a matter of emphasis than of decisive disagreements. Responding in particular to the position of Francis Connell of the Catholic University of America, a Redemptorist who at the time was perhaps America's most influential Catholic theologian, and of the priest-sociologist Paul Hanley Furfey, also of Catholic University, Murray acknowledged the dangers of "indifferentism" in any active cooperation between Catholics and non-Catholics. He also urged, however, that concrete historical conditions, and not only abstract theological principles, govern such encounters. Baptism itself, he pointed out, constitutes common religious ground, and the possibility of finding more extensive ground could not be ruled out.[1]

Emphasis on actual historical situations as a complement to abstract doctrine came to be a crucial point in Murray's ecumenical theology, an implicit rebuke to a kind of Scholasticism which was sometimes criticized as excessively *a priori* and "essentialist," a critique exemplified, for example, in Jacques Maritain's insistence that Thomism is necessarily "existential." (Although American Catholics have taken great pride in Murray's distinctively American contribution to international theology, in the beginning he was overtly developing the ideas of Maritain and of the German theologian Max Pribilla.²)

The key point of dispute between Murray and the traditionalists was his claim that practical cooperation between different religious groups was possible even without doctrinal agreement. Natural law might create a basis for such cooperation, in that people of differing creeds could nonetheless agree on common goals for society, and common ways of attaining them. In the natural order, Christ instituted no new political morality, Murray asserted, and the incompleteness of a purely human society does not thereby render it meaningless.³

By the end of the war Murray was arguing that the principle that even though the Roman Catholic Church is the one true Church (an assertion he did not deny), it was not sufficient in itself to govern either ecumenical relations or the issue of religious freedom.⁴

In Murray's view the salient point of natural law is that God has granted all people freedom with which to reach their supernatural goal, an important corollary of which is that non-Catholics should enjoy civil freedom to worship God in accordance with their consciences. The rights of conscience under natural law are not destroyed under religious law, any more than reason is destroyed by faith. At the same time Murray noted that the obligation to worship God is itself a requirement of the natural law, which demands that human beings not close themselves to whatever revelation God has offered them. Even the state itself has an obligation to "worship" the Creator. Markedly traditional by his own later standards, Murray in 1945 affirmed that the state has a right to suppress atheistic or irreligious propaganda, which has no rights under natural law, and that it refrains from doing so only out of prudence.⁵

Murray's early explorations into the twin themes of ecumenical cooperation and religious liberty were almost all in *Theological Studies*, of which he was editor, a journal mainly read by Catholic theologians. Perhaps sensing the larger significance of his project, beginning late in 1946 he began publishing also in *America*, a journal likewise under Jesuit auspices but aimed at a wider audience and read by non-Catholics interested in a Catholic view of contemporary issues.

Human beings have a dual nature, Murray posited, which is both civil and religious and which cannot be united. The First Amendment to the American constitution is merely a recognition of that fact, made possible by the peculiar historical circumstances of the founding of the

United States. Recognizing the rights of conscience of individuals requires also recognizing their group rights; hence all religious bodies must be tolerated.[6]

His understanding of the "lay" nature of the American state was illustrated in the controversy over public aid to religious schools, which in the post-war years was reaching the Supreme Court for the first time. While parents commonly send their children to religious schools for religious reasons, Murray acknowledged, the lay state can know nothing of this. Instead it should assist such schools merely because they contribute to the common welfare of society. Much of the opposition to such aid, he judged, was Protestant prejudice which could not be countered on the rational level.[7] (Despite his dismissal of this prejudice, his attempt to forge a Catholic argument for religious toleration was probably at least in part motivated by the common charge that the Catholic Church was opposed to democratic freedoms.)

By the end of 1948 Murray was attempting to construct a developed theology of church-state relations based especially on the *De Potestate Regia et Papali* ("Concerning Royal and Papal Power") of the fourteenth-century theologian John of Paris. In the modern state, Murray argued, religious and temporal powers meet only indirectly, in the person of the individual who is both Christian and citizen. The Church forms the consciences of these Christian citizens, who then "prolong" the Church's spiritual authority in the temporal realm. The Church's direct authority extends only to spiritual matters, and it has no right to intervene in temporal affairs. He was critical of the theory of his Jesuit forbear Robert Bellarmine because Bellarmine justified the direct authority of the Church over the state.[8]

Murray also proposed a highly positive view of modern American democracy as based on the autonomous person, a relationship he believed Pius XII himself had recognized as a new historical reality worthy of respect. The First Amendment, he argued, implicitly recognizes the supreme value of religion in forbidding the state to inhibit it in any way. Further, religious liberty as enshrined in the Constitution includes the right of citizens to "impose" on the state the moral demands which their own consciences dictate, provided that they do so through properly political means. His view, Murray insisted, was the authentic Catholic position, resulting from a long process of development, a development which fit with remarkable closeness the actual situation of modern America. Traditionalist hackles were no doubt raised by his consequent dismissal of the medieval idea of church-state relations as "adolescent."[9]

Crucial now to Murray's thought was the distinction of society, state, and government. Society he defined as a "prepolitical matter" to which the state brings a "limited form," a public order directed towards a limited end. Government in turn is only part of the state. A tendency to collapse the three into one was at the root of the traditionalist Catholic error, he thought.[10]

In apparent contrast to what he had affirmed a few years before, Murray in 1949 argued that the state has no obligation to worship God but merely to pursue its own natural end. Apparent modern papal claims that the law of Christ binds states and government, he insisted, are to be understood as reactions to certain false ideas of the lay state prevalent in Europe.[11]

The Church's task, Murray argued, is to protect its members from false teachings and, if the Church is too weak to do so it has no right to expect the state to perform that task. In 1949 he was openly critical of the church-state theories of Msgr. John A. Ryan of Catholic University, noted for his "liberal" positions on social justice but a strong defender of traditional church-state theories. Ryan confused the functions of society, state, and government and even confused the functions of state and church, Murray believed. Ryan had forthrightly argued that in a properly ordered state the government could not tolerate false religious propaganda. To Murray, once again, this was *a priori* reasoning, deduction from a single abstract principle, rather than a respectful approach to the complexity of social existence. Furthermore, Ryan's belief that the state should take responsibility for the full welfare of its citizens logically leads to an intrusive state which does not respect any of its citizens' rights, even to a "Catholic Leviathan."[12]

For the first time in 1949, Murray explicitly repudiated the traditional maxim that "error has no rights," pointing out that only persons, or possibly institutions, have rights and that, even if error has no rights, people in error do. He also attacked the familiar traditionalist distinction between the "thesis"—that truth requires the state to enforce Catholic orthodoxy—and the "hypothesis"—that particular circumstances may render it inexpedient to do so. Such a distinction is facile and misleading, he thought. Earlier theologians such as Bellarmine had made absolute what was once relative—a particular medieval form of society. He argues that, on the contrary, his own version of Catholic teaching—the spiritual and temporal powers as truly distinct and influencing each other only indirectly, through the consciences of the free individuals—is the true Catholic "thesis" by a process of authentic doctrinal development. This idea could not be seen in earlier times because the concrete arrangements of church and state obscured it. Apparent restatements of the medieval view by Leo XIII were explicable, once again, as a reaction to particular historical circumstances in Europe, in which secular governments had propagated a false idea of the "lay state."[13]

Connell did not respond publicly to Murray's thesis until 1948, when he began an exchange that, soon involving others besides himself, laid bare the controversial nature of Murray's ideas and began the process which would lead first to Murray's being for a time silenced on the subject, then to his apparent vindication at the Second Vatican Council.

Connell argued that the state is bound by the law of Christ as well as by the natural law, and the state has a right to suppress error which does spiritual harm to its citizens, since their spiritual good is included in their temporal well being. The state is not based merely on natural law, although he admitted that modern popes, in dealing with the nations of the world, had primarily emphasized such law, recognizing that even that would be a great improvement over sheer political expediency. Unchanging Catholic doctrine requires that governments as well as individuals submit to Christ insofar as they are aware of that duty.[14]

Although Connell was better known, Murray's chief opponent became Msgr. Joseph Clifford Fenton, also of Catholic University of America and editor of the *American Ecclesiastical Review*. Fenton did not name Murray in print until 1950, but some of his earlier writings were obviously directed at the Jesuit theologian.

Fenton saw the Catholic world divided into conservative and liberal (or modernist) camps, each of which is valid up to a point but each of which is also capable of excess. However, integralism—the excess of conservatism—is merely a tendency to mummify traditional teaching and is not inherently wrong, he thought. The excess of liberalism, on the other hand—modernism—is actually a heresy. The liberal aims to make the Faith more acceptable to the larger world, but in the process risks distorting that Faith. Church teachings must be considered adequate statements of Divine Revelation, and dogmas are not mere "instruments" for the preservation of truth but the actual expression of that truth, Fenton insisted.[15]

A vulnerable part of Murray's thesis was his apparent divergence from certain papal encyclicals, and his claim that such encyclicals spoke mainly to particular historical conditions not present in the modern United States. Fenton argued strongly for full and complete assent even to encyclicals which were admittedly not infallible. Attempting to relativize them was for Fenton evidence of a disobedient spirit.[16]

Fenton, along with Connell and another theologian, George W. Shea, argued for the objective duty of the state to offer appropriate worship to the Creator. In a religiously divided society the state may, for prudential reasons, refrain from recognizing the exclusive claims of the true Church and may even show equal favor to all religions. But such is not a theoretically acceptable situation. Like Murray, Fenton admired the American Constitution, but only as a historically conditioned and pragmatic accommodation to a less than ideal situation.[17]

No one, Fenton insisted, believed that the state should coerce consciences in matters of religion, because religious belief is meaningless if not free. Most Catholics would also concede dissenters' rights to live their beliefs privately. The state ought to give special public recognition to the Catholic Faith, however, and might legitimately suppress public manifestations of heresy deemed to be harmful to its citizens. Shea argued that Murray's own earlier writings, with their emphasis on natural law, implied this, since part of the obligation of natural law is precisely the correct worship of the Creator. This, Shea argued, is also the clear position of Canon Law and of the modern popes.[18]

In his responses during the years 1950-54, Murray took as a starting point the classical formulation of Pope Gelasius I in the fifth century—that there are two distinct orders, the spiritual and the temporal, with primacy to the spiritual. But the spiritual cannot be primary, cannot resist the state's inexorable tendency towards political monism, unless the Church is free, which implies a dualism. Church and state must cooperate to achieve the temporal ends of mankind, but the Church does this by creating the appropriate spiritual climate within society.

Murray now began distinguishing more carefully between the state and "the body politic," the state being the means which the latter uses to achieve its ends. The state exists to carry out certain functions, which may change over time. Thus the state is not necessarily obliged to embody all the goods which might be embodied in the larger political and social entities of society and the body politic.[19]

Thus Murray argued that, while Catholic principles of Church-state relations are immutable, they are also "temporalized," which is not mere expediency, as his traditionalist opponents claimed, but a dynamic adaptation to particular historical circumstances. The traditional state church was the result not of immutable Catholic teaching but itself simply an adaptation to particular times and places.[20]

Once again he emphasized that the modern democratic state, especially as found in the United States, is very different from nineteenth-century Continental liberal states which successive popes had condemned. Indeed, Murray argued, modern democracy itself has Christian roots. This new state in fact offers the Church unprecedented opportunities which can only be realized through dynamic and creative adaptation.[21]

Historically, Murray argued, the institution of the state church had not come into being as a deduction from belief in the Catholic Church as the one true Church. On the contrary, because of its own necessary universality, the Church was suspicious of religious establishments which might limit it geographically and politically. The notion of the state church within a particular territory was really a development of Protestantism, following upon the fragmentation of Christendom. Traditionalists err because they identify society and state, and infer that a Christian society requires a Christian state.[22]

Fenton responded by even more forcefully restating the obligation of the state, under natural law, to offer worship to God, and he accused Murray of contradicting papal teaching and the authentic Catholic tradition, which was not historically conditioned in the way Murray claimed.[23] Shea and Connell also returned to the lists against Murray, elaborating their earlier positions.[24] Murray in turn accused Connell of granting too much power to the state, and of not respecting the freedom of the Church, in that he seemed to hold that civil freedom to preach the Gospel is dependent on the state's making a competent judgment that the Gospel is true. He also accused Connell of "pure conceptualism"—arguing solely from premises without regard for the nature of the entities being discussed.[25]

In a series of articles beginning in 1952, Murray undertook a systematic analysis of the relevant statements of Leo XIII, in order to show his own harmony with the pontiff's intentions. The French Revolution had created the new phenomenon of "totalitarian democracy," the product purely of the will of man, with the Church relegated to the status of a mere instrument of popular will. Perennial Catholic doctrine, as expressed by Leo, could be disentangled from polemical concerns inspired by the political conditions of the nineteenth century. When the pope condemned the "separation" of the Church from the state, he was envisioning the totalitarian lay state which had engulfed all of society but had excluded ("separated") the Church from any social role. The American version of church-state separation, leaving the Church completely free to exist within society, is of a wholly different kind, a new phenomenon requiring new theological understanding. Murray went on to claim that Leo had himself developed Catholic theory in a much more adequate direction than the traditionalists. He did this by restricting the state to purely political activity, thus leaving the Church free to influence society. Admittedly, the pope sometimes seemed to envision a paternalistic rather than a minimalist state, but Murray thought this was merely because of the "ignorant masses" who were ceasing to be relevant in the mature modern state.[26]

In 1953, the *American Ecclesiastical Review* published an article by Cardinal Alfredo Ottaviani, the Church's chief guardian of doctrinal orthodoxy in his capacity as prefect of the Sacred Congregation of the Holy Office, criticizing Murray's position.[27] Murray, however, stated privately that he "had it on the highest authority" that Pius XII was not pleased with Ottaviani's essay, and the Msgr. Giovanni Battista Montini, papal pro-secretary of state and the future Paul VI, was cautiously sympathetic to Murray.[28]

In an address at Catholic University in March of 1954, Murray bearded the lions in their den by claiming that the pope had negated the claim that religious toleration was a mere expediency. However, Murray also heard from Roman sources that the pontiff was displeased at some of the criticisms directed at Cardinal Ottaviani. The latter had sent a formal query about Murray to Cardinal Francis J. Spellman of New York. Murray wrote Ottaviani a letter of apology which was not acknowledged.[29]

By early 1955 Murray's Jesuit superiors, based on what they knew of the Roman situation, were warning Murray to exercise caution for the time being, and Jesuit censors in Rome would not approve another of his articles on the thought of Leo XIII. The following year the censors also vetoed the publication in Germany of some of Murray's writings. In effect he had, as rumors were then claiming, been silenced on the subject of church-state relations. As late as 1958 his superiors advised him against trying to publish an article in the Roman Jesuit journal *Civilta Cattolica*. But Murray also received several cautiously friendly communications from the German Jesuit Robert Leiber, a private secretary to Pius XII, telling him among other things that Ottaviani did not have the full support of the pontiff.[30]

The year 1958 also marked the election of John XXIII, and a sudden change of atmosphere in Rome. Murray was permitted once again to resume writing about church-state issues, and in 1960 published his major book on the subject, *We Hold These Truths*,[31] which attracted a good deal of attention outside Catholic circles.

At the Second Vatican Council, which began in 1962, Fenton served as a *peritus* to Cardinal Ottaviani, while Murray was not invited to hold a comparable position. His own belief was that his exclusion was due less to the Roman cardinal than to the Apostolic Delegate to the United States, Archbishop Egidio Vagnozzi, who in the Spring of 1963, while the Council was in session, succeeded in barring Murray and two other theologians from speaking at Catholic University.[32]

However, almost simultaneous with this ban, Murray was invited to the Council to serve as a *peritus* to Cardinal Spellman, an invitation which was formally issued by Vagnozzi's predecessor as Apostolic Delegate, Cardinal Amleto G. Cicognani, now papal Secretary of State. At the Council Murray played an intimate part in the sometimes serpentine maneuvers which led eventually to the Council's proclamation of *Dignitatis Humanae*, its statement on religious liberty. Fenton's resignation as editor of the *American Ecclesiastical Review* early in 1964 perhaps also contributed to Murray's sense of triumph.[33]

Rather surprisingly in view of the American bishops' general reputation for conservatism prior to the Council, and in view of the prestige of some of Murray's opponents, there is evidence that only one American bishop ever opposed his theories. This was only the minor case of Bishop William A. Scully of Albany, chairman of the bishops' committee on film, who feared that some of Murray's strictures against censorship might undermine the Legion of Decency.[34]

As early as 1947, however, Murray had received the private support of the very influential Archbishop John T. McNicholas of Cincinnati, and by the early 1950's he was being actively promoted by Cardinal Edward A. Mooney of Detroit, who in turn tentatively won over the cautious Cardinal Samuel A. Stritch of Chicago. Murray consistently had the support of Cardinal Spellman, and at the opening of the Council was consulted extensively by Archbishop (soon to be Cardinal) Lawrence J. Shehan of Baltimore. At the Council his views were advanced by Bishop John J. Wright of Pittsburgh, at the time considered perhaps the leading intellectual in the American hierarchy, and by Archbishop Patrick A. O'Boyle of Washington, Bishop John J. Carberry of Columbus, and Bishop Ernest J. Primeau of Manchester. During the Council he also wrote speeches for Cardinal Albert G. Meyer of Chicago and several European and Latin American bishops.[35]

The silence imposed on Murray during the 1950's seems mainly to have reflected the caution of his Jesuit superiors, who were generally sympathetic to Murray's project but feared Cardinal Ottaviani. The Vatican had no clear official position at the time, and Murray's superiors correctly assessed the situation when they counselled that a prudent silence would eventually lead to a renewed recognition of his work. As it turned out, Murray's American opponents were arguing for an exercise of ecclesiastical authority which few prelates, either in America or Rome, wanted to exercise.

Within Catholic circles Murray's work attracted surprisingly little attention from people other than theologians, until the time of the Council. Thus a 1950 article on church and state by the Notre Dame professor Heinrich Rommen barely mentioned him,[36] and a 1952 survey on the same subject by several Catholic scholars did not mention him at all.[37] James M. O'Neill, a Catholic professor at a secular college who was the Church's principal public defender against the attacks of the anti-Catholic Paul Blanshard, also made no use of Murray's work in arguing that American Catholics accepted the democratic system.[38] Murray's colleague at the Woodstock School of Theology, Gustave Weigel, did attempt to make Murray's ideas better known,[39] and his work was summarized in a rather neutral manner by another Jesuit, Victor Yanitelli, in a survey of writings on church-state subjects.[40] Another Jesuit, Donald Wolfe, brought Murray's work to Protestant attention in a 1962 article in the *Journal of Church and*

State, a scholarly periodical published under Baptist auspices and generally vigilant against what it considered oppressive Roman Catholic positions.[41] Msgr. John Tracy Ellis, the noted church historian, was a friend of Murray's and defended his thesis, without mentioning him by name.[42] The Vincentian law dean Joseph Tinnelly also published an appreciation.[43]

Outside the United States, Catholic scholars writing on church-state questions do not seem to have made much use of Murray's work prior to the Council,[44] although in 1951 he was strongly criticized by an Italian Jesuit in *Civilta Cattolica*.[45]

The liberal lay journalist John Cogley, an editor of *Commonweal*, praised Murray several times during the 1950's but, despite the alleged growing theological sophistication of the laity, paid little attention to Murray's actual arguments and treated him merely as a symbol of a new enlightenment. Murray, he thought, might "singlehandedly restore the tradition of rational debate to American life," and he credited Murray with striking the proper balance between pluralism and national unity. When the American "holy of holies" is finally unveiled, Cogley interpreted Murray as saying, Americans would discover that it was empty, filled only with the "voices of free debate."[46] A few years later Cogley summed up Murray's contribution as that of calling for "dialogue, not warfare" and argued that such a stance dictated that Catholics cease acting as a "pressure group."[47]

Protestants and Jews also seem to have been rather slow to discover the significance of Murray's work. Will Herberg's celebrated 1956 book *Protestant, Catholic, Jew* did report that Murray was making "brilliant strides" in reconciling Catholic teaching with American society, and claimed that he was being heard "even in the Vatican." However, Herberg's praise was somewhat equivocal in view of his thesis that the three major faiths were compromising their authentic heritages in order to fit into a pluralistic America.[48]

In 1958 the influential liberal Protestant theologian John C. Bennett minimized Murray's originality and described him as "playing off one part of the Catholic tradition against another," taking advantage of the ambiguity of papal pronouncements.[49]

Bennett's somewhat condescending praise was rather typical of Protestants who noticed Murray's work before the Second Vatican Council. In 1961 the Yale theologian George A. Lindbeck conceded Murray's importance only in terms of the shifts he was able to engineer within the Catholic tradition, using methods of argument which Lindbeck dismissed as having no relevance for Protestants or others outside that tradition. In fact Murray's presentation of the natural law idea to the larger society was radically inadequate, Lindbeck concluded, among other things failing to take into account more nuanced ideas of "nature" being developed by European theologians.[50]

In 1959 the Spanish former priest A. E. Carrillo de Albornoz, then on the staff of the World Council of Churches in Geneva, cited Murray in the course of his survey of recent Catholic thinking about church and state, but thought that Murray showed a characteristically American tendency to solve the problem on the juridical and political rather than on the theological level.[51] Six years later, toward the end of the Council, when Murray's genius was being celebrated throughout much of the Catholic world, Albornoz offered an especially harsh judgment on Murray's work, arguing that he was not nearly as liberal as he appeared because he did not directly condemn legal intolerance, as in Spain, and seemed to regard religious liberty and the more basic idea of the dignity of the human person as historically conditioned. Ironically, the liberal Protestant here argued against the Thomist on behalf of an unchanging morality which could escape the vicissitudes of history.[52]

Murray's subject was such that it almost invited evaluation primarily in terms of its ultimate practical results—did he or did he not provide Catholics with plausible arguments for embracing modern pluralistic democracy? Paul Blanshard, after the Council, was generally satisfied with Murray's role, although he noted with disapproval (as had Lindbeck) Murray's support for public aid to religious schools.[53] (The novelist James T. Farrell, famous as a lapsed Catholic, in 1956 saw Murray as a civilized man, in contrast to harsh and repressed American Puritans, and hailed him as an ally in the war against censorship.[54])

The publication of *We Hold These Truths* in 1960 earned Murray an accolade almost unique for either a Jesuit or a theologian: a *Time* magazine cover article in which, with no indication as to whether the editors were being ironic, he was pictured against a background of the *opera omnia* of Robert Bellarmine, the Jesuit predecessor from whose theories he had substantially departed. Noting his basic conservatism, the magazine praised him for his moderation and his commitment to rational discussion and his "realistic" Catholic attitude towards power. The magazine took no apparent position with regard to the Jesuit's proposal that natural law might be the basis for a comprehensive American dialogue but concluded that, if anyone could restore "coherent discourse" to American life, Murray would be the man.[55]

As early as 1958, Murray was aware of John F. Kennedy's candidacy for the presidency, and of the need to clarify the issues such a campaign would raise.[56] *We Hold These Truths* was published in time to influence that debate. Kennedy advisors Theodore Sorenson and Arthur Schlesinger, Jr. both claimed that Kennedy's own formulations of the church-state issue owed much to Murray, Sorenson going so far as to say that he had telephoned Murray to get his approval for the famous speech on the subject which Kennedy gave to a group of Protestant ministers in Houston during the campaign. Murray himself did not comment publicly on these claims. Privately he recalled having spoken with Sorenson but did not recall specifically what was said, and he judged Kennedy's position as more "separationist" than his own.[57]

The Notre Dame political theorist E.A. Goerner, towards the end of the Council, judged Murray's work as an example of "an idea whose time has come" and wondered whether, despite his claim to the contrary, Murray was not in effect canonizing Anglo-Saxon democracy. The Jesuit's view of government was excessively minimalist, Goerner thought, and among other things would not allow for any "great enterprise" which the state might attempt to carry out. The Council, he predicted, would accept some version of Murray's argument, but this in itself would prove to be historically conditioned and in the end too narrow.[58]

John Courtney Murray was a gifted and diligent theologian who tried to discover a perennially valid theory of church and state resting on solid theological foundations. It was perhaps his fate that, because of the urgency of the questions he was called upon to address at the time, the public—both inside and outside the Church—was unprepared to evaluate that effort in all its fullness, and instead judged him hastily on the basis of his timely conclusions.

NOTES

1. Murray, "Current Theology: Christian Co-Operation," *Theological Studies*, III (Sept., 1942), pp. 413-31; "Current Theology: Intercredal Co-Operations,

Some Further Views," *ibid.*, IV (March, 1943), pp. 100-11; "Current Theology: Intercredal Co-Operation, Its Theory and Its Organization," *ibid.*, IV, pp. 267-86. Cf. Connell, "Catholics and 'Interfaith Groups,'" *American Ecclesiastical Review*, CV (Nov., 1941), pp. 336-53; Furfey, "Intercredal Cooperation: Its Limits," *ibid.*, CXI (Sept., 1944), pp. 161-75; "Why Does Rome Discourage Socio-Religious Intercredalism?," *ibid.*, CXII (May, 1945), pp. 364-74.
2. See for example *Theological Studies*, IV, pp. 101, 257-83.
3. "Freedom of Religion, I. The Ethical Problem," *Theological Studies*, VI (June, 1945), pp. 87-90.
4. *Ibid.*
5. *Ibid.*, pp. 240-1.
6. *Ibid.*, pp. 271-2.
7. "Separation of Church and State," *America*, XXVI (Dec. 7, 1946), pp. 261-3; *ibid.*, (Feb. 15, 1947), pp. 541-5; "The Court Upholds Religious Freedom," *ibid.*, LXXVI (Mar. 8, 1947), pp. 628-30; "Religious Liberty: the Concern of All," *America*, LXXVII (Feb. 7, 1948), pp. 513-6; "Dr. Morrison and the First Amendment, I," *ibid.*, (Mar. 6, 1948), pp. 627-9; "Dr. Morrison and the First Amendment, II," *ibid.*, (Mar. 20, 1948), pp. 683-6.
8. "Contemporary Orientation of Catholic Thought on Church and State in the Light of History," *Theological Studies*, X (June, 1949), pp. 177-234; "St. Robert Bellarmine on the Indirect Power," *ibid.*, IX (Dec., 1948), pp. 491-535; "Current Theology: on Religious Freedom," *ibid.*, X (Sept., 1949), pp. 409-32; "Government Repression of Heresy," *Proceedings of the Third Annual Convention of the Catholic Theological Society of America* (1949), pp. 26-98.
9. "Contemporary Orientation," pp. 188, 226; "Bellarmine" p. 530.
10. "Government Repression," p.28.
11. *Ibid.*, pp. 50-2, 30.
12. *Ibid.*, pp. 90-92. Cf. John A. Ryan and Moorhouse F. X. Millar, S.J., *The State and the Church* (New York: Macmillan and Co., 1922).
13. *Ibid.*, p. 83; "Robert Bellarmine," p. 533; "On Religious Freedom," p. 232.
14. "Discussion of Governmental Repression of Heresy," *Proceedings of the Third Annual Convention of the Catholic Theological Society of America* (1949), p. 100; "Christ the King of Civil Rulers," *American Ecclesiastical Review*, CXIX (Oct., 1948), pp. 244-53.
15. "Two Currents in Contemporary Catholic Thought," *American Ecclesiastical Review*, CXIX (Oct., 1948), pp. 294-8; "The Church and Catholic Dogma," *ibid.*, CXX (Feb., 1949), p. 128.
16. "The Doctrinal Authority of Papal Encyclicals, Part I," *ibid.*, XCCI (Aug., 1949), pp. 136-50; "The Doctrinal Authority of Papal Encyclicals, Part II," *ibid.*, CXXI (Sept., 1949), pp. 210-20; "The Religious Assent Due to Papal Encyclicals," *ibid.*, CXXXIII (July, 1950), pp. 59-67.
17. For example, Fenton, "Toleration and the Church-State Controversy," *ibid.*, CXXX (May, 1954), pp. 335, 443; "Principles Underlying Traditional Church-State Doctrine," *ibid.*, CXXVI (June, 1952), p. 455; "The Catholic Church and Freedom of Religion," *ibid.*, CXV, (Oct., 1946), p. 300; "The

Status of a Controversy," *ibid.,* CXXIV (June, 1951), p. 455; "Toleration and the Church-State Controversy," *ibid.,* CXXX (May, 1954), p. 339; Shea, "Catholic Doctrine and the 'Religion of the State,'" *ibid.,* CXXV (Dec., 1951), pp. 405-16; "Spain and Religious Freedom," *ibid.,* CXXVIII (Sept., 1952) pp. 164-6.

18. Shea, "Catholic Doctrine," p. 168; Fenton, "Catholic Church and Freedom," p. 288; Connell, "Theory of Discussion of 'Governmental Repression of Heresy,'" *CTSA Proceedings* (1949), p. 100; "The Theory of the 'Lay State,'" *American Ecclesiastical Review,* CXXV (Jan. 1952), pp. 7-18.
19. "The Problem of the 'Religion of the State,'" *American Ecclesiastical Review,* CXXIV (May, 1951), pp. 327-52; "For the Freedom and Transcendence of the Church," *ibid.,* CXXVI (Jan., 1952), pp. 28-48.
20. "The Problem of State Religion," *Theological Studies,* XII (June, 1951), p. 160.
21. *Ibid.,* p. 163.
22. *Ibid.,* pp. 170, 174.
23. "Status of Controversy," p. 452.
24. Shea, "Catholic Orientation," p. 405; "Spain and Religious Freedom," pp. 169-72; Connell, "Theory of the Lay State," pp. 7-18; "Reply to Father Murray," *American Ecclesiastical Review,* CXXVI (Jan., 1952) pp. 49-59.
25. "For Freedom and Transcendence," p. 28.
26. "The Church and Totalitarian Democracy," *Theological Studies* XIII (December 1952), pp. 147-8.
27. "Church and State: Some Present Problems in the Light of the Teachings of Pope Pius XII," CXXVIII, (May, 1953), pp. 321-34.
28. Donald E. Pelotte, S.S.S., *John Courtney Murray: Theologian in Conflict* (New York: Paulist Press, 1975), pp. 37, 39.
29. *Ibid.,* pp. 46, 49.
30. *Ibid.,* pp. 52, 54, 57-8, 64.
31. (New York: Sheed and Ward).
32. Pelotte, *Theologian in Conflict,* pp. 77, 81, 85, 109.
33. *Ibid.,* pp. 81, 85-100.
34. *Ibid.,* p. 55.
35. *Ibid.,* pp. 16, 39, 40, 74, 82, 110, 93.
36. "Church and State," *Review of Politics,* XII, 3 (July, 1950), pp. 321-40.
37. William F. Lynch, Joseph W. Evans, James M. O'Neill, "Church and State," *Thought,* 103 (Spring, 1952), pp. 581-7.
38. *Catholicism and American Freedom* (New York: Harper's, 1952).
39. "The Church and The Democratic State," *Thought,* XXVII (Summer, 1952), pp. 165-84; "Religious Toleration in a World Society," *America,* XC, 9 (Jan. 9, 1954), pp. 375-6.
40. "A Church-State Controversy," *Thought,* XXVI, 102 (Autumn, 1951), pp. 444-51.
41. "The Unitary Theory of Church-State Relations," (IV, 1 [May, 1962]), pp. 47-64.
42. "Church and State, an American Catholic Tradition," *Harper's,* CCVII (Nov., 1952), pp. 63-7.
43. "The Challenge of John Courtney Murray—Can an American Public Philosophy Be Stated?," *The Catholic Lawyer,* VII, 4 (Autumn, 1961), pp. 270-96.

44. There was no mention of Murray in, for example, *Freedom of Conscience and Religious Freedom*, by the Belgian theologian Louis Janssens (New York: Alba House, 1966—originally published 1960) or in *Conscience and Its Right to Freedom*, by the Australian priest-philosopher Eric D'Arcy (New York: Sheed and Ward, 1961).
45. A. Messinero, S.J., "Democrazia e Liberta Religiosa," (CIIM, 11 1951, pp. 26-37), cited in Yanitelli, "Controversy," p. 444.
46. "In Praise of Father Murray," *Commonweal*, LXV, 10 (Dec. 7, 1956), p. 253.
47. "Person to Person," *ibid.*, LXIX, 15 (Jan. 9, 1959), p. 385.
48. (Garden City: Doubleday, 1956), pp. 14-15, 165, 176.
49. *Christians and the State* (New York: Charles Scribner's Sons, 1958), pp. 85, 266-7.
50. "John Courtney Murray: an Evaluation," *Christianity and Crisis*, XXI, 20 (Nov. 27, 1961), pp. 13, 214-6.
51. *Roman Catholicism and Religious Liberty* (Geneva: World Council of Churches, 1959), pp. 9, 80.
52. "Religious Freedom: Intrinsic or Fortuitous?," *The Christian Century*, LXXXXII, 37 (Oct. 16, 1965), pp. 1122-6.
53. *Paul Blanshard on Vatican II* (Boston: Beacon Press, 1966), pp. 76, 87, 88.
54. "A Jesuit on Censorship," *The New Republic*, CXXXV, 20 (Nov. 12, 1956), p. 18.
55. "City of God and Man" (Dec. 12, 1960), cover, pp. 64-70.
56. Pelotte, *Theologian in Conflict*, p. 58.
57. *Ibid.*, p. 107.
58. *Peter and Caesar: the Catholic Church and Political Authority* (New York: Herder and Herder, 1965), pp. 183-91, 224-6, 273-8.

WE HOLD THESE TRUTHS AND MORE

Criticism of the Murray Thesis

2

John Courtney Murray: The Optimism of the 1950's

by Frederick D. Wilhelmsen

I never knew Fr. John Courtney Murray of the Society of Jesus. But I did know a man who knew him very well: the late Dr. Willmoore Kendall. Kendall had a number of stories to tell about the illustrious Jesuit professor whose political-theological thought engages us in this volume. These stories are hearsay because both men have gone to what I trust is their rewards. Murray as a seminary professor was by no means initially known as the man of the theory of religious liberty of whom we think when his name is mentioned. His earlier specialty was the doctrine of the Blessed Trinity and his mimeographed notes on that central doctrine of the Faith mounted to hundreds of pages of closely written Latin prose, loaded with erudition as well as orthodoxy. He once told Kendall when the vernacular was imposing itself in American Catholic seminaries that "nobody can teach this stuff in English." A herald of a new kind of political theology, he was still rooted in an older order in which a venerable tradition of doctrine was enshrined in the language of the Church. As an apostle of things new, however, Fr. Murray was often lifted into a helicopter and dropped into the Luce family estate where he enjoyed the delights of the American rich before returning to the relative austerity of his seminary surroundings. He was very much at home in both worlds. His thesis certainly reflected the Luce *Time*, *Life*, *Fortune* ethos, one bound up with the United States that emerged from World War II and that spanned the decades running from the mid-forties to the mid-sixties. That time we shall never see again, but it was by no means an ignoble moment in the life of the Republic.

Catholicism, for the first time in the history of the nation, was almost respectable. Msgr. Sheen had converted Clare Booth Luce and that brilliant orator was a media hit, making the transition from radio to television, telling jokes about angels hidden in his splendid cape; Bing Crosby was the quintessential Irish American priest crooning his way to eternity in "Going My Way." It was the time of "The Song of Bernadette," the beauty and talent of the unabashedly Catholic Loretta Young, and of a plethora of motion pictures exulting nuns and priests and always ending with a host of candy-coated triumphs of good over evil. A lot of froth, but good froth! More seriously was the admission of Catholics by the bushel into the F.B.I. because at least one thing about them was known: they were anti-Communist and had never experienced the temptation of the American Left to collaborate with the Soviet Union. For the first time a young man had an edge in Washington if he graduated from Georgetown's famed diplomatic school. The Catholic university system in the land was booming and even the secular academy could not resist the charm and the wisdom of Etienne Gilson. Yale sang his praises. Even though the influence of Chesterton and Belloc was then in decline, American Catholicism seemed capable of handling itself without the aid of their English co-religionists. In a profound sense the Catholic ghetto opened up and culturally Catholics were being accepted in the land. Even that fine old Catholic superstition, the Devil, had a good press as *Time* dedicated an entire issue in 1946 to demonstrating his existence.

It was a time when it was fashionable to be orthodox in religion. Reinhold Niebuhr preached a new neo-Lutheran orthodoxy and the Luce empire lifted his thoughts to instant fame. Will Herberg, in his *Protestant, Catholic, Jew* argued throughout the land that all three religions adhered to a common tradition of civility written into the American constitutional system. The term "The Judeo-Christian" world was coined although nobody had ever heard of it before. I personally listened to Herberg sing the praises of the Catholic understanding of natural law at Stanford. Everything was sweetness and light in the Republic. All we had to do was to refer to the origins of the nation in order to discover that we are what we are, a religious people. And this religious people was wrought out of the catalyst of the unique American experience which synthesized Protestant, Catholic, and Jew into a unity respecting their differences. We were the "virtuous people," Willmoore Kendall trumpeted.

This was the world into which swept John Courtney Murray's *We Hold These Truths* in 1960. A year later the book had undergone five printings. Behind the book's thesis are affirmations that reposed upon the evident prejudice Murray had against the older European Catholic confessional state which he saw as a bad dream disturbing the religious liberty he pushed so assiduously at Vatican II. Murray genuinely thought that the thesis-hypothesis doctrine of an earlier Catholic political theology ought to be reversed: i.e., *not* the confessional state as the norm and the pluralist state with the equality of all creeds as the exception, but the American model as the norm which had outgrown the lineaments of the older Christendom.

Murray was no provincial quasi-puritan American Catholic with no understanding or appreciation for his own European past. *We Hold These Truths* sparkles with a humor that could laugh at the Protestant sensibility which was shocked by a Baroque Rome that issued lists of books the reading of which consigned men to eternal torments even as it tolerated the existence of thousands of licensed prostitutes populating the streets of The Eternal City. He could also be superior to Latin cynicism about American morality. He could joke about both provincialisms in a kind and tolerant tone. But when the chips were down, when the bottom line had to be written, Murray was a quintessential American and a child of his own moment in time.

We Hold These Truths did not hammer home Murray's thesis on the confessional state. The student of his thought has to go to the stacks and look up a plethora of articles published in theological journals. He has to explore the back-door intrigues that swirled in quasi-darkness in Rome behind the decree on religious liberty. I abstract from both tasks in this paper which looks to Murray on natural law and America. The basic proposition of the book which gave the man his public fame is the following. By a felicitous accident of history, the natural law has found a better home on these shores than in the continent that gave it birth. Never denying that barbarism might settle over both sides of the Atlantic, the American Jesuit was highly confident that reason in this nation had incorporated in a consensus a growing body of convictions that validated and even furthered the insights of natural law philosophy. Natural law philosophy in both its articulation and its *praxis* had a better chance to flower in the United States than in Catholic Baroque Europe or, presumably, in South America. Incorporating Walter Lippman's conception of a "public philosophy" into his own thinking, the American Jesuit traced the arrival of natural law philosophy to these shores from the prominent role it played in old English common law and he praised Sir John Fortescue's insistence that the power of the king be specified and tempered by his adherence to a law which did not depend on the caprice of his own will.

Congratulating the American Founding Fathers on a healthy realistic epistemology that was confident in the capacity of human reason to arrive at conclusions concerning the good life which are rooted not in Rousseauistic voluntarism but in the inbuilt capability of the human mind to know first principles and to reason from them to more distant propositions the truths of which are traceable to exigencies written in the script of human nature, Murray continued and insisted that this natural law again is no Stoic document written in a nature which has no author. Coming forth from God, it expresses His Will but I obey that Will because I can understand its reasonableness as it directs my humanity to its proper end. Murray, unlike Herberg, was keenly aware of the voluntarism implicit in much of Protestant and Jewish thought and he never tires of insisting that natural law has found a more comfortable home within the walls of the Catholic Church than beyond them. But with so much said, he was always to insist that the very naturalness of the law, a Catholic discovery, was nonetheless a thoroughly universal human inheritance and it had come home to roost and roost well in the United States of America. Germane to Murray's thesis was his emphasis on the suppleness and plasticity of man's discovery of the law. Never known all at once and proclaimed in any one piece of legislation or constitutional flourish, we come to know the content of the law piece by piece but, also germane to his thesis, the movement is upwards, progressive, admitting of shocking failures here and there historically but advancing in a spiral towards an increasing unfolding of rationality that makes life ever more decent and liveable in political society.

The thesis was melioristic but by no means gnostic. The Barbarian might get us in the end but we do have the tools and the experience to put him off. All we need is the will and the overarching thrust of Murray's thought suggests that he was not only hopeful but reasonably confident that the will would be found, indeed more often than not in our history had been already found. Integral to his thesis is his insistence on a religious pluralism that nonetheless permits of a conversation because Americans are agreed on a number of fundamentals concerning the way in which the business of government is to be undertaken. These fundamentals constitute a still growing consensus or public philosophy the content of which is one with the natural law. Let us put behind us the Battle of the Boyne and King Billy, Oliver Cromwell and the Inquisition, the Spanish Armada and St. Bartholomew's Day—all the old bitterness that hardened into hatred our religious divisions. Let us drop the burden of history and face tomorrow together united in a common conviction that we are all men in the same political boat and that although "religious pluralism is a scandal to God"—his words— it is a political necessity in this nation and even in this largely de-sacralized Western world to which we belong along with Europe.

A man can quarrel here and there with the exhortation, the dream of John Courtney Murray. I bridled when he wrote that Thomas Aquinas was the first Whig as I hold with Samuel Johnson that the honor belongs to the Devil. But then again writers such as Weigel and Novak agree with Murray on the point and possibly Lord Acton would as well. The details, some of them asides, of the development of *We Hold These Truths*, while interesting and reflective of the personality of the author, are not to my point. My question is simpler: Was the man in the whole right or was he wrong? To answer that question I divide the issue into three parts: the history of the book; the history in the book; and, finally and crucially, the theory in the book.

Murray came along at exactly the right moment in American Catholic history as pointed out in my opening observations. Those two decades following World War II represent a kind of peak in both the internal flourishing of the Church in the United States and, more to the point here, of a fairly general acceptance of Catholicism by America at large. The media were friendly to the Church. The government welcomed Catholic graduates into its machinery. And many non-Catholics looked upon the Church as a firm bastion of faith and morality. We were admired and even envied. We seemed to have settled finally into our own country without in any sense waffling or betraying the uniqueness of our religious and intellectual heritage. No one was more patriotic than the typical Catholic. Our universities and colleges flourished and our secondary and primary schools were a wonder in the land. Along with our Protestant, Jewish, and unchurched fellow citizens we were then living an ecumenism before the word was invented. Then a man could easily believe that a common consensus united Americans in their social and political existence. But this moment in history was as ephemeral as it was probably shallow.

A general collapse in public and private morality slammed into the Western world like a hurricane beginning sometime in the seventh decade of this century. I cannot here attempt any exhaustive probe of the causes that decimated our civilization in the past twenty-five years. I can only list my own rosary of secularist beads and any one of you can thread his own: the collapse of the family; the scandal of millions of men and women openly, proudly, cohabiting without benefit of the blessing of either God or State; the spread of the contraceptive mentality threatening to wipe out the white race in Europe and America; the plague of drugs that have decimated our schools, leaving tens of thousands of youngsters, possibly more, huddling in alleys and crack houses, given over to hallucination and the hell of despair; a million and a half unborn babies butchered in the womb in one year; the slaughter of the old hovering like a ghost of Christmas Future over the heads of the elderly; hordes of loathsome homosexuals profaning our streets and badgering the courts for legal recognition of their sins; sacrilege by them in the first Catholic cathedral of the land, St. Patrick's in New York, and the blatant trampling underfoot of the Lord of Hosts—the Cardinal Archbishop in tears and not a single fistful of stout Catholic lads at his side to throw the bastards out; a general epistemological cynicism settling, a plague, into the minds of educators: who can know what is right or wrong?

A sign of this shift in the American sensibility is the massive hostility today to all things Catholic in the media. This has been met by most Catholic politicians and educators not by a stiffening of their backs to hostility but by an accommodation to the world surrounding them. A ticket of success at the polls for a Catholic is often his or her willingness to defy the Church on the abortion issue and thus assure media applause. I need not mention names because they are well known. Catholics today are respectable in the measure of their opposition to their own Church and in the degree of their adherence to a going secularist ethic that is well on the way of sweeping from public life any even minimal adherence to the things of God. This was certainly not true in Murray's time. Catholics were honored for being Catholic in the full integrity of the term and they were so honored more often than not by their non-Catholic fellow citizens. Rome was the bastion. It is difficult to make this ethos understood to young people today because they have never experienced it. Notre Dame was not just football: it was Our Lady and even those who did not share our Faith more often than not admired it. Murray wrote in that very favorable if somewhat odd Indian summer. I was raised then. I grew up then. I knew that time from within and I experienced its effects from without. But it was like a puff of smoke, even the odor of a perfume now dissipated in the air: all gone.

Murray's moment in history is gone, as gone with the wind as was the old South of that famous novel and motion picture. It can be argued that our general assent to the natural law, preached by the Jesuit political philosopher, never existed at all, that those post-war years were a brief late summer night's dream with little or no substance. It can also be argued that possibly once such a reasonable approach to life did exist and that somehow it was grounded in natural law but that now it has disappeared. Argue it either way: it no longer exists.

If the history *of* the book is very much a past, then how about the history *in* the book? *We Hold These Truths*: but we do not! *Roe v. Wade* proves that. Abortion is the law of the land and abortion is the litmus test. Abortion is that "end situation" which the German philosopher Karl Jaspers said ought to be used to test any theory. When re-reading *We Hold These Truths* in preparation for this lecture I hunted everywhere for some reference to abortion, to what the American experience had to say about what Vatican II called "an abominable crime." I could find little and no wonder! No civilized man, and Murray was that, even *thought* about legalizing abortion in 1960. (In the Spain of General Franco a lawyer could argue his case from the natural law and doctorates in law could concentrate upon positive law, canon law, or natural law. Natural law was not precisely written into legislation but an appeal to it could be made *legally* because the regime recognized its authority. The advent of democracy in that land did away with any appeal to natural law in the court. The recognition of a law anterior to all legislation, one rooted in divine authority and human rationality, always involves an appeal to something anterior to constitutionality. This, of course, is the profound meaning of the old adage that princes and governments rule "by the grace of God." I last saw this declaration of God's authority on a coin minted in Spain in 1975. Soon these coins will be collectors' items. Spain has now recognized a right to abortion. Very few polities today recognize any authority more profound than themselves. Our "under God" is a myth.)

When a crime is so blatant and recognized socially as being what it is, an abomination, then positive law does not have to legislate against it. Positive law legislates when crime is a menace upon a society. The abortion case is instructive here because it indicates just how positive law, political power, can answer positively to laws deeper than legislation, how legislation can recognize a system of law rooted in no constitution but in man's nature, to which every constitution ought to conform.

Father Murray saw the natural law tradition as operative in the American political experience from its outset and it is probable that some dose of natural law theory was present in the minds of the men who crafted the American Constitution. At least this proposition has been argued and argued cogitantly by a number of scholars. But what has not been argued cogitantly is precisely how the proposition of a nation "under God" was to be understood. Has this noble affirmation meant throughout our history that political power is subordinate to a divine authority expressing itself through a natural law capable of being penetrated rationally by well-intentioned men? Does it mean that political power is subordinate to something more ultimate than itself? God and His Authority? The "separation of church and state" ideology has vitiated any previous adherence our land might have given to the natural law. If the natural law is *authorized* by God in His creating man and if God is banished from the political forum, then it follows that His law is banished as well. Law, natural and positive, is reasonable but this reasonableness, if it is to be followed, must always be rooted, at least ultimately, in its legitimate Author. Power must locate the source of the wisdom reflected in law and that source is always personal.

Murray never addressed himself to the crucial theoretical distinction between power and authority and their personal character. The terms blur in his analysis as they blur in the analysis of many men and as they have been blurred throughout our entire history.

Power and Authority are two dimensions of political existence which are more often than not confused in their theoretical articulation. I am using the term "confused" in its technical Thomistic sense, *confusio*, which indicates a mixing together of realities or principles which are formally distinct without adverting to these formal distinctions. I follow here the seminal work of Professor Alvaro d'Ors of the University of Navarre in Spain. Authority is the possession of truth socially recognized by the community in which the authority is operative. Authority answers questions put to it by those who exercise power in some fashion within the body politic. Power, in turn, refers to "doing," "acting," and thus lies on the side of being, existence, the font of all power. Power, never encountered in any vacuum, is always specified or determined in the concrete and that determination or limitation is some authority, be it grand or humble. Power asks questions of Authority and Authority answers. Power responds to authority either positively or negatively. I possess a certain power over the use of my money and I ask an authority—let us say, a broker—as to how I ought to exercise that power. He, out of an authority recognized by society that licenses him to act as a broker, gives me advice, counsel. My power over my money is then either specified by his authoritative advice or my power ignores that advice and seeks some other authority, either genuine or fallacious, which will determine the use to which I put the power I possess over my funds. To select another example: I possess power over my own body but I consult a physician concerning the state of my health. He suggests that I need to go on a diet. I either accept his authority or I reject it. My power is specified by his counsel or it is not. If not, that power is specified by some other authority, again either genuine or false. Power in a void is a contradiction in terms. Authority, without a corresponding response in power is frustrated, literally—use*less* because not "put to use" by the power in question.

The symbiosis of power and authority works out their roles in every order of human life and certainly achieve a dramatic culmination in the response public power gives to authority in matters moral. Morality, of course, involves politics and politics involves morality. Beyond morality there repose its metaphysical and epistemological roots: God as the Author of the moral law and our capacity, as human beings, to discover, if not in every detail at least in its broad lineaments, the contents of that law, the law called by the Western tradition "natural."

The American political experience, if quickened and vivified in its sounder dimensions by natural law (an unlikely event), would not by itself be enough to restore order to our world. As a political philosopher I can give no recipes. My role is to point out the disease in its theoretical dimension. The natural law ought to act as an authority specifying and determining the exercise of political power. It matters little in most concrete political situations whether or not this law is written into the positive law of the land. What matters is that this law be respected and obeyed. But a natural law that floats in the air, the private opinion of a handful of university professors themselves besieged in our highly secularist university world, will not cut the ice. That law, as do all laws, requires an authoritative interpreter. All authority is personal, be it the authority of a garage mechanic, a physician, or a professor. The natural law—so beloved by Father Murray—comes from God and the Catholic Church is the interpreter of that law. Unless bedded down to concretion and existentiality, the natural law floats like a gossamer web with neither teeth nor the authority it ought to have.

The identification of political power with ultimate authority—whose theoretician was Jean Bodin—was the charter of independence for modern politics from the authority of God. If the Prince is Sovereign—meaning thereby, the will of the Prince is the law of the land—then the Prince in his power has become the last authority in the land. Through a fairly rapid transmogrification, the will of the Prince became the will of the majority and from this there issued into existence liberal democracy. If a democratic republic adheres to the natural law then a kind of unstable but desirable equilibrium is achieved. If a democratic republic does not adhere to the natural law then those men who would do so have no recourse *if* they have accepted the modern statist assumption that ultimate authority is one with political power. The God of The Fourth of July is ceremonial. His Law and His Authority for that Law must be verified by majorities and if they are not thus verified, then too bad! Bodin himself piously hoped that the Prince would conform his will to God's but if the Prince did not, then the citizenry must suffer the consequences.

What Fr. Murray wanted to do, so it seems to me, was to weave the authority of God into the political order through that order's taking unto itself the demands of the natural law which is God's law for man. This pious hope, however, subtly converts the power of the magistrate into the authority of God, and authority the magistrate now accepts. But if the magistrate does *not* do this, then what happens? Among many other things, *Roe v. Wade* happens. Political power arrogates to itself authority. In confusing these two distinct ontological dimensions of the real, the advocates of this position render any inclusion of the natural law into the body politic something ephemeral. The business is metaphysical nonsense. My power over my body can accept the authority of my physician but that power can never convert itself into the physician's authority. When that occurs, I cure myself. Such cures, as we all know, usually end in death. The man who doctors himself doctors himself into the grave. The polity that does the same faces a similar coffin.

When power and authority—in our case, political power and moral authority—retain their proper distinctiveness, then politics asks questions of authority and does not absorb that authority into itself. The American political experience has wavered between an older order admitting the independent authority of God and His Law and the newer ethos of liberal democracy that identifies all authority with political power. The mythology of one-man, one-vote in matters ultimate abrogates any presumed authority the natural law and its Author might have. God is not one vote among others. Only when a polity offers its power to this authority which is distinct from itself and which ought to specify that power, can that polity be said to correspond to the natural order of things and the Author of that order. I have already pointed out that when the things of God are of the very sinew and muscle of a society, then positive law need not necessarily spell out an adherence to these very things. Where crimes are unthinkable, let them not be thought. But if they are thought, if dangers to the body politic are afoot in the land, then—only then—let political power legislate against them but let political power do so because it responds to that authority beyond and more profound than itself which is the Authority of God and the law He made when He made man.

There is a kind of parallelism in Murray's speculations on this latter issue. On the one hand, he glories in the development of natural law under Catholic auspices. On the other hand, he would cut that development away from Catholic tutelage in the United States where the Church is simply one among several creeds competing for the ultimate allegiance of our citizenry. Murray sees a natural law, a "public philosophy," flourishing in abstraction from its own historical roots in the older Catholic sacral order. His confidence in the good will of a nation the authorities of which are not vivified by grace, not educated in a Scholastic tradition (which swept into itself the best of pagan antiquity and insights come to life thanks to a thousand years and more of speculation on the other side of the Atlantic)—and always quickened by appeals to the ultimate authority, God speaking through His Church—was naive. Murray did not live long enough to see the collapse of our civilization.

Possibly at bottom, Fr. John Courtney Murray was overly optimistic about man's ability to discover the natural law without the positive guide and inspiration of the Church as God's interpreter of that law. This would have fitted well with his general American optimism. He might have pondered those chapters in St. Thomas Aquinas' *Summa Contra Gentiles* where the Common Doctor faced this objection: Why did God reveal so many truths to man which fall within the competence of his own reason? He mentioned specifically the existence of God, the immortality of the soul, *and the moral law.* St. Thomas' answer: what man can know theoretically by the use of his reason he more often does not because of a host of factors including his own moral weaknesses; his exhaustion following the mental labor; his distractions due to other and possibly more fundamental necessities of daily existence and to the downright intellectual mediocrity which is the lot of most men. Thus God reveals what is knowable to human reason, but usually known not at all or only imperfectly. God reveals these truths because man must act by them in order that he might be saved. Even the philosopher who discovers profound verities at age fifty or sixty had better act by these verities when he is a young man of eighteen or twenty. Make with me the transformation of these principles to a society: possibly it can discover these truths by the use of reason alone. It rarely does so and then these truths are mixed in with much error. It were better had this society from its inception been guided by God's law rather than bit by bit discovering its content. The charity inherent in St. Thomas' teaching is hard to make evident to modern democratic man. God wills to save us all and we are under the danger of not being saved if we wait around for decades or centuries to have the law of our own being revealed to us by the exercise of our own reason. God thus hurries us along with this double Revelation, not only of Truths beyond all human reason but those which theoretically are knowable by human reason, which—even when known—are always known in those deficient modes which are inherent in our fallen state. Although not hammered home in these texts, latently operating is the conviction that no law interprets itself, and that the natural law demands that it be interpreted by its Maker, God, who—the Author—"*authorizes*" its very content. We Catholics have always insisted that we have as individuals no red telephone from which we can call God directly. Our interpreter of His Law (which is His Will) is the Church. I suggest that for this reason, among others pointed out, the natural law tradition never took root in the soil of this nation. I also suggest, although the limits of this paper deny my developing the thesis, that Murray's objections to the confessional State, to a society publicly confessing itself Catholic and incarnating the Faith down to its very gestures in every moment of life lack both theological and philosophical delicacy. In fact they do indeed seem to reveal Murray as a quintessential American. He tells us that he wants a "dry" consensus, one purely rational. He holds that we Americans have it—at least he thought we had it in 1960. I have spelled out my reasons why I do not think that we ever had it. We certainly do not have it now. But even if we did, in no way can such a situation be compared favorably to a society in which men sense themselves to be one because they worship before a common Altar and salute one another as brothers in the common Faith of Christendom.

3

John Courtney Murray: Defender of the Myth

by John A. Gueguen

*I*t was George Weigel's *Catholicism and the Renewal of American Democracy* [1] that led me back after so many years to John Courtney Murray and a reconsideration of *We Hold These Truths* from a perspective far different from what was possible thirty years ago at the beginning of my teaching career. At that time my introduction to political philosophy—the intellectual ground to which I will bring Murray's project—was still recent and barely understood. It is astonishing how different a book read in one's youth can be when so many years have been spent in the company of young minds and great books in the effort to deepen one's understanding of political philosophy.

In this paper my intention is to provoke thought and discussion—not only about Murray's project but also about the great issues it raises, issues which have not lost their "sharp urgency."[2]

After reviewing Weigel's book for the *Social Justice Review*, I had already determined to focus upon Murray's intention to show a harmonizing link between a particular religious-cultural tradition on the one hand and a particular social-political experience on the other—between Catholic life and American democracy. A colleague at Georgetown has already posed the question I wish to raise. In a presentation to the American Political Science Association,[3] William Gould confessed to "serious doubts about the soundness of Murray's project—even in the updated version" offered by followers such as Weigel and Richard John Neuhaus.

Gould argues that Murray has not demonstrated [note the word *demonstrated*] the fundamental compatibility of Catholicism and the

American experience; rather, what he has done is to offer an artful, if tendentious, account of their historical relationship which sounds plausible because it skillfully leaves out of the story those elements of both which have traditionally proved [to have] sources of conflict between them. In short, it succeeds in effecting a reconciliation of the two at the expense of misrepresenting them both. And "Murray tends to focus chiefly on those elements of the [Catholic] tradition which find ready parallels in liberalism, while largely ignoring more distinctly Catholic elements." And Murray's "account of the American experience, while certainly correct in some respects, must be viewed, on the whole, as a caricature of the American reality"; it is "a highly idealized portrait." Thus, "Murray never really comes fully to grips with those aspects of the American experience which present a serious challenge to his claims concerning the basic harmony between Catholicism and American life." [4]

Having made this point, Gould then asks the question students of political philosophy are trained to raise whenever they encounter obvious mistakes in carefully conceived books: What could it mean if an author of Murray's "formidable intelligence and powers of discernment" has adopted and defended a position which is open to compelling doubts? "One plausible possibility," Gould goes on, articulating my own observations, "is that Murray was actually less concerned with providing an accurate rendering of the American experience than he was with fashioning a noble myth about that experience which, if widely accepted, could…promote salutary social consequences." [5]

Students of classical and modern political philosophy are well acquainted with precedents for a likely story, fable, or fiction like this alleged compatibility of Catholic and American ways of life. Consider, for example, Plato's myth of the metals and Rousseau's mythical "state of nature." Perhaps, Gould concludes—and this will provide a point of departure for my attempt to develop his insight—perhaps Murray only meant to provide a common ground which he saw as urgently necessary on which Catholics, Protestants, Jews, and secularists might be able to achieve the requisite civic unity.[6]

What this comes to, I think, is that Murray's "Reflections on the American Proposition" must be read as a political manifesto and not as elements of demonstrable theory. Then the very Proposition itself becomes mythical and can be promoted on non-historical and non-philosophical grounds. In a passage where Murray correctly identifies *The Federalist* as a manifesto rather than a treatise in political theory, he suggests his awareness that he is doing something like what Publius did in arguing for the adoption of a particular scheme of government and tailoring his material to that very practical and urgent concern. Murray says there: "It is in the tone of this tradition of American political writing that one would argue for the First Amendment. The arguments will tend to be convincing in proportion as their key of utterance approaches a dry rustle and not a wild ring." And he adds that the arguments he is presenting here "are surely dry enough."[7] The same dryness prevails throughout the essays, and is particularly successful in the final selection, "The Doctrine Lives," where Murray presents a manifesto on behalf of the natural law.

Another recent article which expands on the plausibility of Murray's project and helps to interpret *We Hold These Truths* as a manifesto in defense of a public myth is by Jude Dougherty. Murray was writing, he begins, in a time of "vigorous and self-confident Catholicism." Murray could presuppose "an essentially unified Church...a common outlook with respect to the fundament of law." It was not yet so clear "that the nation was moving from a Christian past to a secular future," although Murray even then "was under no illusion that the U.S. could...develop a public philosophy." But if it could, the Catholic Church, he thought, was the one repository of "the intellectual resources indispensable" to its formulation. Add to this, Dougherty goes on, Murray's judgment that the U.S. of his time was doing badly and his mighty concern about the country's great need for intellectual unity, for a revivified constitutional consensus whereby the people acquire an identity, a sense of purpose, a fundamental agreement about truths, purposes, values. Given Murray's formation, he could not have found grounds for such a consensus anywhere else than in the Church's natural law tradition. Murray was surely aware of the rather checkered path on which that tradition had reached our Founders, Dougherty observes, but he proceeded to emphasize those elements that were consonant with the Catholic tradition while sublimating their Lockean reformulation.[8]

Perhaps the most astonishing mythological achievement in *We Hold These Truths* is Murray's alignment of Locke "with the men of Paris *and* Philadelphia in 1789 [his words, my emphasis]."[9] After recognizing the philosophical innovations of Locke and maintaining that Lockean rationalism, individualism, and nominalism, together with the state-of-nature premise, had by 1960 been discredited, Murray proceeds to argue that Locke had nevertheless "helped to create a stable and vigorous political community largely because he restated...the great political truths that were the medieval heritage...." Even if Locke did this "on philosophically indefensible grounds," still he "asserted in effect the fundamental positions of the natural law philosophy," including popular sovereignty, consent, and participation; it was these truths, and not the ones he devised, that "furnished the essential dynamism of his system."[10] In simpler language, Locke did not know what he was doing, or was doing something he did not himself realize.

But Murray goes even further: The French philosophers of the eighteenth century also "dimly glimpsed" the true natural law of the tradition even as they explored ways of converting the world to a modernized law of nature. "They did not, I say, know that they were looking at natural law....But it was, for all that, natural law that swam before them...."[11]

Thus did Murray fashion the keystone of what Gould and I call the noble myth of "an intellectual tradition confident that the order of nature can be discerned and that what is good for man can be established." And he argued for it as forcefully as he could, employing considerable rhetorical skill along with mastery of language and style.[12] He succeeded in creating a climate of belief in a mythical Proposition which many still find convincing.

Some clerics have a low resistance to the mentality of an American dream, but I do not find this kind of naive clericalism in Murray. Nor can I trace his motive to simple patriotism (though it is apparent that he loved his country more than most) nor to wishful thinking and even less to desperation. Rather, Murray puts one in mind of Archbishop John Ireland, perhaps the first effective promoter of the myth of an American Proposition which could harmonize Catholic and American principles. Ireland belonged to a period which the U.S. Church historian Marvin O'Connell calls the age of assimilation into the dominant American culture. In the second half of the nineteenth century, as Catholics became more literate and more comfortable in America, they began to develop a desire for acceptance—though not yet at the expense of the intellectual and moral integrity of the Catholic tradition. I believe it is against the background of that development, which occurred between the Civil War and World War II as the Church in America advanced from assimilation to incorporation (also O'Connell's term), that we must understand Murray's motive for defending the myth.[13]

For me, this explains how he could see renewal of American democracy as such a pressing necessity that he could consider it permissible to overlook or intentionally misrepresent the historical, philosophical, and theological evidence of serious incompatibilities between Catholic social doctrine and the premises of the American Founding; that he could proceed then to weave so cleverly a persuasive argument that could rescue the mythological Proposition by hitching it to Catholic truth. I think it is necessary to read Murray's essays in the context which led him to apply the principles he inherited from the Scholastic tradition just as he read Leo XIII in the context of the late nineteenth century. Recall that at the end of the Foreword Murray says he wants his book to be useful. To properly interpret him, then, "one must appreciate the extent to which his thought...developed within a fairly well-defined polemical context" as he sought a viable path in between the traditionalist Catholicism of Leo's generation and the liberal Protestantism which was already carrying modern America into secularism.[14] Because of the historical consciousness that was possible to a man like Murray in years like the immediate post-war period, he was able to achieve the last serious defense of the myth which he calls the American Proposition; thereafter reason was overthrown by ideological polarization, by the shrill voices and angry mutterings, the "barbarism" Murray feared was already on the horizon when he put together *We Hold These Truths*.[15]

Men resort to myth when reasoned argument and demonstration is deemed inadequate to deal successfully with a massive crisis of public order. Murray himself says, taking a clue from Chesterton, "there are times and circumstances...when it is necessary to exaggerate [in order] to tell the truth.... These circumstances...are present in America" now.[16] Murray's consciousness of myth is evident in another passage where he refers to "the power of a myth" in connection with the state of nature thesis.[17]

Myth-making circumstances give rise to what St. Augustine understood as "civil theology," or what is sometimes termed "public theology" in Murray's case.[18] My students and I have studied instances of this phenomenon in the history of political thought, and I have treated it in the context of American "civil religion" alongside Robert Bellah.[19] I find public theology or civil religion to be invariably mythological.

In a recent issue of *First Things*, Keith Pavlischek observes that

Murray integrated with "polemical dexterity" three elements of public theology when he sought to give religion an ordering function in society, the undergirding of freedom in society, and the possibility of social justice—even if his overall attempt failed "to create a public theology that could halt 'the secularist drift' of modernity."[20] Perhaps this only means that Murray came too late upon the scene, and not that he lacked expertise as myth-maker. (Varro, too, came too late to save the civil theology of pagan Rome.)

In his *Public Philosophy Reader*, Richard Bishirjian reminds us that "ancient political communities were held together by myths that explained...community life in terms of the actions of the gods....In our era, political philosophy...has supplanted cosmological myth as the representative inquiry into public truth"—in normal times, I would add. But "we still articulate the substance of political order by means of myths that make our noetic understanding socially effective," and again I would add, especially in times of public emergency. Thus even today, Bishirjian concludes, public life cannot do without myth. He states this as one of several principles of public philosophy: "that the public philosophy...articulates the theological truths of our public myths." Plato coined the term *theology* "to express those truths...that would form the public myths." And "like other peoples, Americans share and celebrate the experience that their political order participates in a higher order...."[21]

If one approaches *We Hold These Truths* from this perspective, numerous passages light up a myth-making intention. Here are some examples: "I leave aside the practical issues that have arisen..."; this distinction has "always been difficult to maintain in practice, even when it was affirmed in theory"; "...concrete applications...have presented great historical and legal difficulties"; while a certain proposition may be demonstrable only to an extent, "this is a further question, [one] for the future to answer"; "today we are not looking for forces of dissolution, but for constructive forces.... We want liberty with a positive content...."[22]

It remains for me to provide a list of assumptions and assertions which Murray has woven into his version of the American civil theology—all of them (in my view) dubious and indemonstrable, but in Murray's skillful hands rendered plausible to the reader who shares his concern over the urgency of reuniting the country:

1   "We face a crisis that is new in history" (p. 24).

2 American political experience, unlike Europe's, has been spared ideological struggle (p. 73).

3 Americans are or may be treated as "a people" capable of organizing itself for unified historical action (p. viii).

4 Even more: Contemporary Americans are or may be considered to be the same people the Founding Fathers knew, or even Lincoln knew, when he spoke of "the American Proposition."

5 American citizens in general, and Catholics in particular, can articulate "the fundamental civil question, what are the truths we hold" (p. xi).

6 "The American Proposition" is a continuation of the classical and Christian tradition of civility; the principles of Western classical and Christian culture constitute the core of agreement by which the American people identify themselves. Even more: those principles were "further refined and developed in our own land" (pp. 10-11).

7 Americans no longer believe in the social contract doctrine; all of us take the family (for instance) to be a pre-civil society (p. 7).

8 "Only the theory of natural law is able to give an account of the public experience that is the public consensus" (p. 109).

9 The Scholastic tradition "has been formative of the liberal tradition of the West;" specifically, St. Thomas Aquinas was (in George Weigel's paraphrase of Murray's argument) "the real herald of the American experiment," and not the secularized Protestants who were formed in our colonial history (p. 22). [23]

10 "The American doctrine and project" has put "a new problem" to "the universal Church" in the matter of religious pluralism; in particular, "America has proved by experience that political unity and stability are possible without uniformity of religious belief and practice" (pp. xi, 72).

While Gould faults Murray for making so many undemonstrated assertions, I am simply trying to point out that philosophical demonstration is not germane to a political manifesto. Moreover, a number of the propositions I have just cited were more believable in 1960, and to more Americans, than they would be today.

On the basis of the foregoing assessment of Murray's intention and his achievement, I wish to conclude with some critical reflections.

Murray says that the reasoned dialogue he associates with "civility" is about the *res publica* or the *res populi*, but I submit that it must first deal with the *res aeterna*, the *res Dei*. As Plato shows, clarity about matters of the soul and the afterlife must precede and ground clarity about matters of the city in this life. I can agree with Murray that education is the principal subject of the civil dialogue, but for me it is an education which is more fundamental than the social acculturation that goes on in our schools.[24]

Murray might object that I underestimate what he considers the central fact about America: religious pluralism, and especially estrangement between Catholics and Protestants and between religious people and secularists. An *odium theologicum*, he says, has led to an *odium civile*.[25] I would respond that civility is threatened by something more profound than religious pluralism, seen as a sociological datum. And that is by philosophical error. As I see it, the crisis of America is, in the first instance, and always has been, a philosophical crisis, not a religious one; or rather, the problem of religion has a deeper philosophical root.

I think Murray's preoccupation with doctrinal and cultural pluralism along with freedom of expression and toleration (a great and popular issue at that time) is what threw him off the trail of what should preoccupy us more, that it is principally what causes his mythological project to be defective. It causes him to miss the significance for America of the deeper and more serious philosophical split between classical and modern views of man and society. He is certainly aware of that split and he even speaks of it in ominous tones, but it is nevertheless set aside as a distraction from his purpose. And so he finally argues that we ought to "limit the warfare" between divergent views in the interests of civility.[26] That, I fear, is his worst mistake, for the whole purpose of political philosophy is to enlarge the field of battle between opposing ideas, to illuminate the truth that is at stake. Yet Murray closes his Foreword with an appeal for "nicety" in practicing the civility required of Catholics in a pluralist society.[27] I think boldness is what our situation requires, but boldness need not be uncivil. Anyone who has tried to act as a convinced Catholic in American higher education for thirty years—and has survived to tell of it—knows the meaning of civil boldness and how effective it can be in befriending truth. It is not always polite to call error by its name, but it can be done with Murray's "cool reason," in ordered and friendly dialogue, with the passions well disciplined and narrow self-interest excluded—all of which belong to his notion of "civility."[28]

As Aleksandr Solzhenitsyn has argued, what is most vital to the future of our society is open battle with the Enlightenment program which is rapidly disintegrating as we continue down the path charted by John Dewey and his followers. Jude Dougherty thinks Murray wanted to focus on elements of Modernity which Catholics in America could live with, setting aside "the metaphysical and epistemological difference" between "a Dewey-type instrumentalism and an Aristotelian-Thomistic natural law outlook" in the interest of reaching a working agreement with the non-Catholic majority.

I maintain that a realist cannot "live with" any part of an erroneous philosophical doctrine, and moreover, that if a Catholic attempts to find such *a modus vivendi* he will necessarily eviscerate the practice of the Faith and render its social doctrine irrelevant to contemporary society. For this reason I believe Murray's project was misguided at its inception, no matter how well intended. Today at least, even if Murray and most Catholic intellectuals did not think so thirty years ago, our most pressing concern is not the renewal and defense of American democracy but the renewal and defense of the Catholic Faith in the face of an increasingly militant and unrestrained secular humanist culture which appears to have captured the minds and hearts—and bodies—of a majority of baptized Catholics in the U.S.A.[29] A very different crisis is upon us than the one Murray was reacting to in the l950's. He did detect its early warning signals,[30] but they were not strong enough to affect his project.

The Catholic Faith and philosophical tradition can certainly make a contribution to the reordering of public life in this and in every land, but it will not do this unless formidable minds and effective leaders are able and willing to face, unmask, and dispose of the philosophical errors that are embedded in the American civil religion. This is a task for demonstration, not mythology. The Church's understanding of the law of human nature and her ability to expound it does make her, in Weigel's words, "a potential leader in the search for a new public philosophy,"[31] but this can become actual only if she resorts to it in order to destroy the credibility of the erroneous philosophy of man and society which underlies the American Proposition and the currently reigning gnosis of pragmatism and positivism which grew out of that philosophy. Murray was right to argue for a revival of the natural law teaching, but it would be wrong to use it in effecting a compromise with American principles. Rather the natural law tradition ought to be asserted in its dramatic opposition to those principles.

Murray wanted to argue for a ground which he thought or hoped Catholics could occupy in common with non-Catholics so as to move the whole country closer to a realization of the myth of its foundational ideals. But as Gould points out, in going about this, Murray purposely obscured "important differences and tensions between Catholic social thought and liberal theory," and even more seriously, omitted making reference to "valuable resources within the Catholic tradition…which could serve as correctives to…contemporary liberalism." If the myth he defended "were to become widely accepted as being true, and…American public life became animated by the Catholic tradition of natural law [would this] really constitute the harmonization of Catholic and American principles? Only in a superficial fashion," Gould argues, I think correctly. "Any reconciliation between Catholic and American principles arrived at on such terms could not but be superficial and shallow; and if it were to occur it would almost certainly reflect values and understandings which were more American than Catholic." Even worse, Gould says:

> [T]o the extent that Catholics adopt [Murray's] understanding of the relation between Catholicism and America, they will tend to suppose not only that Catholic and American values are essentially compatible, but that whenever conflicts arise between them, primacy ought to be accorded to the American values. For all along the implication of Murray's insistence on the uniqueness of the American experience was that the wider Church, not excluding the Roman authorities, had much to learn from America.[32]

Perhaps Murray was influenced by the widespread anticipation among Catholic intellectuals that Vatican II was bound to produce a fundamental redirection of the Magisterium, and wanted to move it in a moderate direction on the basis of Catholic experience in America. But it is not exactly in the Jesuit tradition to engage in the construction and defense of myths, and this may be a reason why some Churchmen became suspicious of his intentions and why they may have thought him capable of doing more substantial and more reliable work on behalf of the Church.

If would be unfair to charge Murray with the responsibility for millions of defections of American Catholics and the scandalous public conduct of so many lay people and clerics who seem to think it is the American way to serve mammon *and* God and to render more and more of His things to Caesar as the price of social acceptance and electoral success. Murray would vigorously object to this "Catholicism of convenience,"[33] and even before Vatican II catalyzed the softheartedness that had been accumulating in the Church in the U.S., he was already fearful of a drift toward a greater exclusion of God from public life and morality. Ironically it was also in 1960 that the campaign of John F. Kennedy foreshadowed the secularized Catholic officials of the 80's and 90's who refuse to practice in public what they say they profess in private.

Nevertheless, there was nothing in the recent centuries of Church history that might have alerted Murray (or anyone) to the abrupt "betrayal of the clerks" that was about to occur in America and other Western countries. Hence it is not surprising if Murray was deceived by the external appearances of a solid orthodoxy (even in seminaries and colleges) when substantive commitment to the Faith was already seeping out of the lives of Catholics, lay and cleric. As Dougherty says, the defense of the Faith was not a great concern of Murray, at least in these essays, because he did not think it needed defending and could confidently be presupposed. He could even risk distorting it for his mythological purpose because he saw it as strong and invulnerable.[34]

But perhaps he could be held responsible, as Dougherty agrees, for not noticing that the "ill effects" of secularized pragmatism (he even called it "barbarous") could easily lead to public disaster if not effectively checked. What was more needed than Murray's project was a vigorous challenge of the erroneous premises of which he was aware. Had Murray been temperamentally and intellectually disposed to mount such a challenge he would not have been as popular as he was, and we may not be recalling him now. But perhaps it is simply that Murray was a publicist and not a political philosopher and that he could not have written a treatise as good or as effective as his manifesto.

Murray's lack of optimism "that the West could in the near future recover its patrimony" suggests to Dougherty that Murray suspected such a slippage was possible as did subsequently occur.[35] And so he did the best he could to ward it off by defending the myth (which so evidently needed defense) rather than the Faith (which apparently did not).

It was a gamble, as we can see by looking back upon it, and a gamble lost, in my view. The philosophical patrimony of Catholic tradition is, however, still ready to be called into active service on the battleground of truth. While the America we know today seems far less disposed for this battle than she was in 1960, Gould suggests at the end of his paper that if there is "anything resembling a Catholic moment in American life" today, and if it is "to take advantage of the resources of the Catholic tradition in anything like their fullness, it will…have to go beyond [Murray]—in some respects well beyond him."[36] And Bishirjian adds: "Public philosophy today…must grapple with…the anthropological truth of classical political philosophy [and the] theological truth that God is transcendent."[37] Murray was not disposed to grant the significance of the conflict between those truths and the ones we hold in our civil theology; instead he tried to pacify that conflict.

NOTES

1. George Weigel, *Catholicism and the Renewal of American Democracy* (Mahwah NJ: Paulist Press, 1989), especially Chap. 5: "John Courtney Murray and the Catholic Human Rights Revolution."
2. John Courtney Murray S.J., *We Hold These Truths*: *Catholic Reflections on the American Proposition* (New York: Sheed and Ward, 1960), p. 5.
3. William J. Gould, Jr., "The Challenge of Liberal Political Culture in the Thought of John Courtney Murray," American Political Science Association Annual Meeting, Sept. 1, 1990.
4. *Ibid.*, pp. 18-22.
5. *Ibid.*, p. 23.
6. *Ibid.*, p. 24.
7. Murray, pp. 76-77.
8. Jude P. Dougherty, "Freedom and Virtue: John Courtney Murray on the Truths We Hold," *The World and I*, V, 5 (May 1990) 495-509, pp. 495, 497, 498, 501.
9. Murray, p. 319.
10. *Ibid.*, p. 313.
11. *Ibid.*, p. 317.
12. Dougherty, pp. 498, 502.
13. Rev. Marvin O'Connell, "An Historical Perspective on Evangelization in the United States," Fellowship of Catholic Scholars Annual Convention, Sept. 22, 1990.
14. Keith J. Pavlischek, "The Real John Courtney Murray," *First Things*, 6 (October, 1990), 46-49, p. 49.
15. Murray, p. 12.

16. *Ibid.*, p. 69
17. *Ibid.*, p. 302.
18. Robert W. McElroy, *The Search for an American Public Theology: The Contribution of John Courtney Murray* (Mahwah NJ: Paulist Press, 1989); review by Pavlischek.
19. Robert Bellah, "American Civil Religion," National Endowment for the Humanities Summer Seminar, Berkeley, CA, 1976.
20. Pavlischek, 46, 48-49.
21. Richard J. Bishirjian, "The Nature of Public Philosophy," *A Public Philosophy Reader* (New Rochelle NY: Arlington House, 1978), pp. 17, 23-24; much of the inspiration for this work comes from the philosophical writings of Eric Voegelin.
22. Murray, pp. 48, 64, 67, 72-73, 319. Robert Reilly's contribution to this book offers an excellent example of this same kind of writing.
23. Weigel, pp. 20, 90, 172.
24. Murray, pp. 6-9.
25. *Ibid.*, pp. 15-21.
26. *Ibid.*, p. 23.
27. *Ibid.*, p. xii.
28. *Ibid.*, pp. 6-8.
29. Dougherty, p. 507. On p. 506 he summarizes the core article of this secular faith: The only bond of community is a "civic faith; religion (especially revealed religion) must be banished from the political sphere because of its divisiveness; "civil society is the highest societal form of human life," and "civil law...is the highest form of law"; there is "no eternal order of truth and justice"; there are "no universal verities which command assent, no universal moral law which requires obedience." With respect to the body, Dougherty observes that this analysis of society is "nowhere more evident than in the area of sexual morality. Sexual union has been made a purely personal affair, with society's interest down-played" (p. 499). This helps to explain why sexual morality is the area of Catholic teaching from which Catholics in America chiefly "dissent"—clergy no less than laity. Compromise on that point, on the pretext of being "faithful Americans," initiates further subsequent departures from adherence to the Faith.
30. See Murray, pp. 322 and 327, where he accurately summarizes the theory of "modern evolutionary scientific humanism" and its correlative "ethical relativism."
31. Paraphrased by Robert L. Spaeth in his review of Weigel's book: "Renewing the Civil Public Square," *The World and I*, IV, 5 (May 1989) 421-425, p. 423.
32. Gould, pp. 23, 24.
33. James O'Kane, "The State of Evangelization in the United States: A Sociologist's View," Fellowship of Catholic Scholars Annual Convention, Sept. 21, 1990.
34. Dougherty, pp. 497-498.
35. *Ibid.*, pp. 508, 509.
36. Gould, p. 25.
37. Bishirjian, p. 24.

4

John Courtney Murray and Christopher Dawson: The Pluralist Society or Jerusalem and Babylon?

by John J. Mulloy

*U*pon being asked to compose a paper dealing with John Courtney Murray and Christopher Dawson, I thought of my earlier recollections of Murray from many years ago. That is, that he was a man of very considerable optimism concerning the American Experiment, one who had failed to foresee the general moral collapse in American life which took place in the middle 1960's and thereafter. As I saw it, he had been so intent upon the value and importance of the American achievement in politics that he had not been able to foresee the manner in which America would be perverted to become the center for pornography and abortion, and for the rampant spread of homosexuality, and for the protection of these things by both media and government. He had not anticipated that the United States, which he had seen as inaugurating a new era in world history, would in a few years become the chief agency for the promotion of the killing of unborn infants in other parts of the world which still did not have the benefits of the American democratic experiment. He had not foreseen that the very idea of God and religion would become the object of bitter attack by certain well-financed and well-entrenched lobbying groups in the United States, whose influence was out of all proportions to their numbers. He had not anticipated that the Supreme Court, the unelected arm of our government, would in fact become a kind of super-legislature and be able to overturn whatever State laws it wished, and to impose on the Country at large its own view of what this Nation should become under its judicial oligarchy. Thus, it seemed to me, that Murray, writing in the 1950's (all of the papers in the 1960 volume, *We Hold These Truths*, were written in the preceding decade) had been unaware of the powerful forces at work in our society, which would negate his vision of the unique political achievement of the United States in world history.

Thus I think that John Courtney Murray was far too optimistic in his view of American society, possibly because of the general tendency of the Jesuits to downplay the effect of the Fall of Man on human nature and consequently on human society. I still think that he expected far too much of one particular political development in the history of the world, that of the United States, and that he was, perhaps unconsciously, influenced by the messianic dream which attached itself to America from its very origins.

Christopher Dawson, for example, gives one example of this messianic assertion on a religious context, that of the Puritans as they interpreted the significance of their coming to New England. He quotes a Puritan leader, coming to New England, of the seventeenth century as saying: "Know that this is the place where the Lord will create a new Heaven and a new Earth in new churches and a new Commonwealth together."[1]

Almost a century and a half later, the same note is again sounded, only now from the standpoint of the creation of a liberal Utopia. The following passage is from Thomas Paine's *Common Sense*, the pamphlet which seems to have played a decisive influence in leading the colonies to declare their independence from England. Paine writes:

> O ye that love mankind..., stand forth; every spot of the old world is overcome with oppression. Freedom has been hunted round the globe. Asia, Africa have long expelled her. Europe regards her like a stranger and England has given her warning to depart. O! Receive the fugitive and prepare in time an asylum for mankind.... We have it in our power to begin the world over again. A situation similar to the present hath not happened since the days of Noah until now. The birthday of a new world is at hand, and a race of men perhaps as numerous as all Europe contains are to receive their portion of freedom from the event of a few months.[2]

This conception of America has been shared by many Europeans as well as Americans; one recalls, for example, George Washington's reference to the United States as "the last, best hope of earth," and Thomas Jefferson's second inaugural address in which he sees the United States as bearing the responsibilities of a New Israel. A later statement of this idea is found in Herman Melville's view of the role of America, in a passage cited by Christopher Dawson. "We Americans," Melville writes, "are the peculiar chosen people—the Israel of our time; we bear the ark of the liberties of the world."[3] I have written about other expressions of this conception of America elsewhere.[4] Now against this background, we are perhaps better able to understand the inspiration for such statements as the following by John Courtney Murray:

"The free society...is a unique realization; it has inaugurated a new history. Therefore it might be possible within this new history to lay the ghosts of the past—to forget the ghettos and the autos-de-fe; the Star Chamber and the Committee on Public Safety; Topcliffe with his 'Bloody Question' and Torquemada with his rack," etc.[5]

Is this not in fact a contemporary echo—"Freedom has been hunted round the globe...Europe regards her like a stranger and England has given her warning to depart"—of Thomas Paine? And just as Paine's utopianism eventually had as its nemesis the French Revolution which Paine supported, leading on to the Reign of Terror, so the twentieth-century American dream led on to the killing of far more human lives by abortion than were killed by the French Reign of Terror. And the French people sickened of the Reign of Terror after a few years; but the American people have not sickened of the mass killing in which we are still engaged.

Here is another passage from Fr. Murray which has something of this messianic flavor to it:

> A new problem has been put to the universal Church by the fact of America—by the uniqueness of our social situation, by the genius of our newly conceived constitutional system, by the lessons of our singular national history, which has molded in a special way the consciousness and temper of the American people....[6]

Or, finally:

> America represents a human achievement of a unique kind, not paralleled in history. In a quite different sense from France, America has been revolutionary, the home of a revolution that at least claims to be permanent. The dynamism of this revolution has been an emphasis put by Americans on the assertion, which must be considered sincere and surely has been constant, of certain human values.[7]

There is no awareness here of the fact that slavery was an accepted institution of America for two hundred years, that it was maintained in America even after it had been abolished in other parts of the Western world, and that it was only brought to an end here by a bloody and fratricidal civil war. There is no anticipation of the blood of unborn infants into which the nation was to plunge itself in less than a decade and a half after his book was published. There is no thought that the "certain human values" to which Fr. Murray refers could easily be perverted to protect the sale of pornography and the sovereign right of the woman to kill the child in her womb. Are these indeed parts of the "new problem" which America was "to put to the universal Church," and which was to weigh heavily on the deliberations of Vatican Council II? Or was it the idea that America's conception of human values and their promotion must now be accepted as forming a unique achievement in world history, which the rest of the world, and the Church within it, must now be prepared to imitate? In better reality, of course, many of the countries of Europe and elsewhere have imitated the example we afforded them of the wholesale killing of the unborn. And in the case of the Third World we have pressured their governments to adopt this special form of murder.

Incidentally, was the proof of Murray's thesis dependent on using the example of France as the opposite of America, and ignoring political developments in England? It was, after all, from Great Britain that we borrowed many of the features of our constitutional government, including the bicameral legislature and a limited monarchy (the American president is a more powerful limited monarch than the English monarch soon became). It was from England that we derived many of our constitutional safeguards, including the idea of a Bill of Rights. And it was the English view that pure democracy may override personal freedom which led the Founding Fathers to hedge around both the Senate and the Presidency with certain barriers to direct democratic control. So, in judging the character and alleged uniqueness of the American Proposition, we must not allow our minds to be dominated by the polar opposites which Murray sets up of the American Proposition on the one hand and French Jacobinism on the other.

It is true that in certain parts of his work Murray recognizes the great importance of natural law and of the rights of man as derived from God. But I think he underestimates the way in which the drive for equality can overturn those human values which he cherishes. It would have been well, therefore, if he had reflected on the example afforded by English political life, and how, in the past, it had served to protect the rights of the individual against the leveling down tendency which Tocqueville saw as one of the chief dangers of America. Concerning this example Christopher Dawson wrote:

> The English tradition attaches far more importance to freedom and toleration than does the continental; it developed in defense of individual liberty (and also class privilege) against the State. Continental democracy, on the other hand, was essentially the affirmation of the supremacy of the General Will as against class privilege. It attached more importance to equality [than] to freedom and to the sovereignty of the people than to the toleration of minorities.[8]

Dawson continues on the need to maintain these values while adapting them to the changed social situation with which we are faced today:

> The English state in the past has been the classical example of that mixed constitution which was the political ideal of St. Thomas Aquinas. And just as it succeeded in developing self-government without abandoning the historic tradition of monarchy, so too English democracy must preserve the vital elements of the aristocratic tradition in so far as they can be adapted and reinterpreted according to the needs of our time. Above all the principles of personal honor and individual responsibility, which have always been the life blood of freedom in the ancient world and in medieval and modern Europe alike, must be preserved at all costs, if democracy is to be a community of free men and not an inhuman anonymous servile State.[9]

I should now like to note certain statements of Murray concerning the American Proposition with which I find Dawson to be in general agreement. Here is one of them:

> The first truth to which the American Proposition makes appeal is stated in that landmark of Western political theory, the Declaration of Independence. It is a truth that lies beyond politics; it imparts to politics a fundamental human meaning. I mean the sovereignty of God over nations as well as over individual men. This is the principle that radically distinguishes the conserva-

tive Christian tradition of America from the Jacobin laicist tradition of Continental Europe.[10]

He then gives quotations from presidential proclamations of John Adams and Abraham Lincoln to show how this view manifested itself in times of crisis. He might also have mentioned the powerful statement of this belief found in Lincoln's Second Inaugural Address, in which Lincoln sees the Civil War as a punishment upon both North and South for having allowed the existence of slavery in the nation for so long a time in our history. He might also have noted Jefferson's statement, "I tremble for our country when I consider that God is just," when he reflected upon the controversy over slavery at the time of the Missouri Compromise.

A second statement of Murray runs as follows:

> [T]he fact [is] that the American political community was organized in an era when the tradition of natural law and natural rights was still vigorous.... It still commanded universal acceptance. And it furnished the basic materials for the American consensus.[11]

Finally, there is this passage:

> Formally and in the first instance this consensus was political, that is, it embraced a whole constellation of principles bearing upon the origin and nature of society, the function of the state as the legal order of society, and the scope and limitations of government.[12]

Now to the degree that the principles on which the American Proposition is founded go back to the traditions of the Middle Ages and even to the time of Cicero, as Murray recognizes, the political institutions of America are much less new than he at times makes them out to be. Even the particular structures by which the United States attempted to realize these principles have their origins in European models. Thus there is a certain conflict between Murray's strong sense of the historical roots of the principles of the Founding Fathers and his messianic impulse to make out the United States and its institutions as something completely new in human history. I think this cleavage or conflict in Murray's thought is to be found in other aspects of it also.

Following is a statement of Christopher Dawson which parallels what we have quoted from John Courtney Murray:

> The American ideology on which the Constitution was based involved two essential and related concepts—in the first place the philosophy of Natural Law and Natural Rights and secondly the limitations of the

by which New England democracy had vindicated the rights of man.¹⁶ But I think the chief matter on which Dawson parts company with Murray is in Dawson's conception of the overwhelming pressure for the secularization of culture exerted by the modern technological order. He sees that pressure as the fundamental fact with which both social freedom and religious faith are confronted. Where Murray in some respects seems to be back in the eighteenth century, with society to be explained on the basis of rational principles, and the civil exchange of views among different parties as deciding policies, Dawson is much more aware of the irrational and non-rational elements in human society and he recognizes the strength of their influence upon the direction which society decides to take. It is true that Murray tells us that he is not "maintaining that civil society is a purely rational form of association." [17] But this disclaimer means little when we listen to his views concerning politics and how it is different from other elements in society. He writes:

The specifying note of political association is its rational deliberative quality, its dependence for its permanent cohesiveness on argument among men. In this it differs from all other forms of association found on earth.[18]

Or again he writes, "Hence the climate of the City is likewise distinctive. It is not feral or familial but forensic.... It is cool and dry, with the coolness and dryness that characterize good argument among informed and responsible men." [19] And further, "If then society is civil when it is formed by men locked together in argument, the question rises, what is the argument about?"[20]

Or he tells us, "On both of these titles, as a heritage and as a public philosophy, the American consensus needs to be constantly argued." [21] He implies in his next sentence that, unless this is done, it will die out. But surely a constant process of argument about fundamental principles, such as is embodied in "a heritage and a political philosophy," is quite likely to undermine them. Why should one not come to doubt those basic principles, as constant argument about them casts doubt on their validity? Hasn't Murray become so enchanted with the idea of rational argumentation that he fails to see that there are definite limits to it, beyond which it leads to skepticism?

This is one part of Murray's analysis of what he thinks American society *is* based upon. But when we look further at his description of the elements that constitute the American social scene, we find very little correspondence to this "cool and dry" attitude which he claims should constitute American politics and civil society. When we read his description of the different contending groups he identifies and the quite different views they have of how society should be organized, and the distrust and often animosity with which they regard other's beliefs, we are bound to ask: How does John Courtney Murray erect this super-structure of cool rationalism on the welter of hotly contending forces which lie just underneath it as its foundation? It is Murray's identification of these other elements, described in realistic terms, which makes us wonder if this is not something schizophrenic about Murray's conception of American society. I mentioned at the beginning of this paper my idea, based on past reading of his work and now recollected many years later, that Murray was unduly optimistic about the nature of American society, but in fact there would seem to be two Murrays, each one clashing with the other, in his chapter in *We Hold These Truths* on "The Civilization of the Pluralist Society." We have the eighteenth century rationalist on the one hand and the twentieth century realist on the other. As an example of the latter, consider the following statements:

> This is the pluralist society as it is encountered on the level of intellectual experience. We have no common universe of discourse. In particular, diverse mental equivalents attach to all the words in which the constitutional consensus must finally be discussed—truth, freedom, justice, prudence, order, law, authority, power, knowledge, certainty, unity, peace [etc.].... Our intellectual experience is one of sheer confusion, in which soliloquy succeeds to argument.[22]

Or consider another factor that goes counter to cool and intelligent discussion:

> We more or less share the short segment of history known as America. But all of us have had longer histories, spiritual and intellectual.[23]

He also says the following:

> The fact of our discrepant histories creates the second experience of the pluralist society. We are aware that we not only hold different views but have become different kinds of men as we have lived our several histories. Our styles of thought and of interior life are as discrepant as

our histories. The more deeply they are experienced and the more fully they are measured, the more do the differences among us appear to be almost unbridgeable.[24]

Or, as we recall that civility is necessary for the rational argument which Murray thinks constitutes the political City, consider this analysis which appears to make any such argument impossible:

> The fact is that among us civility—or civic unity or civic amity, as you will—is a thing of the surface. It is quite easy to break through it. And when you do, you catch a glimpse of the factual reality of the pluralist society...our pluralist society has received its structure through wars and...wars are still going on beneath a fragile surface of more or less forced urbanity.... We are not really a group of men singly engaged in the search for truth, relying solely on the means of persuasion, entering into dignified communication with each other, content politely to correct opinion with which we do not agree. As a matter of fact, the variant ideas and allegiances among us are entrenched as social powers; they occupy ground; they have developed interests, and they possess the means to fight for them.[25]

If one were to seek for someone to combat the ideas which Fr. Murray has advanced concerning the rational argument which constitutes political association, could he have found a better adversary to controvert this view than Murray himself and what he here tells us? How does one explain such a complete contradiction in Murray's thought on American society? Did he suddenly realize the abstraction of his view of politics as rational argument? Was this his reason, in writing his Introduction, for deciding to throw in a considerable amount of realism to counterbalance it? Whatever the explanation, the contradiction between one and the other view seems irreconcilable.

Or take this statement of Murray's on what is needed for the effective working out of democratic government, a statement which seems true enough, but is seemingly impossible to attain if one is dealing with entrenched interests to whom moral principles are no more than counters in a game. Murray writes:

> In any phase civil society demands order. In its highest phase of freedom it demands that order should not be imposed from the top down, as it were, but should spontaneously flower outward from the free obedience to the restraints and imperatives that stem from inwardly

possessed moral principle. In this sense democracy is more than a political experiment; it is a spiritual and moral enterprise. And its success depends upon the virtue of the people who undertake it. Men who would be politically free must discipline themselves.... Political freedom is endangered in its foundations as soon as the universal moral values, upon whose shared possession the self-discipline of a free society depends, are no longer vigorous enough to restrain the passions and shatter the selfish inertia of men.[26]

If that is what democracy requires, does it not seem obvious that there exists no such possession of shared moral values in America today? Why, then, speak about rational argument as though this in fact constitutes the political City today when its very foundations have been destroyed? What shared moral values does the Christian have with the pornographer, the homosexual, and the murderer of unborn children? Is not the appearance of social order merely a facade covering up the bitterness of ideological warfare which already counts its unborn victim in the millions, and its spiritual casualties in who knows how many lives ruined by pornography, homosexuality and the promotion of sexual activity through the public schools?

It is for this reason that I think Murray's own realistic analysis shows us that ours is not really a pluralist society as he sought to describe it. It is not a matter of Catholic, Protestant, Jew and secularist being the four major elements in society, each striving to achieve some kind of reconciliation with the other. What we have is not four different conspiracies, as Murray calls them, but a spiritual life and death struggle for the soul of America between secularism on the one hand and the Judaeo-Christian tradition on the other. And, as Catholics know only too well from their experience in the post-Vatican II period, the disciples of a secularized culture and a secularized religion are quite active and prominent within the Church herself. The same division is also present in other religious communities, whether Protestant or Jewish, so that the issue of basic religious values versus the surrender to the world cuts across the lines of all religious denominations. So, while there are important differences still dividing Protestant and Catholic, and Christian and Jew, they have become far less important than this fundamental line of cleavage on whether God or the spirit of the world is to have our primary allegiance.

And here it is, I think, that Dawson's work brings out the nature of that conflict and what are the stakes involved in it, far more than does the thought of John Courtney Murray. Writing in the same decade as that in which the Murray articles were published which form the basis for *We Hold These Truths*—that is, the decade of the l950's—Dawson was aware of the tremendous pressure for conformity to the world which modern secularized culture places upon any religious group. And, as a corollary to that, he was aware of the fact that most Christians and Jews are deeply secularized in their outlook upon life, because of the social environment in which they live and breathe. And this applies also to some degree even to those who wish to remain faithful to their religious traditions.

Following is a passage from an article published in 1954, in which Dawson takes issue with the idea of a pluralist society, an idea not restricted to John Courtney Murray, but having a much wider acceptance:

> For modern culture is not pluralistic in character, as some social scientists have assumed; on the contrary, it is more unitary, more uniform, and more highly centralized and organized than any culture the world has known hitherto. And modern education has been one of the major forces in producing this, since it brings the whole of the younger generation under the same influences and ideas during the most impressionable period of their lives....
>
> Now the problem is that while culture and society are unitary, *religion* is pluralistic, most of all perhaps in the United States, and this makes it exceedingly difficult for any particular religion like Catholicism to stand out against the pervasive and overwhelming pressure of the "common way of life." This is why the problem of Christian culture is of such paramount importance, for unless Christians are able to defend their cultural traditions they will not be able to survive. It is necessary not only to show the dangers to human values inherent in our modern unitary culture, but also the positive values of the Christian cultural tradition and its universal significance.
>
> Thus a realistic approach to the problem demands first and foremost a clear recognition of the contradiction and conflict between our unitary culture and our Christian tradition. For in this unitary culture there is little room for the concepts which are fundamental to the

Catholic or Christian view—the supernatural, spiritual authority, God and the soul—in fact, the whole notion of the transcendent. So, unless students can learn something of Christian culture as a whole—the world of Christian thought and the Christian way of life and the norms of the Christian community—they are placed in a position of cultural estrangement—the social inferiority of the ghetto without its old self-containedness and self-sufficiency.[27]

If the situation is such as Dawson here describes it— and remember that this was written well before the sexual revolution of the 1960's and 1970's had brought about the moral collapse of our society—then we are faced with quite a different condition than that which Fr. Murray's rational argument between civilly contending groups projects for us. As Murray himself recognized in his more realistic phase of analysis of American society, the contending parties are much more strongly opposed to each other and much less given to civility in dealing with ideas opposed to their own, than Murray's "Civilization of the Pluralist Society" would lead us to expect. What has happened in the last thirty years has been an intense sharpening of the conflict and the advocacy of policies and practices which in the past would have been regarded as an outrageous violation of all civilized norms. Who then would have thought that homosexuality would be held up as an acceptable alternative lifestyle and efforts made to have it promoted by means of government policy and public school support of it? Who then would have expected that Catholic priests would in large numbers be charged with homosexual practice, and that these or other priests would be speaking of the vileness of homosexual erotic activity as an enriching spiritual experience? Who would have expected that the killing of unborn infants would have become a standard part of the American way of life, and that any attempt to change this would be bitterly resisted as an infringement on the woman's right of free choice—that is, her choice to kill the child in the womb? To see how much the pressure of secularized culture has made abortion seem more acceptable, go back to the statements of some thirty leading cardinals and bishops on the morrow of the Supreme Court decision to legalize abortion (these were printed in the *Wanderer* in early February 1973), with their sense of moral outrage and imminent disaster for our nation; and then compare with the reluctance and unwillingness of many if not indeed most American bishops today to mount any effective action against pro-abortionists, whether in politics or in the medical industry that makes its livelihood from abortion. This is a living witness to how much a secularized civilization exercises an eroding influence on the moral conscience of Christians, even on those whose position gives them the opportunity for moral leadership and the forceful expression of what has been consistent Christian teaching throughout the ages.

I think the scene has shifted so enormously and so radically since John Courtney Murray wrote these articles in the 1950's that we need to think of a quite different model in order to understand the position of Christianity in our society. That model was suggested by Christopher Dawson in this same decade of the 1950's. He wrote:

> The margin between the old forms of liberal or social democracy and this new Leviathan is growing narrower every year. Hence we can hardly doubt that when ultimately a conflict takes place between the new state and the Christian church, it will be far more severe in character than anything that has been known before....
>
> Here again the trend of events is following the same pattern as in the early days of Christianity. Nothing was clearer to the Christians of that age than the imminence of a tremendous trial, in which the mystery of iniquity that was already at work in the world would come out into the open and claim to stand in the place of God Himself. It was with the constant awareness of this coming catastrophe that the new Christian way of life took form, and it was this that made the Christian belief in a new life and in the coming of a new world, not an expression of other-worldly pietism, but an active preparation for vast and immediate historical changes.[28]

If this is the case, then our most immediate task must be to deepen our sense of the Christian way of life, of Christian culture as a social reality which stands forth against the secularization of modern culture and which meets and responds to the secular ideologies at every point in which they challenge the Christian Faith. Because of the weakness of the institutional Church, its failure to give effective leadership and its deep infiltration by the values of the secular city, we must be prepared to act with some degree of independence in this matter. We must be prepared to form associations on our own that will reinforce the practice of the Christian way of life and deepen our understanding of it on the intellectual and historical-cultural levels as well as the spiritual one. Whether this is to be accomplished through family life apostolate, home schooling, discussion groups, colleges and universities faithful to the Magisterium of the Church, sound Catholic publishing houses, participation in the pro-life effort or efforts to prevent the spread of pornography—such choices will depend upon the particular talents and opportunities of the individual person. But at the center of all these activities and giving unifying purpose to them, there must be the reinforcement of the Christian family and its commitment to the practice of the Christian way of life. There can be no effective witness of Christianity in society if the family is given over to secularized purposes and pursuits. Consequently, the family is where the battle for the future of American society will be fought out. It will be no easy battle and the odds against it seem great. In fact, the existence of the Church in this country may well depend upon its outcome. Christopher Dawson points out what is at stake:

> In the past, as for instance under the Roman Empire, the family formed an independent society which was almost immune from the state, so that it could become the primary cell of an unrecognized Christian society or culture. But today the very existence of the family as a social unit is threatened by the all pervasive influence of the state and the secular mass culture. Yet without the Christian family there can be no Christian community life and indeed no church in the traditional sense of the word: only a few scattered individuals who maintain an isolated prophetic witness, like Elias in the wilderness.[29]

But if the Christian family does survive, by deepening its awareness of the riches of Christian culture, and thus countering the attempts of the mass media and the mass culture to subvert it, then a new prospect opens up before us. Christopher Dawson describes what that prospect is:

> If society were once again to become Christian, after a generation or two or after ten or twenty generations, this sacred tradition [of the Faith] would once more flow out into the world and fertilize the culture of societies yet unborn. Thus the movement toward Christian culture is at one and the same time a voyage into the unknown, in the course of which new worlds of human experience will be discovered, and a return to our own fatherland—to the sacred tradition of the Christian past which flows underneath the streets and cinemas and skyscrapers of the new Babylon as the tradition of the patriarchs and

prophets flowed beneath the palaces and amphitheaters of Imperial Rome.[30]

NOTES

1. Quoted in Dawson, Christopher, *Understanding Europe* (New York and London: Sheed and Ward, 1952), p. 161.
2. *Ibid.*, p. 167, quote.
3. *Ibid.*, p. 174.
4. See Mulloy, John J., "The American Revolution and the French Revolution, *The Wanderer*, July 27, 1989 & Aug. 3, 1989.
5. Murray, John Courtney, *We Hold These Truths: Catholic Reflections on the American Proposition.* (New York and London: Sheed and Ward, 1960), p. 24.
6. *Ibid.*, p. 27.
7. *Ibid.*, p. 177.
8. Dawson, Christopher, *Beyond Politics* (New York and London: Sheed and Ward, 1939), p. 41.
9. *Ibid.*, pp. 48-49.
10. Murray, p. 28.
11. *Ibid.*, p. 30.
12. *Ibid.*, p. 31.
13. Dawson, Christopher, *The Crisis of Western Education* (New York and London: Sheed and Ward, 1961; Steubenville, OH: Franciscan University Press, 1989), p. 183.
14. *Ibid.*, p. 185.
15. Dawson, Christopher, "Europe and Christendom," *The Dublin Review*, Oct. 1941.
16. Dawson, Christopher, *The Gods of Revolution* (New York: New York University Press, 1972), p. 46.
17. Murray, p. 7.
18. *Ibid.*, p. 6.
19. *Ibid.*, p. 7.
20. *Ibid.*, p. 8.
21. *Ibid.*, p. 11.
22. *Ibid.*, p. 16.
23. *Ibid.*
24. *Ibid.*, p. 17.
25. *Ibid.*, pp. 18-19.
26. *Ibid.*, pp. 36-37.
27. *The Crisis of Western Education*, pp. 146-147.
28. Dawson, Christopher, *The Historic Reality of Christian Culture* (New York: Harper and Row, 1960), p. 27.
29. *Ibid.*, p. 42.
30. *Ibid.*, pp. 29-30.

5

We Hold These Truths and More: Further Catholic Reflections on the American Proposition

*By Donald J. D'Elia**

When Ralph Waldo Emerson was visiting England in 1848, the American poet tells us in his book, *English Traits*, he was asked by Thomas Carlyle and other friends "whether there were any Americans?—any with an American idea—any theory of the right future of that country?"[1]

Englishmen, Frenchmen, Italians, it has been said, do not feel compelled to explain what their countries are all about—what John Courtney Murray would call their national "Proposition." But they do expect a self-justification of America; and on that summer day in 1848 Emerson felt compelled to give one to Carlyle and his circle of brilliant friends. Other thoughtful Americans do too; and this has never been more the case than today when the United States has become for millions and millions of people simply a place to live and pay taxes.

One can hardly imagine an Emerson or a Carlyle discussing the "American idea" and the "right future" of the United States in the world of the late twentieth century; or even men with the remarkable personalities of an Emerson or a Carlyle. The Hegelian God-state or, better, God-society has triumphed. State and society exist for themselves, not for God and man, giving man—in Hegelian terms—whatever "worth" or "spiritual reality" he possesses.[2]

There is no moral law, universal and immutable, no Emersonian conscience to guide man. Instead, as the founder of American legal pragmatism and Hegelian, Justice Oliver Wendell Holmes, Jr. decreed, there is only the morality of the community, what Will Herberg was later to call the democratic religion of "the American Way" of life.

---

*The author of this paper is indebted to Dr. John J. Mulloy, who introduced so many of us to the thought of Christopher Dawson.

What Murray and others feared, the complete "loss of identity," seems to have taken place. American national existence has become an end in itself, its own absolute. No longer can America claim with the Pilgrims and the countless millions who have lived here to be the New Israel, knowing only one Absolute, one God.[3]

But in 1776, when Emerson's grandfather was a Congregationalist minister and zealous patriot in Concord, the whole Revolutionary generation was asking itself Thomas Carlyle's question of "whether there were any Americans?—any with an American idea—any theory of the right future of the country?"

What was the "American idea" in 1776? Or, to use the language of John Courtney Murray almost two centuries later, "What were the truths Americans held at the founding of the nation?"[4] What was and is the "American Proposition?" What is the real patrimony of the American Revolution? When we put aside historicism and all the modern relativisms that rob the events of our national past of their proper character, only then can we begin to understand the meaning of America in 1776—and today. This may be "the most difficult thing in the world," as Hilaire Belloc cautions us, but we must try to see events as contemporaries saw them, otherwise the past will be distorted beyond all recognition, as is pretty much the case already in our textbooks. "Anybody can make history," said Oscar Wilde, "only a great man can write it."

Father John Courtney Murray's *We Hold These Truths: Catholic Reflections on the American Proposition*, appeared in the year the first Catholic, John Fitzgerald Kennedy, was elected President of the United States.[5] This fact, whatever else is said, makes Murray's collection of thirteen previously published occasional essays a rewarding study in political and religious sociology. Moreover, there is a polemical dimension to his writing, and this should be taken into account in any evaluation of the book.

But the question I should like to address as a historian is much simpler. It is the question about the "American idea," i.e., the question about what conception the American people had at the Founding that, in Murray's words, "constituted us a people organized for action in history."[6] My comments will have to be brief and somewhat impressionistic, given the limitations of space. But it is my hope that they will reflect many years of study in the field of the American Revolution and have heuristic value for other students.

The contents of the public consensus at the time of the American Founding, writes Murray, were the "principles and doctrines" of "Western constitutionalism, classic and Christian."[7] These truths are our patrimony, and their vitality can be preserved in the public mind only by argument. "In the public argument there must consequently be a continued recurrence to first principles," he goes on. "Otherwise the consensus may come to seem simply a projection of ephemeral experience, a passing shadow on the vanishing backdrop of some given historical scene, without the permanence proper to truths that are 'held.'"[8]

That the principles and doctrines of Western constitutionalism, as seen in the Declaration of Independence and the federal and state constitutions, and a public philosophy resting on a realist epistemology inspired the American Founding cannot be doubted. And perhaps Murray was right to think in the days before *Roe v. Wade* that the Catholic Church could best contribute to public ethical discourse in an increasingly de-Christianized society by appealing to philosophy alone, rather than to faith, reason, and the ancient pre-Reformation fullness of the Church's tradition.[9]

But it is also true, as John A. Coleman, S.J., notably has suggested, that Murray, by not including religious symbolism and biblical imagery, and arguing only from the tradition of reason in his discussion of the American Proposition, has exaggerated the influence of liberal public philosophy and individualism in the creation of the American nation.[10] The fact is, to take Coleman's point further, that the Christian faith, religious symbolism and theological discourse of the Revolutionary generation have not only been neglected by the author of *We Hold These Truths*, even though he was—after all—a theologian. American historians of the 18th century, who should know better, continue even today to impose their own highly secularized, reductionist categories of understanding on the rich American past.[11]

Having made these preliminary observations, that the Murray thesis errs in reading too much into the public philosophy of the Founding generation and leaving out altogether the public theology, I will use the time that remains to suggest the importance of the latter in the shaping of the "American idea." But in all this we should keep in mind that Murray's argument, that America needs a public philosophy based on natural law, does not stand or fall with his interpretation of the Founding Fathers.[12]

It is anachronistic to think, as Murray seems to do, that the founding generation did not believe that government must submit to divine positive law. Here the author confuses the Enlightenment minimalistic natural law views of Thomas Jefferson and a relatively small group of Founders with the consensus of the overwhelming majority of the American people in 1776 and 1789 that the state indeed has an obligation to worship God or perish. The Declaration of Independence and the Federal Constitution, as well as the state constitutions, however they may be celebrated and interpreted in liberal historiography today, were seen at the time as having meaning only within the much larger "oral constitution" of what was a Christian culture—not an Enlightenment culture![13] These charters, important as they were, were never intended to be made into absolutes. The Declaration of Independence, for example, was seldom invoked at the Constitutional Convention, in the pages of the *Federalist Papers*, or by delegates to the ratifying conventions.[14] The point is, that for practically everyone in that generation, it was still their Christian culture that endowed documents with meaning.

Dr. Benjamin Rush (1745-1813) of Philadelphia signed the Declaration of Independence, but his understanding of its meaning as an evangelical Protestant was very different from that of his secular-minded friend, Thomas Jefferson. The "unalienable Rights" of the Declaration, Rush believed with many, many other Americans, were bestowed on man not mediately by some abstraction called nature in the Jeffersonian and Lockean sense, but directly and immediately by the living God. This was no dogmatic individualism! "Self-existence," he protested against the eighteenth century spirit of presumption that would culminate in the French Revolution, "belongs only to God." The "language" of American independence, Rush wrote in 1783 to his English Quaker friend, Granville Sharp,

> has for many years appeared to me to be the same as that of the heavenly host that announced the birth of the Saviour of mankind. It proclaims "glory to God in the highest—on earth peace—good will to man." [15]

How foolish it was, how presumptuous it was, to think that some autonomous Jeffersonian man had brought this about, relying only on natural reason! Fulton J. Sheen was much closer to the truth about the meaning of the Declaration of Independence to the American people at the nation's Founding. While no friend of Catholicism, such as he understood it, Dr. Rush would have agreed with the Bishop's characterization of the Declaration of Independence as also a Declaration of Dependence. "The Declaration of Independence," Sheen had the historical insight to realize, "asserts a double dependence: dependence on God, and dependence on law as derived from God….

> Read the Declaration of Independence and there find the answer: [I might add to the nature of the "American idea"] "We hold these truths to be self-evident, that all men are created equal, that they are *endowed by their Creator* with certain unalienable Rights, that among these are Life, Liberty and the pursuit of Happiness." Notice these words: *The Creator has endowed men with rights and liberties*; men got them from God! In other words, we are dependent *on God*, and that initial dependence is the foundation of our independence. [16]

Everyone in the country in 1776, except for a decided minority of men like Jefferson and Thomas Paine who mocked revealed religion, understood the Declaration and the constitution of the United States, including the Federal charter, in this way. Rush believed that the hand of God was to be seen in the Federal Constitution, as much as it had been in His dividing the Red Sea to give a passage to the children of Israel.[17] The divine character of the new government of the United States was professed from a thousand pulpits, and one did not have to look far to see this confirmed in newspapers and magazines.

M.E. Bradford has shown that, out of the fifty-five men who signed the proposed Federal Constitution in 1787, no fewer than fifty were members of established Christian communions. Nearly thirty of them were not just active, but extremely active in the administration and growth of their churches.[18] Benjamin Franklin proclaimed himself a deist, but he was no Thomas Paine, and the good Doctor urged public prayer at the Philadelphia Convention, attended religious services, and was generous in contributing to the many churches in the City. "If men are so wicked as we now see them *with religion*," he told a would-be author, probably Paine, who was attacking organized religion, "what would they be if *without it*?" "Talking against religion is unchaining a tiger," Dr. Franklin liked to say, "the beast let loose may worry his deliverer."[19] Even "deists," a very imprecise term in any case that has been much over-used, generally accepted traditional Christian metaphysics and epistemology in a pre-Kantian American culture.

Except for the few Catholics—perhaps as many as 20,000 out of a population of less than 5,000,000—Americans were not men of the ancient Faith. But there was still in eighteenth century America much that was left of the historic reality of Christian culture.[20] Antinomianism, with its Hutchinsonian theology of continuous revelation, was ever threatening; yet it was still held in check, as Alexis de Tocqueville was later to point out, by public opinion.[21] The social way of life, to use Christopher Dawson's standard for a Christian culture, was still largely based on the Christian faith.[22] Most Americans, fragmented as they were in their sectarianism, possessed even in schism that "rich and vivid vision of reality" which is the hallmark of Christian culture.[23] The "American Proposition," I have been arguing right along, simply cannot be understood in its integrity without that Christian vision of reality. The social and political symbols of the American Founding took their meaning from it.

The swelling numbers of the bourgeoisie, with their "stale and superficial" world-view, had not yet succeeded completely in separating faith and reason, religion and culture.[24] When that happened, it was Thomas Jefferson's American Revolution that became normative—not Benjamin Rush's. What John Henry Newman called the "goodly framework of society which is the creating of Christianity" was still in place in the period of the nation's Founding.[25] Religion was the "bond of society," and real law of the land, not, what was often ridiculed as "parchment" constitutionalism. Tocqueville was right to say, and many years had passed from the creating of the Republic when he said it, that the Christian religion was "the foremost of the *political* institutions of the United States (my italics).[26] The "conscious moral effort" of American society in 1776 and 1789 was, in any case, largely "inspired by Christian ideas and directed to Christian ends," to borrow the words of Christopher Dawson in his description of Christian England. As in that country, secular Liberalism was soon to triumph, with its principle of utility.[27]

In 1776, though, Dr. Benjamin Rush was representative of the great majority of Americans in giving explicit Christian and biblical meaning to the Declaration of Independence and all the other national and state charters that were to follow. They were covenants, having a solemn religious character as among the ancient Hebrews, no mere secular contracts or Lockean compacts. Their model, whether consciously realized or not, was that of the Pilgrim Fathers in 1620, applying ideas of church government to civil government. Only the Anglicans to some extent, were exempted from what Perry Miller has called the "Federal or Covenant Theology," the American people's intense awareness of their being "a chosen race, entered into specific covenant with God, by the terms of which they would be proportionately punished for their sins."[28] The symbols of the covenant and "jeremiad," that popular recital of the Chosen People's sins, were what mattered. Even "British liberties" and the social and political philosophy of John Locke made sense only within this *Gestalt*.[29]

Liberal as well as pietist Calvinists hailed the Continental Congress' appeal to the states to encourage "true religion and good morals."[30] On June 12, 1775 the Congress recommended to the states that July 20 be set aside as "a day of public humiliation, fasting, and prayer."

> …that we may with united hearts and voices unfeignedly confess and deplore our many sins, and offer up our joint supplications to the all-wise, omnipotent, and merciful Disposer of all events: humbly beseeching Him to forgive our iniquities, to remove our present calamities, to avert those desolating judgments with which we are threatened….[31]

No less than three times during the war Congress declared Fast Days for prayers and contrition.[32] Only a crude Marxist could dismiss this as a clever manipulation of the Christian belief system.[33]

Clearly, something other than Jefferson's "cold philosophy" of the Enlightenment was involved here. Benjamin Rush's public theology, if you will, was shared to a large degree by the American people at large, who sought "to discover and communicate the socially significant meanings of Christian symbols and tradition."[34] Their doctrine of man, for example, derived not from Enlightenment rationalism but from the biblical sources of the Great Awakening and the older Aristotelian-Thomist tradition of the West.[35]

Man for Rush and most of his Revolutionary generation was made for God in the Hebrew and Augustinian sense that, without Him, the human person was incomplete and even deformed. Consciously or not, Christ for them was the ideal man on whom they must model themselves. In Rush's view, the American Revolution was to be the historic opportunity for regenerated men, men like himself of "new heart" and "new spirit," to found the New Jerusalem here in America, as Jonathan

Edwards and other holy men of the Great Awakening had prophesied.[36]

There was no "right to life" in the Lockean and Jeffersonian manner of speaking, nor were there autonomous rights to liberty and the pursuit of happiness. Christ was the " 'life of the world,' 'the prince of life,' and 'Life' Itself, in the New Testament," Rush wrote in his *Three Lectures Upon Animal Life*.[37] Man did not exist in himself: he was a relation to God. Rush, while more articulate in his political anthropology than millions of his compatriots, was like them in still thinking of man as made in the Image and Likeness of God, absolutely dependent upon His life-breath, and subject to His government.[38]

Jefferson, on the other hand, as a Modern thinker according to the classic definition of Romano Guardini, was untypical of Americans at the time in his ancient Greek and Renaissance understanding of man in the abstract.[39] This presumptuous way of thinking about man as an absolute would find its bloody climax in the French Revolution which, as Ross J.S. Hoffman so very well points out, must not be confused with the conservative American Revolution.[40] Jefferson's philosophical friend, English-born Tom Paine, may have written the *Age of Reason*: Benjamin Rush's in-law and president of the Continental Congress, Elias Boudinot, answered Paine and other deists with his *The Age of Revelation*.[41] This is important to know.

As for the "right to liberty," this too was to be understood according to the ultimate, religious norm of the society. "Where the Spirit of the Lord is, there is liberty" (2 Cor. 3). Central to this political anthropology was the biblical love of God and one's fellow man as the absolute criterion of all human life. The Jeffersonian language of the Declaration was understood by most Americans in the Judeo-Christian context of man's recognition of his dependence on God, rather than the Enlightenment's of making man "a limited god in opposition to God—a rebellion he could not accomplish if he were not free, or if there were no God."[42]

We cannot address here the serious problem of reconciling this "freedom," indispensable to democracy, with orthodox Calvinism—a problem that Isaac Hecker saw very clearly in the next century.[43]

Rush found his solution in the doctrine of Universalism.[44] The great majority of Americans never seem to have confronted the problem, or avoided it altogether by embracing Arminianism as a substitute for the Catholic doctrine of free will.

I have discussed Rush's political and social theology at length elsewhere, a theology in which the new republican government and progressive evangelization of America would lead to the restoration of all things in Christ and the millennial reign of Love Himself.[45] Jonathan Edwards and the other Great Awakeners had also called for a new Christendom in the land to be established by re-born men who made up the "Party of Christ."[46] The Christian ethos of love, declared one prominent evangelical minister in 1784, in the Great Awakening tradition, would soon create "ONE GREAT REPUBLIC," with "ONE HEART AND ONE LIFE."[47] Alan Heimert in his encyclopedic, *Religion and the American Mind: From the Great Awakening to the Revolution* (1966), has demonstrated just how widespread these views were among evangelical nationalists.[48]

Indeed, Rush harkened back to seventeenth century Puritanism in describing himself at the end of the century as not a Republican or a Federalist but a "Christocrat," a latter-day Fifth Monarchyman who believed that the Holy Community, with Christ as its Head, would soon be realized in America.[49] Any number of articles in contemporary magazines and newspapers like the *American Museum* and the *Pennsylvania Packet*, written by both ministers and laymen, reveal how strong millennialism was *vis-a-vis* Enlightenment rationalism and naturalism. Even as late as 1831, Tocqueville saw that the pulpit was the "most powerful single force in America for the creation and control of public opinion,"[50] and there is a whole literature of travel accounts by Europeans that supports this. Americans interpreted events, political and otherwise, in the biblical images, language, and style of their seventeenth century forefathers. The ultimate norms of American society remained moral and religious, but the trend to secularization was growing fast. Politics and economics were not yet autonomous.

Writing of the "translation of the conception of the Holy Community from an ecclesiastical ideal to a principle of revolutionary political action" during the Cromwellian Commonwealth, Christopher Dawson argued that Puritanism's

> religious impulse opened the way for a new type of civilization based on the freedom of the person and of conscience as rights conferred absolutely by God and Nature. The connection is seen most clearly in America where the Congregationalist Calvinism of New England which was a parallel development to the Independent

power of the State which left the individual citizen free to lead his own life and organize his economic and cultural activities.[13]

A little further on, Dawson remarks:
> The study of Christian culture in the American Catholic college...should devote special attention to the problem of the Enlightenment and the way in which the doctrines of natural law and the theory of the limited state had their original roots in the Christian tradition.[14]

Then there is another passage by Dawson, written about 1941, in which he seems to go far towards agreement with Murray on the importance and newness of what America was striving to realize:
> It is true that the actual founders of the United States were men of the Enlightenment, and it is easy to interpret the Declaration of Independence and the State Constitutions exclusively in terms of eighteenth century rationalism. Nevertheless, the fact remains that the fundamental principle of the whole American system is a religious one—the divine right of the human person against political power and social privilege and economic interests.
>
> It was on the basis of this principle that the United States established their new order—an order which was intended to give every man political freedom and an opportunity of a full human life—a good life in the Aristotelian sense. And consequently, during the nineteenth century, America was the promised land of all the oppressed and disinherited peoples and classes and individuals in Europe. It was literally a New World in which the injustices and inequalities of the Old World were redressed. It is only during the present century that the closing of the frontiers and the contracting of space by the new modes of transport have brought Americans back into the Old World to face the same problems as the rest of us.[15]

It is true that Dawson is not always so inclined to praise the social achievement of America. Speaking of the French intelligentsia of the eighteenth century Enlightenment and their desire to see in America the ideal society of their own utopian hopes, Dawson writes:
> [They envisioned] a social order based on natural principles and inspired by a spirit of fraternity and equality. They forgot the mob law, the tarrings and featherings, and the ruthless proscription of minorities

Puritanism of England, developing from the same roots in a different environment, leads on directly to the assertion of the Rights of Man in the constitutions of the North American States and to the rise of political democracy.[51]

It was this "new type of civilization," republican and constitutional, that Orestes Brownson had enthusiastically pronounced compatible with Catholicism.[52]

The Enlightenment, Murray and liberal historiography notwithstanding, was not as important as Christianity in the founding of the American nation. At least three-quarters of the American people at the time of the Revolution came from Puritan families.[53] And, as Christopher Dawson early pointed out, Calvinism, like Catholicism and unlike Lutheranism, asserted that the state must be under the spiritual power.[54] Americans accepted Calvin's view of church-state relations in 1776 and 1789; consistently following his and traditional teaching that natural law and moral law were one and the same, and that together they constituted the norm revealed by mankind's reason and conscience. This was the norm to which men and governments must conform.[55] As one New England minister put it, "Christ confirms the law of nature." [56]

In a true sense, the American Revolution was justified more in terms of public theology than Enlightenment philosophy. Eighteenth-century Americans held many truths, not just the few mentioned by name in the Declaration of Independence and the other founding charters. The Declaration itself says this, otherwise many men probably would not have signed it. "We hold these Truths to be self-evident" ["sacred," Jefferson wrote in the original draft],

> that all men are created equal, that they are endowed by their *Creator* with certain unalienable Rights, that *among these* are Life, Liberty, and the pursuit of Happiness [my italics]. [57]

The Truths and Rights, natural and supernatural, that Americans held at the time were too numerous to be listed in any document; moreover, it would have been thought absurd even to try.

It was unnecessary to put in writing, nor could it be done, the Truths and Rights that had created Western civilization itself and continued to inspire Christians and Jews. The ultimate Truth of Eighteenth century American society, cherished above all other Truths and Rights, was the Truth of Christianity. And the ultimate Right, which included all others, was the Right to be a Christian, with all that entailed to Protestant Christians, separated from Rome but the Church's wards all the same. This is the patrimony that Father Murray, with all good intentions, has minimized. This is the history of the American Founding that we must reclaim. For, surely, the American people believed at the creation of the Republic, as they had always believed, that the loss of God was the beginning of tyranny.

If we must search for the meaning of the "American Proposition," it is here, in the Christian origins of the American nation. The American Founding was a prophetic and messianic movement, drawing from the depths of the Christian experience of God, as well as a "Proposition." These are the Truths we hold. It is here that our true identity as a nation lies.

NOTES

1. Howard Mumford Jones, ed., (Cambridge, Mass., 1966), pp. 185-186. Quoted in Milton R. Konvitz, *Judaism and the American Idea* (Ithaca and London: Cornell University Press, 1978), pp. 15-16.
2. G.W.F. Hegel, *The Philosophy of Right* (Chicago: Encyclopedia Britannica Great Books, 1952), Vol. XLVI, p. 171. Quoted in John A. Abbo, *Political Thought: Men and Ideas* (Westminster, Md., 1960), p. 300.
3. *Ibid.*, 301: cf. Martin Buber's "The Gods of the Nations and God," in *Israel and the World* (New York, 1948), pp. 197-198. See Charles E. Rice, "Some Reasons for a Restoration of Natural Law Jurisprudence," *Social Justice Review* 81 No. 7-8 (July-August 1990), pp. 125-127; *et passim*: John Courtney Murray, *We Hold These Truths: Catholic Reflections on the American Proposition* (New York, 1960), pp. 5-6; Will Herberg, *Protestant, Catholic, Jew: An Essay in American Religious Sociology* (New York, 1960).
4. Murray, pp. "Foreword," pp. vii-xii.
5. The quotations are from Hilaire Belloc, *The Great Heresies* and Oscar Wilde's *Aphorisms*. On the political timing of Murray's book, see Henry J. Schmandt's review in *Thought* 36 (Spring 1961), pp. 149-150. Important is Thomas T. Love, *John Courtney Murray: Contemporary Church-State Theory* (Garden City, 1965). For some judicious observations on the writing of history, in this instance by St. Augustine, see Marthinus Versfeld, *A Guide to the City of God* (New York, 1958), pp. 66-70, *et passim*.
6. Murray, p. viii. C.f. Keith J. Pavlischek, "The Real John Courtney Murray," *First Things: A Monthly Journal of Religion and Public Life* 6 (October 1990), pp. 46-49.
7. *Ibid.*, 10.

8. *Ibid.*, 11. On the importance of first principles in the education of the Founding Fathers, see James J. Walsh, *Education of the Founding Fathers: Scholasticism in the Colonial Colleges. A Neglected Chapter in the History of American Education* (New York, 1935), c.f. George Weigel, "The Achievement of John Courtney Murray S.J.: John Courtney Murray and the American Proposition," *Catholicism in Crisis* 3 (Nov. 1985) pp. 8-13.
9. On the role of the Treaty of Westphalia (1648) in giving over to civil government the power to interpret divine and natural law, see Joseph McSorley, *An Outline History of the Church by Centuries (from St. Peter to Pius XII)* (St. Louis, Mo., l945), pp. 630-631, *et passim.*
10. "A Possible Role for Biblical Religion in Public Life," in David Hollenbach, S.J., "Theology and Philosophy in Public: A Symposium on John Courtney Murray's Unfinished Agenda," *Theological Studies* 40 (December 1979), pp. 701-706; and Father Coleman's *An American Strategic Theology* (New York, 1982), pp. 193-198.
11. Nobody understood this better than George Washington, i.e., the great importance of morality and religion as political and social factors, as witnessed by his and Alexander Hamilton's *Farewell Address to the People of the United States* (1796), Edward F. Humphrey, *Nationalism and Religion in America, 1774-1789* (New York, 1965), pp. 4-5. This book is essential: as are works by Emile Durkheim, Robert A. Nisbet, Robert Bellah, and Peter Berger for what the latter calls the "sacred canopy," the Weberian symbols of legitimacy that every authority system requires.
12. Schmandt, p. 150; John A. Rohr, "John Courtney Murray's Theology of Our Founding Fathers' 'Faith': Freedom," in Francis A. Eigo, O.S.A., editor, and Silvio E. Fittipaldi, O.S.A., associate editor, *Christian Spirituality in the United States: Independence and Interdependence* (Villanova, l978), p. 30.
13. On the United States Constitution as a symbol, an expression of the Higher Law, a classic is Edward S. Corwin, *The "Higher Law" Background of American Constitutional Law* (Ithaca, 1957), originally published in 1928-1929.
14. Philip F. Detweiler, "The Changing Reputation of the Declaration of Independence: The First Fifty Years," *William and Mary Quarterly*, 3rd. ser., 19 (1962), pp. 557-574. As Marshall Smelser points out, it is hard to understand why Thomas Jefferson and the Declaration of Independence loom so large in our thinking about the constitutional revolution, especially in that Jefferson was in France until 1789 and missed the Constitutional Convention, ("The Reconciliation of Liberty and Authority in the American Revolution," in George N. Shuster, ed., *Freedom and Authority in the West* [Notre Dame, 1976], p. 101). This is another example, we might add, of the exaggerated importance assigned to the Enlightenment in American historiography.
15. John A. Woods, ed., "The Correspondence of Benjamin Rush and Granville Sharp 1773-1809," *Journal of American Studies* l (April 1967), p. 17. The seminal work for understanding the Enlightenment and the Modern Age is Romano Guardini, *The End of the Modern World*, edited, with an Introduction by Frederick Wilhelmsen (Chicago, 1968). For the American Revolution as a "work of reformation," a recurring theme of the times, see Cushing

Strout, *The New Heavens and New Earth: Political Religion in America* (New York, l974), p. 67 *et passim*.
16. *A Declaration of Dependence* (Milwaukee, 1941), pp. 121-122.
17. Quoted in D.J. D'Elia, *Benjamin Rush: Philosopher of the American Revolution* (Philadelphia, 1974), p. 56. On Jefferson, see *idem.*, *The Spirits of '76: A Catholic Inquiry* (Front Royal, Va., l983), ch. i, pp. 9-23; *idem.*, "The Real Bicentennial: the Continual Quest for a Therapy of Order," *Faith and Reason* 13, No. 4 (1986), pp. 353-362.
18. *A Worthy Company: Brief Lives of the Framers of the United States Constitution* (Marlborough, N.H., 1982), Introduction, pp. viii-ix.
19. Quoted in D'Elia, *The Spirits of '76*, p. 140.
20. Lagging behind Europe in terms of secularization, the Americans could carry out their dynamically conservative Revolution, while the rationalists and liberals of the "Heavenly City" plunged Europe into destruction: see, e.g., Ross J. Hoffman, *The Spirit of Politics and the Future of Freedom* (Milwaukee, 1950), pp. 12-30.
21. *Democracy in America*, Phillips Bradley, ed., (2 vols., New York, 1945), II, pp. 27-28.
22. *The Historic Reality of Christian Culture: A Way to the Renewal of Human Life* (Harper Torchbooks ed. of R.N. Anshen's edition of the vol. in the *Religious Perspectives Series*: New York, 1960), p. 14.
23. *Ibid.*, 16.
24. *Ibid.*
25. Quoted in Christopher Dawson, "The Trend to Secularism," in James Oliver and Christina Scott, eds., *Religion and World History: A Selection from the Works of Christopher Dawson* (Garden City, N.Y., 1975), p. 290.
26. De Tocqueville, I., p. 305, *et passim*. "The sacred rights of mankind," Alexander Hamilton wrote in 1775, "are not to be rummaged for among old parchments or musty records. They are written as with a sunbeam, in the whole *volume* of human nature, by the hand of the Divinity itself, and can never be erased or obscured by mortal power….," *The Farmer Refuted: Or, A More Impartial and Comprehensive View of the Dispute between Great Britain and the Colonies*, in Richard B. Morris, ed., *The Basic Ideas of Alexander Hamilton* (New York, 1956), p. 9.
27. Dawson, "The Trend to Secularism," p. 290. "A living religion always aspires to be the centre round which the whole culture revolves, so that whatever is most vital in social institutions and activities is brought into relation with religion and receives a religious function," *idem.*, *The Dynamics of World History*, ed. by John J. Mulloy (New York, 1956).
28. "From the Covenant to the Revival," in James Ward Smith and A. Leland Jamison, eds., *The Shaping of American Religion*, vol. I of *Religion in American Life* (4 vols.: Princeton, New Jersey, l961), pp. 325, 339.
29. *Ibid.*, 328. "Our mental image of the religious patriot," Perry Miller observed of the orations of the day, "is distorted because modern accounts do treat the political paragraphs as a series of theoretical expositions of Locke, separated from what precedes and follows. When these orations are read as wholes, they immediately reveal that the sociological sections are structural parts of

a rhetorical pattern. Embedded in their contexts, these are not abstractions but inherent parts of a theology. It was for this reason that they had so energizing an effect upon their religious auditors," *ibid.*, p. 342.
30. Quoted, in Strout, p. 67.
31. Quoted in Miller, 322.
32. Strout, p. 68. As President, Jefferson refused to follow the precedent of recommending to the people of the United States a day of thanksgiving and prayer, *ibid.*, p. 97.
33. Important is Werner Stark, *The Macrosociology of Religion* (3 vols., New York, 1967).
34. Coleman, "A possible Role for Biblical Religion in Public Life," p. 714.
35. See, e.g., Hoffman, pp. 13-14.
36. D'Elia, *Benjamin Rush*, pp. 88-89. *et passim*. On the nature of the Judeo-Christian view of man, still widely held in the Colonies, see Dom Wulston Mork, O.S.B., *The Biblical Meaning of Man* (Milwaukee, 1967). For a comparison and analysis of Rush's and Jefferson's radically different understandings of God, man, nature, and society, see D.J. D'Elia, "Jefferson, Rush, and the Limits of Philosophical Friendship," *Proceedings of the American Philosophical Society*, 117, No. 5 (October 1973), pp. 333-343.
37. *Medical Inquiries and Observations* (5th ed., 2 vols., Philadelphia, 1818), I, pp. 53-54. For the influence of David Hartley on Rush's thought, see D.J. D'Elia, "Benjamin Rush, David Hartley, and the Revolutionary Uses of Psychology." *Proceedings of the American Philosophical Society*, 114, No. 2 (April 1970), pp. 109-118. Not surprisingly, Fulton J. Sheen recognized the importance of Hartley (1705-1757) in his *Philosophy of Religion: the Impact of Modern Knowledge on Religion* (New York, 1948), pp. 15, 17.
38. Rush's doctrine, ultimately deriving from the Hebrew *ruach*, i.e., God's outgoing Life or breath, was an articulate version of what he and so many other young men and women had learned in the school of Christendom, intensified by the Great Awakening in which so many of them had been formed, see D.J. D'Elia, "The Republican Theology of Benjamin Rush," *Pennsylvania History*, 33, (April, 1966). pp. 194-196.
39. Mork, p. 23.
40. *The Spirit of Politics and the Future of Freedom*, pp. 14-22. American statesmen, said Orestes Brownson, "did not destroy or deface the work of Providence, but accepted it and organized the government in harmony with the real order, the real elements given them. They suffered themselves in all their essential work to be governed by reality, not by theories and speculation. In this they proved themselves statesmen, and their work survives," *The American Republic* (New York, 1866), p. 271, quoted by Hoffman, p. 26.
41. Humphrey, p. 103.
42. Sheen, *Philosophy of Religion*, p. 243.
43. Margaret Mary Reher, *Catholic Intellectual Life in America: A Historical Study of Persons and Movements* [vol. III in C.J. Kauffman, ed., *The Bicentennial History of the Catholic Church in America*] (New York, 1989), p. 49.
44. D'Elia, "The Republican Theology of Benjamin Rush," pp. 190-203.
45. *Ibid.*

46. E.g., Samuel Finley, *Christ Triumphing, and Satan Raging. A Sermon on Matthew XII, 28. Wherein is Proved, That the Kingdom of God is come unto Us at This Day....January 20, 1740* (Philadelphia, 1741), p. 27. An excellent study is Ernest Lee Tuveson, *Redeemer Nation: The Idea of America's Millennial Role* (Chicago, 1968).
47. Quoted in Strout, p. 67.
48. Cambridge, 1966, *et passim.*
49. April 2, 1799, Woods, ed., "The Correspondence of Benjamin Rush and Granville Sharp 1773-1809," p. 33.
50. Humphrey, p. 4. "Christianity is in fact understood to be, though not the legally established religion, yet the national religion.... Religion and Conscience have been constantly active forces in the American Commonwealth...by which moral and political evils have been held at bay, and in the long run generally overcome," James Bryce, *American Commonwealth* (888), quoted in *ibid.*
51. *The Judgment of the Nations* (New York, 1943), pp. 33-34.
52. Reher, p. 40. Cf. Jacques Maritain, *Reflections on America* (NY: Charles Scribner's Sons, l958), p. 132, for an "insidious" naturalism in America.
53. Sydney E. Ahlstrom, *A Religious History of the American People* (2 vols., Garden City, N.Y., 1975), I, p. 174.
54. Dawson, *The Judgment of the Nations*, p. 31.
55. *Ibid.*, p. 35: Stark, pp. 11, 14.
56. "Our natural and constitutional privileges," said Jonathan Parsons, a New Light Presbyterian minister from Massachusetts, are "a legacy left us by Christ, the purchase of His blood," quoted in Strout, p. 72.
57. On the Declaration itself, see Carl L. Becker, *The Declaration of Independence* (New York, 1922).

Defense of Murray and The Murray Thesis

6

The Truths They Held: The Christian and Natural Law Background to the American Constitution

by Robert R. Reilly

*W*as the Founding of America rooted in the Christian heritage and natural law? Or, is it a product of the Enlightenment, infused with the idea of the perfectibility of man, and therefore inimical to the Christian conception of reality and to the world view that natural law implies? Was the Founding fatally flawed in its origins? If so, are present day evils simply a logical working-out of this fatal flaw? Or do current maladies result from a fundamentally sound proposition gone awry? The answers to these questions determine whether America is founded on basic principles that are true and just—ones which we can unqualifiedly support—or whether our republic is based on ideas that are false and unavoidably lead to corporate and individual evil. If the United States is, as I believe it is, founded on the highest moral principles of any government that ever existed, then we owe her and the principles on which she was founded our grateful support. If, on the other hand, America is founded on principles that are malign, then we are actually complicitous in anything we do to advance America's two hundred-year-old experiment in democracy.

So, where does the truth lie? There is no denying that the Enlightenment influenced the Founders, but does a partial influence make American political origins solely a product of the Enlightenment? To answer this and other questions we have asked, we must grapple with yet another: How much of the Constitution is derived from concepts of the Enlightenment and how much implies the Christian world view and a respect for natural law? A close reading of the Constitution lends any fair-minded reader to the inescapable conclusion: divorced from

Christianity, Natural Law and the Constitution

natural law and Christian principles, the Constitution would be utterly incomprehensible—a philosophical mish-mash devoid of cogent argument, compelling moral vision, or unifying principles.

However, the proof for this thesis is somewhat indirect because there are no Christian principles *per se* embedded in the Constitution: rather, the Constitution is embedded in Christianity. The Constitution does not declare principles, it provides for their implementation. It considers the principles on which America is founded so self-evident that it does not even name much less defend them. In its short Preamble the Constitution briefly mentions, without defining, justice, general welfare and the blessings of liberty, clearly indicating that these are already accepted ends.

In fact, what is not in the Constitution is, in some ways, more interesting than what is. More interesting still are the presuppositions that these omissions suggest. I do not mean things already contained in the Declaration of Independence, but those that are not mentioned at all, things that might be considered truisms. But the problem with truisms, as G.K. Chesterton once said, is that people forget that they are true. So, the truisms that the Constitution omits because it takes them for granted, can tell us much more about what the Founding Fathers intended than we might think. Indeed, the Constitution is implicitly Christian—in fact, I will argue—so deeply Christian—taking its Christianity so much for granted—that its framers felt no need to make their reliance on Christian tenets explicit.

The unstated premises, without which the Constitution is incomprehensible, derive respectively from Jerusalem, Athens and Rome. From Jerusalem: monotheism; the fundamental goodness and reliability of creation; and a rational universe created by a rational God. From Athens: the immutability of nature; the existence of human nature; and the existence and immortality of the human soul. From Rome: the dedivinization of the world, salvation history, and a personal God. It is beyond the scope of this essay to substantiate these sweeping claims. One can only briefly outline the support for them in the history of Western thought. One can also point to the fact that nothing similar to the U.S. Constitution has ever arisen where these premises are lacking.

To grasp these fundamental concepts which the Constitution presupposes, one must look back to the distant past, to ancient Greece, to the pre-philosophical world, to the cosmological empires of the Mesopotamians, the Egyptians and other ancients. For instance, in the ancient pre-philosophical world, when a dog wagged its tail, one simply said "That is the way of a dog." When the Egyptians buried their dead in brightly painted caskets, one said, "That is the way of the Egyptians." The ancients did not discriminate between nature and convention. They did not have the means even of distinguishing that what the dog does grows out of its nature, whereas the Egyptians buried their dead in painted boxes because that is simply a convention they made up.

Another related distinction was also missing in the ancient world. There was no demarcation between the civic order and religious life. In the cosmological empires of, for example, the Pharaohs, the empire was supposedly an analog of the divine order. This was replicated, point by point, by the divinity of the Pharaohs and then, in rippling concentric circles, by the order of society and the political schema, which derived their importance from their proximity to the Pharaoh. Since there was no distinction between the political and the religious, participating in religious life was essentially a civic duty. The local gods upheld the city and the ruler ruled because he had a special relationship with them. In other words, in cosmological empires, a personal relationship with God was not possible. One participated in the divine scheme of things by fulfilling one's role in the empire, centered on the person of the semi-divine ruler.

Therefore, in the ancient world, the worst possible punishment was exile. It was worse than death because it meant banishment from the source of order and meaning. Worse still, by being separated from participation in the empire one was automatically cut off from the ruler and the order he had established—thus, one was cut off from the gods as well. Exile was, *in esse*, existential, as well as physical banishment. Perhaps this is one reason that Socrates chose hemlock rather than exile.

The importance of the gods was by no means merely cosmetic. For example when the Egyptians sallied forth to conquer another city, they would also defeat the gods of that city. After all, the Egyptians reasoned, what are the local gods for if not to protect their votaries? If a city lost at war, the ancients assumed that its gods had been defeated and subjugated by the greater powers of the gods worshipped by the victor.

The gods also played a crucial role in what we would think of as history—a concept that was far from the modern meaning of the term.

How did the ancients define history? For them, history was simply the cyclical repetition of events. Empires rose and fell repeatedly—all empires were fated to end, but once all possibilities had been exhausted, others were fated to take their place: endless cycles of rise and fall. Creation, in the sense in which they understood it, resulted from a battle between the gods. This creation was neither *ex nihilo* nor entirely good; a god of light and a god of darkness struggled for supremacy, and the resultant chaos erupting in life and nature manifested the struggle of these demiurges. Consequently, instability constantly threatened to overwhelm the very tentative order of things with the chaos from which it came. Matter was often identified with evil itself in battle with the principle of light or goodness. Far from transcending the universe, the divine order was part of it: literally the heavens themselves.

In the ancient world, one tribe, the Jews, located in the Middle East, regularly beaten by other tribes, formulated a far different cosmogeny. Even when the Jews were defeated in battle, they did not consider their God defeated. The Israelites' developing consciousness of their God, revealed throughout the Old Testament, implies a God who is transcendent, omniscient—moreover one who creates *ex nihilo* and creates what is always good. "He Who Is," Yahweh, is not just a tribal god. He is the God of all people and all things. *Genesis* makes it clear that Yahweh is a sovereign Creator who makes everything and makes it well: Nothing exists which He did not make and all of it is *good*. Yahweh's creation is not threatened by some evil demiurge who is equal with Him.

Also, God's handiwork is so well made that man can come to know the Creator by studying His works. The *Book of Wisdom* called "naturally stupid" those men, who "from the good things that are seen, have not been able to discover Him-who-is, or who, although studying those works, fail to recognize the Artificer" (Wis. 13:1-2). So this well-made creation offers an invitation to natural theology, (an invitation later taken up by the Declaration of Independence). The *Book of Wisdom* also makes it clear that the Creator who reveals Himself in His works has called His creatures and works into being out of love. The Scripture says of God: "You love all that exists, you hold nothing of what you have made in abhorrence, for had you hated anything, you would not have formed it. And how, had you not willed it, could a thing persist, how be conserved if not called forth by you? You spare all things because all things are yours, Lord, lover of life, you whose imperishable spirit is in all" (Wis. 11:24-27).

Our familiarity with these texts, or at least with their assertions, has robbed us of the astonishing uniqueness of the biblical idea that creation is good. Since all that exists is good because it was made by God, creation is stable and reliable. Man can count on it.

The absolute supremacy of the God of the Israelites, in short monotheism, provided an assurance against the Manichean bifurcation of creation into coequal forces of good and evil. A good and stable creation can be confidently built upon. It provides the necessary requisite for man's enterprise and exploration. It is impossible to find a comparable vision of creation expressed in the Assyrian, Babylonian, or in any other ancient creation myth. In contrast, all of them invoke the principle of evil, often considering it as the Manicheans do, matter itself. Moreover, in such creation myths, this evil threatens to overwhelm the universe which would then dissolve into primeval chaos. *Genesis*, on the other hand, makes it very clear that evil is derived not from God, but from man. Therefore, according to the Judeo-Christian vision of being, man himself is responsible for disorder in creation, which originally resulted from his disobedience which, in turn, was caused by disordered will. Naturally, such a situation called for response by a Creator who is all good and so, as the Bible tells us, God undertook to "re-create" man and to remedy his disordered will by promising to send a Savior to restore creation and redeem man. The promise of the redemption created salvation history, which is the foundation of all modern history. For the first time, history became linear instead of cyclical. It moved with purpose toward a consummation.

The Athenian vision of man, his nature, and how he came to be was starkly different from that enclosed in Judaic culture. In a sense, it is true to say that the ancient Greeks discovered the idea of the human soul as well as the concept of human nature. They recognized that human nature enables man to recognize another person as a human being. In most of the ancient world, there was no sense of man's common humanity. When one people conquered another, the typical *modus operandi* was mass execution or enslavement. It was the most natural thing in the world for the victors to enslave or slaughter everyone in an enemy city. They were not killed because they were human beings, but because they were simply members of an opposing tribe. Significantly, there was no word for human being, no concept of personhood.

This situation still exists today in certain tribes in Africa, or in specific regions in South America. Such tribes define themselves in terms of their gods, not in terms of their own common personhood. These tribes name themselves, and other tribes, but they have no term to refer to human beings. Consequently, they cannot recognize themselves or other people as human beings. Indeed, their own wives are often slaves.

We owe the extraordinary discovery of personhood to the Greek philosophers. They were the philosophical pioneers who first announced that there is such a thing as human nature. Even more impressive than the discovery of human nature and personhood was the Greeks' recognition that man alone in all creation is endowed with an immortal soul. In Socrates, moreover, we read that the human soul has a typical order. What does human nature mean? It means that human beings are fundamentally the same in their very essence. Socrates and Aristotle said that men's souls are ordered to the good and that there is a single standard of justice which transcends the political standards of the city. There should not be one standard of justice for Athenians and another for Spartans. There is only one justice and this justice is above the political order. It is the same at all times, everywhere. Socrates was executed for this impiety—for suggesting that there could be a standard of justice independent of the city's gods. The Athenians considered this idea blasphemous, and, according to their understanding of the world, it was an impious affront to the gods and the old order.

Socrates' great discovery was that man's soul cannot be satisfied through political means. Politics cannot meet the needs of the human soul, for it cannot achieve perfect justice. Therefore, the Greek philosophers realized that one must look beyond politics for the fulfillment for which man hungers. Socrates showed that any attempt to fulfill the soul's ultimate desires through politics—by trying to achieve perfect justice—would transform the state into a totalitarian enterprise engaged in eugenics. Such a state would destroy the family, militarize its citizens, and do away with privacy. Socrates' discovery was that the soul may not be subsumed by political ends. The soul is inviolate and supersedes the political order. There is something essential in man's makeup that finds its end outside of politics and that can only be reached by the divine or the transcendent.

Therefore, Socrates argues for the immortality of the soul. He believes that justice requires the immortality of the soul since the demands of justice cannot be met in this life. In one of the most moving passages of political philosophy ever written, Socrates says: "In heaven there is laid up a pattern of it [the ideal city] methinks, which he who desires may behold, and beholding may set his own house in order. But whether such a one exists, or ever will exist in fact, does not matter; for he will live after the manner of that city, having nothing to do with any other" (*The Republic*, 592B). In other words, the good and the wise will live according to a spiritual order that transcends the actual order as well as the particular in which the individual lives. Indeed, Socrates' transcendent view beautifully adumbrates St. Paul's prophecy: "As you well know, we have our true citizenship in heaven."

I do not mention either St. Paul or heaven adventitiously, for the idea of heaven—or the city of God—is the ultimate, yet transcendent political order because it is so ordered by God Himself who is (among many other things) Order itself. Moreover, He is, according to the Christian view, not only ultimate order but also the ultimate Ruler and His kingdom (heaven) the perfect *polis* or city. Thus, the great Christian contribution to the question of man's nature and his ultimate end is the revelation that man's soul is not only, as Socrates said, drawn to the good but to goodness itself which is God.

Of course, the Christian revelation only begins there, unfolding like Dante's multifoliate verse, into further revelations connected not only with God's goodness but with His triune nature. The coming of Christ, the second person of the Trinity, totally revolutionized the ancient world. In fact, in the West, we consider the Incarnation that event that decisively divides time: cutting ancient times from our own Christian era—designated as A.D., *Anno Domini*, in the year of our Lord. The Incarnation was an earth-shaking event in an ancient world diffused with pantheism, divine energy, with spirits inhabiting trees and groves and grottos. Everything was animated by spirit, its own god. But, as Father Stanley Jaki so brilliantly points out, St. John testifies that Christ is the "only-begotten" of the Father, *only*-begotten. God did not beget anything, *but* Christ. He did not *beget* the world. The world is not made up of God, but made by Him and is separate from Him. The universe itself cannot be divine. Thus, the Incarnation makes pantheism impossible. Matter is not eternal. This doctrine delivered the *coup de grace* to the ancient world. The world owes its existence to a free act of God but is not a necessary part of Him. As a result, Pan was dead and the world de-divinized.

An infinite distance opened between God and His creation, because this God is an infinite God. But at the same time man became infinitely distant from God, he grew intimately close, because across this infinite distance came Christ Himself, God incarnate, through whom contingent creation, flawed through man's sin, is saved. Since Christ is a personal savior, interested in each individual soul, in love with each human being, each person could participate in the divine order of salvation as an individual, not through his participation as a citizen of his state, not through the mediation of a semi-divine ruler, but through union with Christ. As the Romans implicitly recognized when they sentenced to death Christians who would not sacrifice to the emperor as a god, Christ's identity as a personal savior was totally incompatible with the ancient cosmological view of the universe.

The vision out of which our Founding Fathers operated was based on the discoveries and revelations that we have just mentioned that grew out of the cultures of Jerusalem, Athens and Rome—to wit, the world was created *ex nihilo* by a good God and this world is *in esse* good. Moreover, each soul created by God is uniquely dear to Him. So dear, in fact, that when man, as a result of cunningly misusing his free will, fell, thereby ushering evil into the world, God sent Christ, His only-begotten Son, to save man. That salvation not only redeems man and creation, but also offers each individual salvation through personal union with Christ. Jerusalem revealed the name of the one God to whom all are ordered. Athens discovered the nature of man's immortal soul that directs him to a transcendent God. Rome was when the identity of the God sought and the seeker meet in the person of Christ.

Ironically, by offering a vision that transcends politics, Christianity enabled politics to focus on its proper study—how best to govern man in this world. As Fr. James Schall writes in *The Politics of Heaven and Hell*, "Christianity was vital to the very structure of classical political thought because it was able to give a reason why politics did not have to be concerned with man's highest destiny or virtue. Resurrection and the Kingdom of God suggested both that man's deepest desires would be fulfilled and that politics could, consequently, pursue a temporal good in a human, finite fashion." Since man's ultimate human happiness lies in God, and a transcendent God is, by definition, outside of history, man cannot make his home in this world. Thus, politics is not the salvific engine for the transformation of mankind and the elimination of evil. Christ is. This is what ultimately limits (and therefore makes possible) politics. Without this limiting view of politics, constitutional thinking is not possible. Only such a vision as this gives impetus to the effort to restrain political power.

The Founders were deeply grounded in these beliefs. They proclaimed in the Declaration of Independence that American independence is based upon total dependence on God. This is why the Constitution contains no solution to the problem of evil. The Constitution implicitly recognizes that politics cannot, and should not, attempt to spiritually transform man or turn the world into a terrestrial paradise. The more limited goal of politics is to arrange the material circumstances of man's life to mitigate the effects of evil so that he can pursue virtue and, in so doing, achieve the ultimate happiness which lies beyond politics. The primacy of the person, unthinkable without the foundation of Christian truth, defines the very order of the Constitution.

The American Constitution makes no sense divorced from these presuppositions. If man lives in a world of which he can make no sense, a world that is a plaything of the gods, an irrational world, he can choose only to surrender to fate or to despair. In such a state and such circumstances, he will not go about writing constitutions, for constitutions by their very nature imply a belief in order, in man's reasonability, and in his ability to formulate and establish a rational mode of government, grounded in a rational creation. Law is reason, as John Courtney Murray said, which is why we discuss reasons for laws. Ultimately, law is reason because God is *Nus*.

If man is not a political creature endowed with reason in a world accessible to his mind, why attempt to order political life based upon deliberation and representation? If man does not have free will, deliberating over what he ought to do is superfluous. If reason is simply an excrescence of material or physiological forces, then deliberations are meaningless. Freedom, obviously, is a hollow idea if free will and reason do not exist. These faculties themselves only make sense in an order of nature which directs man toward ends that make him fully human. This is the perspective that formed our Founders, and that infuses the Declaration of Independence, the Constitution and the Founding Fathers' ancillary writings.

Of course, this view of the Founders has not gone unchallenged in the world of constitutional scholarship. In that forum, it is the fashion to present the American Founding as an outgrowth of the Enlightenment, as a Hobbesian or as a Lockean enterprise, that somehow co-opts the American experiment into the ideological endeavor to transform man. This interpretation, which, I believe, is politically motivated, cannot be historically substantiated or even philosophically justified.

A study, done by Lutz and Hyneman, supports this case. They examined the references cited by our Founding Fathers from 1760 to 1805. Of 3,154 items cited by the Founding Fathers, 34% came from the Bible. Nine percent were from classical authors like Cicero, Plutarch, Livy, and Plato. Thus, 1,356 citations came from the Bible and the classics, making up forty-three percent of the citations. Eighteen percent were from Whig writers, 11% derived from English common law, and 18% from so-called Enlightenment thinkers. Significantly, Montesquieu, the author of *The Spirit of the Laws*, was most frequently cited, three times as often as John Locke.

John Adams' habit of annotating the books he read, making his reading like a living dialogue, offers interesting insight as to how he reacted as he read various texts. The margins are full of his comments on and to the authors. One of the books Adams read in this manner was *The Progress of the Human Mind* by the Marquis de Condorcet, one of the leading lights of the French Enlightenment. One of the Marquis' sentences epitomizes the spirit of the Enlightenment: "The results of my work will be to show from reasoning and from facts, that no bounds have been fixed to the improvement of the human faculties, that the perfectibility of man is absolutely indefinite." Condorcet goes on to argue that the state provides the vehicle for organizing and implementing man's self-perfection.

As one would expect, Condorcet attacked organized religion, claiming that priests had become dupes of their own fables and that kings and priests waged a continual war against the truth. In the margin by that statement, Adams wrote, "Just as you and yours have become the dupes of your own atheism and profligacy, your nonsensical notions of liberty, equality, and fraternity.... Your philosophy, Condorcet, has waged a more cruel war against truth than was ever attempted by king or priest." When the Marquis complained that true genius had been suppressed by organized religion, Adams retorted, "But was there no genius among the Hebrews, none among the Christians? I understand you, Condorcet, it is atheistical genius alone that you would honor or tolerate." And when the Marquis insisted on the natural equality of mankind as the foundation of morality, Adams wrote, "There is no such thing without a supposition of a God. There is no right or wrong in the universe without the supposition of a moral government and an intellectual and moral governor."

Clearly, Condorcet's views and those of his Enlightenment *confreres* were inimical to those of Adams and most of the other Founding Fathers. These distinguished men had a keen appreciation of the ill effects of original sin both in individuals and in groups. Moreover, they realized that any document describing how men should govern and be governed must make ample provision for man's basically flawed nature and his unfortunate propensities. The Constitution implicitly recognizes this nature and these propensities when it advocates the separation of powers. Furthermore, the Constitution implicitly acknowledges original sin and its baneful effects when it insists on a wise system of checks and balances. This is why, as we have already mentioned, the Constitution does not offer any solution to the problem of evil. Our Founding Fathers clearly considered this solution beyond the realm of politics and beyond their own individual competence. But this does not mean that they did not think that a solution had been provided. Indeed, they believed that the "solution"—in the form of Christianity—was so widely known and accepted by them and their fellow countrymen that there was no need to make it explicit. It is telling that they dated the Constitution *"Anno Domini"* in light of the later French Revolution which presumed to date its inception as the year "zero," thus constituting a completely new beginning for man in time.

Lest one think that Adams and the other Founding Fathers objected exclusively to Condorcet rather than the ideas he and other figures of the "Enlightenment" endorsed, I would like to mention Adams' rather sharp marginalia addressed to David Hume. As is well known, this British philosopher is often credited with having had a decisive impact on the American Founding. Reading a book which praised Hume, Adams wrote that the famous Englishman "was a greater blockhead than he pronounced Mr. Locke to be. If ever there existed a wise fool, a learned idiot, a profound deep thinking coxcomb, it was David Hume...."

As interesting as these marginalia are, Adams did not confine himself to mute debate with figures of the Enlightenment. In his intriguing correspondence with Thomas Jefferson, Adams specified what he believed were the ideas that those who drafted our foundational documents took for granted. Writing about the basic concepts on which the Fathers achieved independence, Adams asked:

> And what were these principles? I answer, the general principles of Christianity in which all those sects were united and the general principles of English and American liberty in which all these young men united. Now I will avow that I then believed and now believe that those general principles of Christianity are as eternal and immutable as the existence and attributes of God. And that those principles of liberty are as unalterable as human nature. ...I could, therefore, safely say consistently with all my then and present information, that I believe they would never make discoveries in contradiction to these general principles.

In this remarkable passage Adams implicitly acknowledges the various presuppositions from the ancient past that we have mentioned: the immutability of human nature; the constancy of the universe; the basic goodness of creation; the existence of a good God; the divinity of Christ; and His identity as man's savior.

The fact that the American Revolution was not an exclusive product of the Enlightenment is even clearer in contrast to the real revolution of the Enlightenment—the French Revolution. In one great act of Enlightenment in 1789, the French revolutionaries broke into the Church of St. Etienne du Mont near the Pantheon, the burial site of St. Genevieve, the patron saint of Paris. The revolutionaries desecrated St. Genevieve's grave, took the remains into the square and burned them. Later they proceeded to Notre Dame where they overthrew the main altar and constructed a huge mound of earth on which they enthroned the Goddess of Reason, a naked woman, who happened also to be a whore. This was their Goddess of Reason.

Proposed laws in the French Assembly would have made all buildings in France equal. No building could be taller than another. This would have required the leveling of every steeple in France. Other laws advocated a national uniform for everyone and a calendar to begin anew in 1793 as the first year of the new era.

Although many of these laws were not put into practice in eighteenth-century France, many of them bore weird fruit in our own time in places like China, the Soviet Union, and Cambodia. All of them consider or have considered the state the secular vehicle of salvation. In these countries, the whole burden of salvation falls on politics. As a result, politics becomes the engine of salvation. Happily, the United States has been protected from such a situation by the Constitution, as well as by the vision of which the Constitution is a part. If we lose that vision we will lose our communities, we will lose our families, we will lose our unborn children, and eventually, we will lose ourselves.

That vision is already under attack and seriously eroded by *Roe v. Wade*. This Supreme Court decision challenges ideas on which the Constitution and Western civilization itself are based. Making it legal to kill unborn children in the name of freedom challenges the idea that each of us as a human being has a fundamental duty and responsibility to all other human beings. Ironically, by legalizing the slaughter of infants who happen to be unwanted, we throw into question not only the humanity of those destroyed but also that of those who allow that destruction. Furthermore, such wanton destruction threatens our very understanding of human nature. As we have said earlier, the discovery of human nature gave man the ability to recognize another person as a human being. Ironically, we, the most modern of modern countries and certainly the most sophisticated and richest, are in danger of losing sight of that ancient discovery. *Roe v. Wade* suggests either that the unborn person is not a human being, or that if he or she is, he or she is not as human as his or her mother. In other words, the Court has basically admitted that it cannot distinguish between the human and the nonhuman. Ironically, however, the very authority of the Court is based upon the distinction between the human and the nonhuman, for it is impossible to adjudicate human rights if one cannot tell what a human being is.

With *Roe v. Wade*, the members of the Court have declared that: by the power invested in us by the virtue of our humanity, we do not know what a human being is. In taking this absurd position, the Court not only opened the gate to the massacre of the innocents, it undermined the most fundamental basis of constitutional government. The *Roe v. Wade* decision has given impetus to the process of the rebarbarization of man in the twentieth century, because it has the effect of impairing our ability to recognize each other as human beings.

Earlier stages of this process were clear enough in the writings of Marx and Lenin. One is not a human being, but a member of the working class. It is clear enough in *Mein Kampf* that one is not a human being, but a Caucasian. It is only our Declaration of Independence that appeals to all men everywhere in the same way because it appeals to the principles of truth which transcend history. Calvin Coolidge aptly expressed this idea in relation to our Founding documents. He observed:

> It is often asserted that the world has made a great deal of progress since 1776, that we have had new thoughts and new experiences which have given us a great advance over the people of that day, and that we may therefore very well discard their conclusions for something more modern. But that reasoning cannot be applied to [the Declaration of Independence]. If all men are created equal, that is final. If governments derive their just powers from the consent of the governed, that is final. No advance, no progress can be made beyond these propositions. If anyone wishes to deny their truth or their soundness, the only direction in which he can proceed historically is not forward, but backward toward the time when there was no equality, no rights of the individual, no rule of the people. Those who wish to proceed in this direction cannot claim to progress, they are reactionary.

Coolidge's words obviously counter the theory that everything needs to be updated and implicitly suggests that cultural relativism can be a menace. Unfortunately, the brightest students in U.S. universities have been thoroughly infected with this notion. Frequently they are incapable of defending anything about the Western civilization that they have been trained to denigrate. "On what grounds could one possibly advance the notion of the superiority of Western civilization?" they ask. Even asking such a question is ridiculed as ethnocentric hubris. I once asked a student who held this view how he felt about the human sacrifices of the Aztecs, who sometimes slaughtered tens of thousands of slaves on special occasions. The student uncomfortably complained that he was being forced into being a relativist. In fact, he was being shown that he *wasn't*, for if he objected to human sacrifice, he clearly had some idea of the sanctity of human life. The Aztecs probably did not have a word for human being, because they had no concept of human beings as persons. They did not have the means to recognize another person as a human being.

To me, at least, it does not seem chauvinistic to assert that a civilization that has a word for "human being" is likely to be better than one that does not.

A case can and should be made for Western civilization. In British-ruled India, for example, the British governor was confronted with Indian elders who protested violently against the government's order outlawing the burning of widows on the funeral pyres of their husbands. The elders came to the British governor and said, "How dare you invade and desecrate our culture by banning the burning of widows. This happens to be *our way*." And the British governor replied, "Well, if you put it like that, it's *our way* to hang people who burn widows on funeral pyres."

If everything is reduced to cultural relativism, and there is no appeal to principles which transcend this cultural relativism; there can be no truth, and where there is no truth force rather than right reason rules. The relativists do not realize—when they celebrate the multi-cultural milieu they favor and deride Western civilization as the source of all evil—that they are unwittingly advocating force when they deny the possibility of appealing through reason to truths that transcend history and culture.

These truths alone are universally relevant and in respect to them all else *is* relative. Cardinal Biffi put this pithily: "That which is eternal is not only more important, but is, in fact, more incisively contemporary than that which is merely contemporary, and that which is substantial and absolute is capable of influencing history more effectively than that which is above all relative to present circumstances."

The Cardinal's words accurately describe the greatness of the gift that we have inherited. The Constitution takes it for granted that the verities on which it is based are immutable, transcendent, and eternal. Moreover, our Founding Fathers believed that God Himself was the Author of these truths and that He had written them in the hearts of all man as natural law. We will keep that great gift only if we maintain that enormous vision of which it is a part.

7

Murray's Transformation of the American Proposition

by Peter Augustine Lawler

We Hold These Truths is the great work of political philosophy written by an American Catholic. It has had an enormous influence and is widely respected as authoritative. But it is still not well understood.

There is a Murray revival of sorts today, and with it a revival of the suspicions Murray's project aroused among some Catholics when and before the book was published. Murray is usually praised and blamed for attempting to reconcile Catholic with American thought, and with good reason. But he is also praised and blamed for attempting to remove from Catholic thought all opposition to what Americans regard as self-evident. That he did not do. His project of reconciliation is based in a reinterpretation of America, and not a reinterpretation of the Church. Murray is, in other words, often praised and blamed for a project that originates with American Catholic liberals and some neoconservatives, for one that is not his own.[1]

Murray's writing is being employed today for a variety of polemical purposes, some of which are not his own. His own writing must be viewed in its polemical or partisan context. Murray always wrote for or against a certain position and for a certain audience. He never, despite his undeniable gifts, wrote a comprehensive, theoretical work. He is most well known for arguing against the position that it would be better, in principle, if American government promoted true religion. His limited and nuanced dissent from some of the details of the Church's official position on religious liberty, which seemed no longer to be dissent after Vatican II's *Dignitatis Humanae*, is understood by political and religious liberals to have paved the way for the general legitimation of theological dissent within the Church.[2]

But Murray did not argue that the Church should be structured in the same way as the American political community, because the purposes of the two communities are not the same. He saw that the political affirmation of religious pluralism, under American circumstances, is undeniably salutary if properly interpreted. It keeps the peace and limits the "monistic" pretensions of politics (56-58).[3] Murray also says that religious pluralism, lamentably, is "the human condition," and hence an inevitable part of human history (23, 70). But pluralism is not the model for the community which is the Church.

Human liberty, Murray argued, is to be understood as freedom from the political order for the "freedom of the Church," which is freedom for membership in a "genuine intellectual community" (21), an "order of culture" (35) that transcends politics and resists politicization. This "intellectual community," to remain a community, must not, especially in a pluralistic democracy, look for its definition from the political order, which is barely, at best, a community at all. The Church is the "order of culture" that limits and justifies democracy's pluralistic tendency toward relativism by defining human dignity or sacredness against the humanly unworthy claims of "flat majoritarianism" and the anxious impotence of moral relativism or nihilism (13).

Murray's bold claim is that American liberal democracy has no choice but to define itself in deference to the freedom of the Church, and not that the Church needs to redefine itself in the light of liberal democracy's success and self-evident goodness. Murray sees, in fact, the self-evident failure of American democracy today to make sense of itself. One of his most insistent claims is that the procedures of liberal democracy do not represent or produce the whole human good. He refuses to affirm their goodness unless their purpose and limits are well understood. A purely procedural consensus is no consensus at all (85).

Murray's political project was to deepen and even transform American thought by incorporating it within the Catholic tradition of natural law. He says that "[m]y proposition is that only the theory of natural law is able to give an account of the public moral experience that is a moral consensus" (102). Hence he writes to conform the American Proposition to his own, one characteristic of the Catholic tradition of thought. He hoped to begin a refounding of America on a more secure foundation. He begins his book by comparing his project to Lincoln's, with the intention of showing why his must be more profound or radical. We must begin by becoming aware of how politically ambitious his "Catholic reflections" are, and of how his ambition is conditioned by his view of the depth of the crisis America and the world faces. His refounding is not only of America, but of a world perplexed and anxious with the exhaustion of the modern experiment in politics. He intends to participate in the origination of the "postmodern" world (198, 216).

Murray describes the need for his political, transformative project in the "Foreword" to *We Hold These Truths*. There he traces the "thread of unity" that makes his book more than a collection of essays written for a variety of occasions and purposes. That unity, he says, in each essay's exploration of the "American Proposition," is "otherwise called...the public consensus or public philosophy of America." The questions of greatest urgency raised by this exploration are "whether and to what extent this nation, now no longer new, still remains dedicated to the conception that first constituted us as a people organized for action in history" (viii). The questions are those of the concerned American citizen who wonders whether his people are still a people properly speaking, united by dedication to the same idea or purpose.

Murray's work of political philosophy begins with the perspective of the citizen. His answers to the citizen's questions are negative. He shows, in Lincolnian fashion, that our dedication has declined over time, and, far more indirectly, that this decadence is caused by the fact that the people were never fully and properly constituted.

Murray's reconstitution is, in part, a new constitution. His first assertion is: "It is classic American doctrine, immortally asserted by Abraham Lincoln, that the new nation which our Fathers brought forth on this continent was dedicated to a 'proposition' " (viii). With this close paraphrase of the Gettysburg Address, Murray calls attention to Lincoln's most ambitious attempt to transform what our Founders or "Fathers" had given us. The word "proposition" is Lincoln's, not theirs. It made much more definite and central one particular nation's dedication to equality. Our Founders also would not, in their opposition to uncritical traditionalism, want to be called "our Fathers," to be confused with the Biblical patriarchs and even God the Father.[4]

Lincoln's blurring of the sacred imagery of the biblical tradition and the Declaration of Independence suggests a criticism of the Founders' rather abstract and secularistic rationalism as inadequate as an object of human dedication. This criticism is ultimately one of their excessive reliance on the individualism of the Lockean law of nature. Murray later makes it clear it is perfectly in accord with the doctrine of natural law (320).

Lincoln went on and aimed to create, for this nation, a "political religion."[5] The fact that Lincoln's transformative project is now "classic American doctrine" suggests the magnitude of his success. He was able, to some great extent, to become the authoritative interpreter of what "our Fathers" had given us, partly because he identified his doctrine so beautifully and persuasively with theirs. Lincoln's criticism of their work, which is far from insignificant, was necessarily quite muted in order that he might establish, for Americans, an improved but still more sacred tradition.

Murray follows Lincoln's example by interpreting Lincoln's transformative project in light of his own. He also imitates Lincoln by attributing his innovative doctrine, not without reason but sometimes more than is reasonable, to our Fathers. It is Murray's post-modern interpretation of the American Proposition that now must replace Lincoln's as "classic American doctrine."

Murray prepares us for this conclusion by using "proposition," allegedly following Lincoln, "with conceptual propriety." Proposition means both "the statement of a truth to be demonstrated" and "the statement of an operation to be performed." The American Proposition, as a result, is "at once" a doctrinal or theoretical "affirmation" and practical "intention." It means to be an "organized political project that aims at historical success" rooted in "a coherent structure of thought" (vii). The coherence of the structure of thought seems to be a necessary if not sufficient cause for enduring practical success.

But the proposition, Murray goes on, never reaches perfection as either theory or practice. It is never "a finished thing." It requires "development on penalty of decadence" (vii). We cannot rest content with what our Fathers have given us.

Dedication to the tradition established by the American Proposition does not call forth, primarily, the piety of uncritical traditionalism, although Murray does not hesitate to appeal to that piety to support his cause. The proposition cannot be accepted, at least by those who, in their wisdom, are called to accept political responsibility (119), as merely a "patrimony" (12). For them, it should become "a personal acquisition" (85-86). Genuine devotion to our Fathers' affirmation and intention requires their "enlargement" (vii).

Lincoln's enlargement of their proposition, Murray goes on, was "[i]n a moment of national crisis." He "asserted the imperilled part of the theorem and gave impetus to the impeded part of the project in the noble utterance, at once declaratory and imperative: 'All men are created equal'" (vii-viii). Americans came to doubt the truth of human equality. But they did not doubt that a political community could have a theoretical foundation.

Lincoln's solution was to assert, or strengthen through willful resolution, the part of the proposition that was "imperilled" by doubt and "impeded" by lack of dedication. He saw that there was a close connection between the doubt and lack of dedication. He gave "impetus" to the nation's affirmation of equality, producing a unity which overcame the nation's crisis.

Murray emphasizes the partiality and particularity of this crisis and its solution. The crisis involved only part of the proposition, and a particular nation. Its solution, as assertion, was also partial and particular. It was, to repeat, a criticism of the excessively theoretical or deracinated character of our Fathers' declaration, which was, finally the cause of the crisis.

The crisis Murray confronts, by contrast, is in several senses universal.[6] "[C]ivil war," he begins, "has become the basic fact of world society." The American fact of Lincoln's presidency has become a global one. Every "element" of the theoretical dimension of the proposition, moreover, is "menaced by active negation." The intellectual credibility of the proposition is aggressively denied across the board. Finally, each part of the historical or political project rooted in its theory "meet[s] with powerful opposition" (viii). Not only American in particular, but all government dedicated to equality in liberty, is embattled.

Lincoln's crisis, in its particularity, was perhaps best met with assertion. But, for Murray, his solution did not correct the root deficiency of our Fathers' work. Our crisis, in its radicality and universality, must be met, first of all, with an argument, one which is partly an affirmation and partly a correction of our Fathers' argument. This argument must incorporate but go beyond Lincoln's criticism of their individualism.

Murray's argument suggests a criticism of Lincoln's propensity to attribute "ultimate" or religious significance to the merely political project of this particular nation. Murray takes from Lincoln the phrase "ancient faith" (xii). Devotion to the duties of faith moderates, at least, the modern, including our Fathers', individualistic obsession with rights. For Lincoln, that faith is our Fathers' egalitarian political devotion. For Murray, it is the faith of "the Fathers of the Church," in which our political Fathers shared more than they knew (30, 43). This particular nation, Murray shows, must interpret itself in light of "the universal Church" (xi), a community which transcends the limits of politics and includes all human beings.

Both the theory of natural law and the faith of our spiritual fathers point away from the assertiveness implied in Lincoln's political religion and our political Fathers' individualistic doctrine of rights and toward the creature's existential situation of dutiful subordination before his or her Creator and a moral order which exists independently of human making (215, 329).[7] Part of the American Proposition, Murray says, "has been the profound conviction that only a virtuous people can be free." But the "possibility" of freedom with virtue "can be realized only when the people as a whole are inwardly governed by the recognized imperatives of the universal moral law" (36). The theory of natural law is, first of all, "a metaphysics of right," not rights, because "objective law has primacy over subjective rights" (327). Murray is perfectly aware, of course, that our political Fathers did not clearly or even unambiguously affirm this conclusion, but neither did they decisively and unequivocally reject it.

Murray does not abandon Lincoln's concern with dedication to the way established by our political Fathers. He makes that concern his own. It is only from the superficial, misanthropic perspective of Lockean or disembodied rationalism that one can recommend a wholly new beginning (305-06). Tradition is indispensable for human existence, and political reform is best understood as renewal of a nation's dedication to its original, constituting self-conception (11-12, 85). Murray uses Lincoln's rhetoric of innovating traditionalism, and the sound insights about human nature that inform that rhetoric, to his advantage.

But Murray's argument is still that our crisis cannot be resolved by human or political assertion. We must make, he says, "a metaphysical decision" about "the nature of man" (321). He means that our choice or decision, our enlargement of the proposition must be, and be understood to be, reasonable, or in accord with the truth we perceive about the dignity or sacredness of free, rational, and social creatures.

The core of Murray's innovating traditionalism is his rescue of the "central" idea of the American Proposition by showing its indispensability and its reasonableness, by accomplishing what our Fathers believed they had done but, in truth, had not. Such a rescue, paradoxically enough, is what is required by times so untraditional that we have no choice but to confront "the nature and structure of reality itself," a confrontation our Fathers thought they had made, but had not (199). "Our reflections," Murray asserts, "cannot be merely political." They must be "much more profound" than our Fathers' (321). We, finally, must affirm natural law not as tradition but as theory, as part of a new or post-modern beginning.[8]

Every proposition which is "argued," Murray contends, presupposes an "epistemology." The American Proposition, from its origination, has been, most fundamentally, an argument. Murray learned from Lincoln (30) that "the Constitution...has to be read in light of the Declaration of Independence."[9] The Declaration, in its elementary affirmations about God and nature, is the source of the American Proposition's theory. But Murray points to a different "famous phrase" of the Declaration as its core. It is the "realist epistemology" asserted in "We hold these truths." Murray says that "[i]f this assertion is denied...the American Proposition is eviscerated in one stroke." This assertion is based on our Fathers' "conviction" that good or just government "is founded...on a certain body of objective truths...accessible to the reason of man" (viii-ix). For Murray, this conviction is reasonable. But our Fathers, contrary to their intention and belief, did not argue convincingly for why it is so. Murray holds that the self-evidence of what our Fathers held to be true may be "legitimately questioned." From the perspective of reason, it may be illegitimate now not to question it, because "the serene and often naive certainties of the eighteenth century have crumbled"(viii). Our theorists, for good reason, no longer hold our Fathers' truths to be true. Americans, they believe, no longer have an argument to support their dedication. But, according to our Fathers, the dedication is unworthy unless the argument is true. Hence we have a crisis. We no longer have any clear or convincing answer to the "fundamental civil question" of what truths we as citizens hold in common (xi).

Our Fathers' certainties, Murray finally explains clearly in his concluding and most theoretical chapter, were those of the eighteenth century, English version of "Locke's individualistic law of nature."

What strikes Murray most about this doctrine is its incoherence and superficiality. The English had too much of "the more human medieval tradition" deposited in their "institutions," and hence their "intelligences," to "work out" in theory or practice all of the law of nature's "logical social consequences" (306-07, 317).

The English, including our Fathers (38), remained incoherently, "very superficially Christian" (317). They were more wed to a tradition they prided themselves in rejecting than they knew. They did not accept or, more precisely, see all the consequences of Locke's "rationalistic secularism" (316) to which they were attracted in principle. In this obtuseness they followed Locke himself. Locke, Murray says, could be a political liberal only because he "did not draw out all the implications from his theory" (308).

The French, Murray observes, had the theoretical merit of understanding Locke's individualistic or asocial law of nature more consistently than he did himself. They understood that its "naked essence" reduced politics to a question of power. With it, the individual lost any perspective, either theoretical or practical, by which he might oppose the power of the state. The result was the "monism" or politically-imposed unity of the "totalitarian democracy" of the French Revolution and its theorist Rousseau (308).

Lockean theory culminates in the denial of human liberty and, more particularly, the denial of the freedom of the person and of the Church from political domination. The human being is reduced to the citizen and nothing more, and religion is reduced to "civil religion" and nothing more (309-10). The American Founders, in their incoherence and superficial, residual Christianity, were far from affirming this conclusion.[10] But, for Murray, their superiority to the French here is not theoretical.

Not only has the modern experiment in the working out of the consequences of Lockean doctrine been discredited by its totalitarian culmination. It has been shown, through the "genuine and true [critical] insights" of "Darwin, Freud, and Marx" to be radically unsound or unempirical as an account of human existence. These "systems," whatever their monistic shortcomings, have the theoretical merit of "destroying the Lockean idea of man" (309), of showing that he does not describe the nature of human beings. Our Fathers' epistemology, which was at least partly Lockean, can no longer be taken "with any philosophical seriousness." It is, as our theorists say, undeniably "dated" (311).

For Locke, human liberty was a problem because its seems, by its nature, to be only negative. The individual pursues freedom from all constraints for nothing in particular (126-28, 200). The problem could only be solved, finally, by denying that human liberty really exists. The tendency of the modern experiment, contrary to its original, liberal intention but not to its misanthropic core, has been to destroy everything which is distinctively human. Its effect, of course, has not been to raise man up to divinity, but to reduce him in theory to an indistinguishable part of some deterministic system and in practice to an indistinguishable part of some "monistic" social whole (130-31). "Communism," Murray notes, "is political modernity carried to its logical conclusion," because it solves the problem presented by Lockean individualism (211).

The strength and weakness of that individualism is that it is merely destructive. The undeniable achievement of the modern experiment has been "to destroy an order of political privilege and inaugurate an order of political equality" (319). This achievement, from the perspective of natural law, is based on the fundamentally Christian denial that "the people are the great beast of aristocratic theory" (181). Thomistic theory is distinctively Christian, or different from Aristotle's, in the weight it places upon consent (33-34, 315).[11]

But modern destructiveness went beyond political equality toward a comprehensive egalitarianism which aims at the root of human liberty or distinctiveness as such. We now know that the modern experiment will never "erect an order of social justice or inaugurate an order of freedom" (319). One difference between Murray's project and Lincoln's is that Murray holds it is now time to defend freedom and order against the promiscuous leveling of egalitarianism, to show that America is dedicated to more than equality. In his limited affirmation of and criticisms of the excesses of egalitarianism Murray, as a political thinker, reminds us, above all, of Alexis de Tocqueville.[12]

Murray says that communism is the end of modern history, and not the end of history as such. Its failure, which was clear enough to Murray and undeniable to us, points to the beginning of post-modern history.[13] Modern destructiveness has not really been able to destroy human liberty, or to solve the problem it presents to human thought. Its apparent success in communism was an illusion, because it came with the unempirical or merely theoretical abolition of human liberty, with a theory that could not become reality. The end of history to which modern theory points is a "mirage" (215).

Still, if human liberty is not for anything in particular, it is not experienced as a human good. The modern experiment has never been able to give a satisfying account of the purpose of human liberty. We now search for a "definition of freedom," for the "positive content" of liberty, for "ordered liberty" (319). We seek to fill "a spiritual vacuum" the failure of the modern experiment reveals "at the heart of human existence" (216). In this search, Murray holds that we should be guided by our post-modern knowledge that all "philosophies which bear too heavily the stamp of modernity" (198) are discredited.

We must, most fundamentally, reject the unempirical individualism of the Lockean state of nature and be open to the "metaphysical" claims of Thomistic natural law. Natural law, in opposition to the idea of the state of nature, recognizes that the human person, by his nature, cannot sustain his transpolitical liberty or dignity outside a community of thought and belief (313).[14] This liberty, understood coherently as a human good, can only be freedom for the community which is the Church. The modern experiment in freedom, Murray says, has been, from one perspective, the search for a "secular substitute" for all that is implied in the idea of freedom of the Church. We now know that there is no such substitute (201).

Returning to the "Foreword," it is at this point in the argument that Murray introduces himself, as "a citizen" and "a Catholic" (x). He says that only the Catholic natural law tradition or community of thought can give American citizens what they most urgently need today to enlarge and hence perpetuate, legitimately, their unifying proposition. Murray concludes that Catholic thinkers, in this sense, are at least potentially the best American citizens.

But Murray's "Catholic reflections" are not, first of all, those of a citizen. He does not even call them reflections of a "Catholic American." He "knows that the principles of Catholic faith and morality stand superior to, and in control of, the whole order of social life." Hence he asks not "whether Catholicism is compatible with American democracy," as the American citizen as citizen would do. He asks "whether American democracy is compatible with Catholicism," as the American Catholic must do (x). He answers the latter question affirmatively, but only by interpreting American democracy in light of the Catholic tradition. Today's definitions of democracy, both the popular ones and the ones put forth by our theorists, will not do.

Any particular interpretation of this democracy's proposition must confront "the problem of pluralism." Murray's primary criticism of American theorists, from the beginning but especially today, is that they do not see how problematic the fact and theory of pluralism are. Pluralism, for Murray, means fundamental disagreement over the answers to the "religious" or "ultimate questions" for human beings (XI). The problem, Murray later explains, is that the "coexistence" of such "incompatible views" is "inherently disintegrative of all consensus and community" (73, emphasis added). From the citizen's and the proposition's perspective, the problem is that religious pluralism which is too extreme makes political community and consensus impossible (117).

Murray says that American pluralism, as it now exists, is an "intellectual experience" of "sheer confusion" (16). There is no American intellectual community. The American university "long since bade a quiet goodbye to the whole notion of an American consensus" (40). Our theorists, to repeat, see our Fathers' argument as discredited, and they know of no replacement.

Outside the university, the American experience is not simply chaotic. It is "a structure of war." The "urbanity" of pluralist doctrine barely masks religious conflict rooted in theoretical disagreement and historical distrust (18-21).

Americans do seem to agree on the goodness of the great document of American pluralism, the First Amendment. But they disagree, radically, on how it is to be understood, on how its "doctrine" is to be defined. The Catholics, at one extreme, see it as protecting the freedom of the Church to define itself as a "community of thought" superior to the political order. The secularists, at the other, see it as protecting Americans from any organized force, especially the Church, that would disrupt the "community of democratic thought" (21).

The Protestants distrust the extremism of both the secularists and Catholics, but the latter more than the former. They see the Catholics as covertly promoting "clericalism" as an "instrument of tyranny" (20). They doubt their devotion to the Amendment, believing that they affirm it, for now, only out of expediency.

The Catholic partisans of natural law hold, in turn, that the apparent Protestant moderation is actually incoherence. It contributes, as such, to the dissolution of the civilization rooted in the rational, Christian tradition (20) and points toward the misanthropic monism of consistent secularism. Protestant theory, history has shown, has not been able to sustain itself over time. Its individualism, from its beginning, owes too much to Lockeanism and its derivatives. Murray participates unreservedly in the Catholic critique of the antirealistic extremism of Protestant Kantianism, which puts form in the place of content and sincerity in the place of the truth. He emphatically denies that the First Amendment has a Protestant interpretation which can make sense out of our Fathers' assertion that our proposition is, most fundamentally, a convincing argument about the nature of man (276-79, 290).

Americans seem to disagree too radically on the purpose of religious liberty to form a political community or consensus. Murray's transformative task is to show that the Catholic, natural law interpretation of the First Amendment alone provides the unity that would reduce the chaos and war of American pluralism to some intelligibility and hence some genuine public consensus (136). He has to calm, first of all, the Protestant suspicions (17). He has to show that Catholic thought is not alien to American principle of religious liberty, that Catholics do not regard the American Proposition as hostile to their own.

The Catholic affirmation of the First Amendment can be unreserved, because the Catholic tradition of thought, properly understood, also rejects the principle of clericalism in politics. For one thing, the Church's "spiritual freedom... demands that she should not be compromised in her essential mission by engagement in the inevitable uncertainties that attend every directly political and economic manoeuvre."[15] Murray asserts that his tradition is the source of the distinction between state and society, which is, more precisely, the distinction between the order of politics and the order of culture, or State and Church.

Murray even hopes to incorporate American secularism into the Christian, natural law consensus. He shows the secularist that his affirmation of the First Amendment's dualistic, more than pluralistic, doctrine of liberty also is necessarily rooted in his affirmation of "Christian values" (52). A consistent secularism is always a monism. Pre- and post-Christian thought and practice both deny the person's transpolitical dignity (15, 133, 322-26). The First Amendment, in its protection of that dignity, must be "a product of Christian history" in the decisive sense (39). The misanthropic consistency of rationalistic secularism is alien to the American Proposition.

Murray sketches the limits to religious pluralism required to make sense out of the American Proposition. Americans must agree, if their proposition is intelligible, that human beings, in their dignity and sacredness, transcend political life for participation in the Church or religious community. They must affirm, finally, a metaphysical view about the nature of man that depends upon a Christian insight, even while they remain in disagreement over which Church is, truly, the universal one. The absence of this limited but public agreement on religion creates a vacuum which, history has shown, will be filled, one way or another, by "secular civil religion," with a public, monistic denial of the person's transcendence of political order.

Murray says at one point that "the whole [American] consensus has its ultimate root" in this Christian conception of personal sacredness (81). Despite our Fathers' ambiguity, incoherence, and superficiality, their Declaration of Independence and First Amendment are decisively part of the "conservative Christian tradition," because their "idea is that man has certain original responsibilities primarily as man, antecedent to his status as citizen" (30). The person protected by the Bill of Rights, "whether he knows it or not," is "the Christian man" (36). That our Fathers were not properly aware of their Christian, Thomistic dependence simply means that they built better than they knew.

Murray claims to understand what our Fathers accomplished better than they did. He is aware, as a result of deficiencies in their self-understanding. They were far from clear, especially, in understanding that the transpolitical dignity they defended, which they characteristically called freedom of conscience, can only flourish within transpolitical community. The isolated conscience protected by what Murray calls Madison's principled "anti-ecclesiaticism" cannot bear the weight placed upon it in defense of human liberty or dignity (65, 69-72, 315). Murray agrees with Lincoln that the American Proposition is vulnerable because it owes too much to Lockean individualism. But his criticism of individualism is much less political than Lincoln's. It is barely political at all, because he, against Lincoln, shares the Founders' distrust, on behalf of human liberty, of civil theology.[16]

Murray is aware, of course, that other interpretations of our Fathers' theoretical and practical accomplishments are possible, precisely because of their incoherence. His method of interpreting the Declaration, for example, is simply to identify "Nature's God" with the "Creator," to attribute to that great statement of the American Proposition a consistent, Thomistic theology. But the Declaration, plainly, can also be viewed as purposely incoherent in the name of revolutionary unity, as a mixture of orthodox Christian and secular, Deistic theologies.[17] Murray, again imitating Lincoln, chooses the interpretation which is most in accord with the truth about human liberty or dignity. His choice, of course, is a transformative one, a deliberate improvement upon what our Fathers had chosen.

It will not quite do to agree with E. A. Goerner that Murray's history is a "noble, Platonic tale," because it is far from simply untrue.[18] The American experiment is different from the French. It is less modern or rationalistic, and more "integrally human" or rational (319). The Declaration and the First Amendment do affirm human freedom under God, even if the unamended Constitution does not.[19] Properly interpreted, these differences between the American incoherence and the French consistency are decisive. The American tradition can be rescued by its transformation, by making sense of it in a certain way by incorporating it into the tradition of natural law.

NOTES

1. See, for example, John Gueguen's review of George Weigel's *Catholicism and the Renewal of American Democracy* (*Social Justice Review* 80 (November/December, 1989): 192-94. Weigel often cites Murray as an authority, but most of Gueguen's criticisms of Weigel's project do not apply to Murray's. Murray is, for example, far from uncritical of the American Founders, and he explicitly and consistently understands America in light of the universal Church. Also missing from Weigel's thought is a nuanced and profound understanding of why natural law theory points to the solution to the crisis of our time. Gueguen misleads us when he blames Murray for the neoconservative Americanism of Weigel.
2. Even Murray's moderate Jesuit friend, Richard Regan, concluded in the wake of Vatican II that "the long-suffering chorus of dissent within the Church was vindicated in the Declaration [on Religious Freedom]. As a result, dissenters in other matters of theological opinion are more likely to find an open forum of expression" (*Conflict and Consensus: Religious Freedom and the Vatican Council* [New York: Macmillan, 1967], 185).

 But Gueguen, I think rightly, contends, against Weigel, that Murray's position was never really in dissent. Weigel, he says, "is apparently unaware that the universal Church has always taught that the human person has religious liberty by natural right. Once again Weigel has trouble distinguishing the authentic teaching of the Church from pronouncements of authoritarian bureaucrats and theologians who have held misguided views concerning human liberty...." *Dignitatis Humanae* is best understood as in continuity with "the universal tradition of the Church" (193).

For a brief account of Murray's dissent from some of the argument (but not from the conclusions) of the Vatican II *Declaration*, see Francis J. Canavan, "Murray on Vatican II's *Declaration on Religious Freedom*," *Communio* 9 (1982): 404-05. The *Declaration*, in Murray's view, remained too anchored in the rights of a sincere conscience, and not in the dignity of the human person as a moral subject. In other words, the *Declaration* was too American or modern or Madisonian in its argument.

3. All page references in the text refer to John Courtney Murray, *We Hold These Truths* (New York: Sheed and Ward, 1960). Consider here that Frederick D. Wilhelmsen's criticism of both Murray and the American Founders seems to downplay peace as so central of a political goal. See his *Citizen of Rome* (LaSalle, IL: Sherwood Sudgen, 1980), 61-62, 139-40. Wilhelmsen writes, with irony, that the American Founders "brought forth the only great power in history that has not been guilty of anything so indecent as a religious war" (140). The problem with his position is that it ignores the danger that a certain kind of intensity of conviction can readily produce such war. He thus seems to dislike one of the important principles that characterized the thinking of both Murray and the Founding Fathers. This is why he places Murray's Catholic moderation in the same camp as Protestantism and secularism.

4. My interpretation of Lincoln's transformative project is drawn from Harry Jaffa, *Crisis of the House Divided* (Chicago: University of Chicago Press, 1982), especially 226-31.

5. The phrase "political religion" comes from Lincoln's Address to the Young Men's Lyceum (1838).

6. On the primacy of spiritual crisis for Murray's thought, see Robert W. McElroy, *The Search for an American Public Theology: The Contribution of John Courtney Murray* (New York: Paulist Press, 1989), Chapter 1.

7. On Murray's subtle and distinctively Christian understanding of natural law. See my "Murray's Natural Law Articulation of the American Proposition," *John Courtney Murray and the American Civil Conversation*, ed. K. Grasso and R. Hunt (Grand Rapids, MI: Eerdmans, 1991). See also my "Natural Law and the American Regime: Murray's *We Hold These Truths*," *Communio* 9 (1982): 368-89.

8. On this point, Murray's post-modernism would be less traditional than that of Richard John Neuhaus, who often cites with approval but still criticizes Murray's natural law theory. See my "Thoughts on America's Catholic Moment," *The Political Science Reviewer* 17 (1988): 163-96. The Catholic moderation of Murray's thought undoubtedly made a strong contribution to Neuhaus's recent conversion.

For a strongly Catholic criticism of Neuhaus's postmodern traditionalism or communalism or contextualism, see J. Brian Benestad, "On Richard John

Neuhaus's *The Catholic Moment*," *Communio* 15 (Winter, 1988): 490, 494-95. Murray would agree with this criticism, as Neuhaus would admit.

Benestad criticizes Neuhaus for relying on Murray's account of the American Proposition as "a product of Christian history or the medieval Natural Law tradition." Our Founders, Benestad contends, are more properly understood as "Enlightenment thinkers who had serious quarrels with Catholic natural law thinking" (495). Murray, as I show below, agrees with Benestad's characterization of the Founders while denying that their break with Christianity or the natural law tradition was total or even decisive. His evaluation of their theory is much more ambivalent than Benestad or even Neuhaus allows. Neuhaus, by the way, does not view the American Founding as part of the medieval natural law tradition, but that is a story for another day.

9. John Courtney Murray, "Leo XIII: Separation of Church and State," *Theological Studies* 14 (1953): 151-68.
10. On Jefferson's incoherent, superficial Christianity, see my "Classical Ethics, Jefferson's Christian Epicureanism, and American Morality," *Perspectives on Political Science* (January, 1991).
11. See William Baumgarth and Richard J. Regan, S.J., "Introduction," *Saint Thomas Aquinas: On Law, Morality, and Politics* (Indianapolis, IN: Hackett, 1988), xix-xx.
12. Murray, like Tocqueville, presents himself as a friendly critic of democracy on behalf of human liberty or dignity. Tocqueville and Murray are both, theoretically, critics, above all, of the misanthropic consistency of secularist rationalism. See my "Tocqueville's Elusive Moderation," *Polity* 22 (1989): 181-89 with my "Was Tocqueville a Philosopher?" *Interpretation: A Journal of Political Philosophy* 17 (1990): 401-14. Consider the reference to Tocqueville as historian in *We Hold These Truths*, 67. Did Murray model his history of human liberty on Tocqueville's?
13. Consider *We Hold These Truths*, 80: "[I]f the Communist empire were to fall apart tomorrow, and if the Communist ideology were to disintegrate with it, our problems would not be solved. In fact, they would be worse in many ways."
14. For more on this thought, see my "Murray's Natural Law Articulation." It is also at the foundation of Tocqueville's defense of religion from the perspective of the individual in Volume 2 of *Democracy in America*.
15. John Courtney Murray, "Toward a Theology for the Layman: The Problem of Finality," *Theological Studies* 5 (1944): 70.
16. On the Founders' distrust of civil theology, consider the extreme tentativeness of *Federalist* 49's promotion of constitutional veneration. Also consider the now well-established fact that at least the primary authors and defenders of the Constitution opposed the "classical republican" or "civic humanist" tradition. See my "James Madison and the Metaphysics of Modern Politics," *Review of Politics* 48 (1986): 92-115.
17. See Michael Zuckert, "Self-Evident Truth and the Declaration of Independence," *Review of Politics* 49 (1987): 319-39.
18. E. A. Goerner, *Caesar and Peter* (New York: Herder and Herder, 1962), 82.
19. For a convincing defense of the position that the First Amendment was intended to protect freedom for religion, see Gary Glenn, "Forgotten Purposes of the First Amendment Religion Clauses," *Review of Politics* 49 (1987): 340-67.

8

Personal Recollections of John Courtney Murray, S.J. and Some Reflections

By Msgr. George A. Kelly

Introduction

*J*ohn Courtney Murray and I had a good number of contacts over the years, although I was not a close friend. During his lifetime priests like me maintained a great regard for him and were his staunch supporters in his controversy over church and state. John Courtney Murray was not a simple man. He had his successes and his failures during a shortened life, but he did play a very important role in the modern history of the Church. And he did have the favor of the American bishops, I might add. In the Second Vatican Council he also won a very large victory. No one can gainsay him that. The following is what I remember best about him.

Our Final Visit

My last visit with Fr. Murray occurred several weeks before he died. At the time he was, as I remember, the head of the John LaFarge Institute operating out of the America House in New York. One day he called to ask if I would come to an ecumenical dialogue, and I did. The other Catholic guest was the President of Manhattanville College, which by that time had almost alienated itself from the Church. Two Jewish rabbis and two Protestant ministers were also in attendance, discussing with us certain areas of religious tensions in the City. During the course of a two-hour afternoon session, the nun in question began to sound bitterly anti-Catholic, highly critical of bishops and was almost insulting about the state of the Church. It was an embarrassment to be there as an official of the Archdiocese of New York, and I wondered in my own mind why the blazes John Courtney Murray had engaged me in such a dialogue. Nothing very concrete came out of the meeting itself, and I was happy to leave. At that point Fr. Murray stopped me to ask, "Are you doing anything tonight?" I asked, "What do you have in mind?" He said, "I'd like to go to supper with you." We ended up in New York's University Club where we spent two hours, during which the Jesuit vented his fury at this religious woman, not only for the embarrassment she was to him, but for the injury she had inflicted on the Church. As the evening went on he began to talk about the Jesuits, about their contemplated move from Woodstock to New York where they became a tragedy. By 1967 Murray wasn't a well man, and he was highly upset at what he saw going on among scholastics there. He might have been a hero to the bishops but by this time he was considered "old hat" by younger Jesuits. I was touched by his sincerity and by his great sense of the Church.

As the meeting was drawing to a close, I asked him: "Do you recall going to Dunwoodie in 1941?" He said, "No." I reminded him: "Well you came up to Dunwoodie just about the time I was to be ordained a priest for a day of recollection, as I remember. You gave us a meditation on the virtue of fidelity, and the reason that you chose that topic, you said, was because you thought fidelity was a virtue in short supply among diocesan priests, that we diocesan priests were not faithful to each other, nor faithful to our pastors nor to our bishops. Before you finished you held up as a model of fidelity your own Jesuit community." Murray looked at me and departed saying, "I could not do that today."

Murray and His Antagonists

Most of my young contemporaries bought his intuition that the Catholic position on Church and state needed refinement *and* in the direction of Murray's argumentation. We looked upon his antagonists, Fr. Francis Connell, as a saintly priest, but wrong—and Fr. Joseph Fenton as too rambunctious and equally wrong.

Nor did any of us young Turks think a major matter of *revealed Catholic doctrine* was involved—merely a *long-standing political arrangement* that grew out of historical circumstance, satisfactory for many centuries to Church authorities, if not necessarily or always beneficial to the Church's well-being.

Throughout his controversial years, and in the face of severe criticism, more from academicians than from Church authorities, *Fr. Murray conducted himself as a good priest and a loyal son of the Church.*

In line with his conversations with me, his own notes of Commentary to Vatican II's *Declaration on Religious Freedom* (Abbot Edition) demonstrate that at Council's end he thought no differently than any modern Pope. I cite here his own statements:[1]

1. *Objective Truth and Moral Order*: The correlative of the principle of human freedom is, he said, "the order of duty and obligation. In it man acts freely indeed, but under moral imperatives which bind in conscience. No man may plead 'rights' in the face of the truth or 'claim' 'freedom' from the moral law." Religious freedom, therefore, "is not a pretext for moral anarchy."

2. *The Church is the Source from Christ of Religious Truth*: "For the Catholic 'truth' . . . subsists in the Church, is taught by the Church, is believed by the Church." Religious truth has been "given by Christ to His true Church, the true religion [which] remains the one way in which all men are bound to serve God and save themselves."

3. *Truth and Good Source of Rights*: "Neither error nor evil can be the object of a right, only what is true and good."

4. *Conscience Does Not Determine Good or Right*: The Vatican II *Declaration on Religious Freedom* does not base its conclusions on "*freedom of conscience.*" This is "perilous theory"—subjectivism—to think that people have a right to do what their conscience tells them, that personal conscience, not objective truth, determines what is right or wrong, true or false.

5. *Church Has A Unique Mandate*: The Catholic Church has a "divine mandate laid upon her by Christ Himself," one that no other Church or Community may claim to possess in all its fullness, a mandate also to insist on freedom to conduct her ministry.

6. The establishment of a state religion, "at least from the Catholic point of view, is a matter of historical circumstance, not of theological doctrine."

7. Church Authority: Christian faithful are "urged to form their consciences under the guidance of the authority of the Church."

8. It would be "perilous" to confuse religious freedom as a principle of civil order and Christian freedom inside the Church.

John Courtney Murray, the Elder

During the debate over religious freedom and the civil order, a form of argumentation developed which, however proper and useful in redirecting the Church's legal-political determinations of long standing, eventually caused damage to the Church's spiritual life. This occurred once the argumentation began to be used to cast doubt on matters of faith and morals about which the Church had taught authoritatively throughout the centuries of her existence.

Even John Courtney Murray, who was precise in the application and limits of his methodology to Church-state relations, and in spite of his own cautions in explicating their relevance to his favorite subject, began to suggest at the end of his life that the Church might also need updating in her reading of Christian sexual norms.

In his commentary on the Council's *Declaration on Religious Freedom*, Fr. Murray called upon the Church to alter its Church-state position because of (l) "the rise of man's personal consciousness, his sense of self-hood," and (2) "the Council's intention to 'develop' Catholic doctrine."

During the Council other theologians began to apply these same principles to advance the relaxation of the Church's attitude toward contraception. Murray's convictions about the historical conditioning of the Church-state position were transposed to raise doubts about the Catholic understanding of the Ten Commandments. One commentator expressed the Murray framework as follows: "Can one depend on the inherited words (of Church formulas) themselves or must one look behind them for a dynamic but constant intent whose relevancy to changing circumstances demands periodically revised formulations?"[2]

At the time (1964) Murray made his argument consistent with Church teaching and applied it only to an area in which he thought a theologian free to experiment. This was clear when Chicago's Albert Cardinal Meyer, pressured by some diocesan officials to issue a statement on the birth control issue, found himself opposed by the diocesan theologian who thought the proposed statement compromised Catholic teaching. The officials in question thinking this position too narrow, sought counsel for the Cardinal from Fr. Murray who to their surprise supported the diocesan theologian, without his knowing the theologian's position. Since Meyer died in April 1965—six months before the Council's end—Murray's mind at the time on sexual ethics is clear.

Other theologians had a different agenda in mind, challenging not only the Church's political posture, but also her understanding of human nature, the nature of marriage, and the nature of sexuality itself. These are subjects about which the Church had spoken doctrinally and with substantial authority for the better part of two millennia. It did not take some theologians long to relativize further on historical grounds the Church's positions on Christ's divine nature, His establishment of the Church and the priesthood, and His statements on marital indissolubility. There are some indications that very late in his life, Murray was similarly weakening on his commitment to the orthodox teaching of the Church. Following the Council and before he died, he was overheard in the staff house of the United States Catholic Conference criticizing Fr. John Ford, then the Church's great defender of *Casti Connubii*. Three months before he died (May 5, 1967), Murray also used "historical consciousness" to criticize the minority report of the Pope's Birth Control Commission, arguing that on the matter of contraception "the Church reached for too much certainty, too soon, went too far." Shortly after his death a Jesuit here and there could be heard saying that Murray was even wavering on marital indissolubility.

It is Murray the Elder that has been used by dissenting theologians to turn Moses' Ten Commandments into what Bishop Austin Vaughan says have become for many "the Ten Suggestions."

There is little doubt that virulent dissent has ravaged the post-Vatican II Church doctrinally, morally, and in her discipline. The *skepticism* created by the misapplication of the *historico-critical method* and by the *philosophical assumptions* taken for granted by its practitioners, eventually discredited or eviscerated the meaning of Catholic doctrinal formulations or moral absolutes, even the idea of revelation as "the Word of God."

Not so surprising is the manner in which John Courtney Murray, prior to Vatican II, rejected such skepticism, calling it the "new secular faith [which] produced a new revelation with regard to the nature and destiny of man." With confidence Murray the Younger asserted that "history does not alter the basic structure of human nature." He also severely criticized the "corrosive skepticism and positivism and relativism—all the other isms that are abroad today in the intellectual world."[3] These are the intellectual vices, I might add, which self-proclaimed disciples of Murray have introduced into Catholic academic life, and which today underpin the thinking of masses of our people.

Some Reflections

With the picture of John Courtney Murray in mind as I remember it, I would like to reflect on the thinking associated with post-Vatican II theologians. It is important that we go beyond Murray and ponder, not what this or that theologian thinks, but the mind of the Church:

1. If the Catholic Church is not the Church of Christ, but only one among others in the process of becoming such; and if the Church does not have the ability to decide whether her affirmed universal teachings are true, i.e., those which pertain to God's revelation through Jesus Christ and the eternal salvation of mankind; and if the Church can revise those affirmed universal teachings from one historical period to the next to the point of contradiction. . . then the Church not only lacks religious authority, but has no credibility as the Church of Christ. (*Development* of Catholic doctrine is *one thing*, but *contradicting* such doctrine or *eviscerating* its content is *another*, whether that emptying is accomplished by *denial*, by *deceitful nuancing*, or by *simple neglect*.)

2. Because the Church's priority is the worship of God and the salvation of souls, any development of the Church's understanding of God's Word or any reform of ecclesiastical institutions based on doctrine or in its corollaries, must always take place in orderly fashion under the authority of the College of Bishops in union with the Pope or of the Pope alone. No one is exempt from submission to this authority—neither clergy, nor religious, nor Catholic institutions, not even academics.

3. If John Courtney Murray, caught up in an ever widening circle of dissenting peers, expressed at some point the beginnings of his own dissent in a minor way and mostly privately in small groups, then it might be better for academics to look at the larger figure of Henri DeLubac. Henri DeLubac certainly wrote more and more deeply on more theological subjects than John Courtney Murray. Like DeLubac himself, we priests of my generation did not suffer at the hands of Church authority and we lived under very tough bishops. Those who protest their anguish about living under superiors exaggerate their travail. Michael Harrington, the ex-Catholic socialist, author of *The Other America*—the book which became the basis of LBJ's "War on Poverty"—wrote another book *Fragments of a Century*, in which he described his meeting with Martin Luther King, Jr. He said to King, "Dr. King, have you read my book?" And King said, "Yes," to which response Harrington asked further, "What did you think of it?" King replied finally, "I didn't know I was so poor until I read your book." Most of the people I now hear talk about their suffering didn't really know they suffered so much until someone told them they were suffering.

4. Movements of Catholic development and/or reform must find their motivation and energy in the Church's sacramental charism, from her own close union with God, and in the greater holiness of her people. Neither development nor reform derives from worship of false idols or from undue accommodation to social circumstance, over which believers have little influence or control.

5. The hierarchy of the Church, above all other Catholics, is responsible for legitimizing development and reform—and for censuring heresy and schism. This pastoral responsibility at times involves sanctions of approval for those who build up the Body of Christ, and of disapproval for those who disedify and scandalize the "little ones" of Christ. One conundrum of our time is the assumption that bishops are not supposed to sanction, that they are not supposed to give approval to the faithful followers, and they are not at any cost to censure unfaithful followers holding key institutional positions. If there is any group worthy of close scrutiny by bishops it is contemporary academics. All one has to do is to live in the university world long enough to discover who gets hired and who does not, who gets promoted or not, and in our time who rails against magisterial political

control of institutions (which owe their identity to the approval or toleration of bishops).

One of my first experiences as Secretary for Education to Cardinal Spellman was an assignment to meet a group of rabbis from the City University of New York, who wanted him to intervene in the internal administration of CCNY because politicians, not faculty, had become the driving force for admissions, examinations and of the courses students were required to take. I had to tell the rabbis that there was no Catholic stake in the issue, but I knew well that the university world was not simply academic.

I can give you names, some of which you know, of men and women who have been sanctioned in the academic world of our time simply because they fully professed the Catholic Faith. Dissenting academics today seek privileged sanctuary from bishops, while they use bishops' support to underpin their continued control of institutions that are at best erratically Catholic, and at worst a menace to the Body of Christ. The president of Manhattanville College, who embarrassed Fr. Murray, headed an institution replanted and subsidized by the Archbishop of New York. She eventually abandoned the presidency and the religious order, but *in situ* still sat in judgment on bishops. The balance of authority in Fr. Murray's day tipped in favor of the common good, of the objective moral, civil, and ecclesiastical order, and within Catholic circles in favor of eternal verities. Today the balance tips the other way, to the detriment of the Church.

Conclusion

The controversies that preoccupied the John Courtney Murrays are really old stories.

St. Paul once told the Philippians (4: 7-9)
> Your thoughts should be wholly directed to all that is true. All that is honest, pure, admirable, decent virtues worthy of praise.
> Live according to what you have learned and accepted. What you have heard me say and do. Then will the peace of God be with you.

Ours is a hierarchical Church, one whose origin is in God. There is no way we can mediate God's Word to mean something opposite to what His revelation has always been understood to mean by the

Magisterium. We of the twentieth century depend on Christ's work as it has been preached by His Vicars.

Consider St. Gregory the Great's Homily on the Gospels in the seventh century, dealing with heretics and an interfering emperor:

> I speak of our absorption in external affairs;
> We accept the duties of office.
> But by our actions we show that we
>   are attentive to other things.
> We abandon the ministry of preaching
>   and, in my opinion, are called
>   bishops to our detriment.
> For we retain the honorable office
> But fail to practice the virtues proper to it.
> Those who have been entrusted to us
>   abandon God
> And we are silent
> They fall into sin
> And we do not extend a hand or rebuke. [4]

NOTES

1. Walter M. Abbot, S.J., and Joseph Gallagher, eds., *The Documents of Vatican II*, America Press, 1966, pp. 672-696.
2. Donald E. Pelotte, SSS, *John Courtney Murray: Theologian in Conflict,* Paulist Press, 1965, p. 89.
3. Robert W. McElroy, *The Search for an American Public Theology,* Paulist Press, 1989, pp. 27, 59, 69.
4. *Homily on the Gospels.* (P.L. 76: 1139, 1140, 1146).

WE HOLD THESE TRUTHS AND MORE

Murray and Religious Freedom

9

John Courtney Murray and the Privatization of American Religion

by Gerard V. Bradley

Anecdotal evidence of the privatization of American religion is hardly scarce. And anecdotal evidence can be enough, even for those drunk on statistics. It all depends on how revealing, how typical, the anecdotes are. There are lots of anecdotes of Catholic politicians assuring voters that their Catholicism leaves them personally opposed to abortion, but that such religious convictions are irrelevant to lawmaking.

Maybe abortion is atypical. It *is* uniquely controversial, however revealing. How about some anecdotes from our only national "town" meeting, the quadrennial ordeal of Presidential campaigning? Our Catholic politicians may take their cue from John Kennedy, the first and only Roman Catholic President. Kennedy insisted that his religion was a purely private matter that would not affect his public decisions. But maybe Kennedy's is also an atypical case. Roman Catholic Americans, unlike other Christians and only faintly paralleled these days by Jews with Israel, have always endured charges of disloyalty, of subservience to a foreign prince. Perhaps they, but not other believers, need to conspicuously strut their privatized religion. And Nixon hardly helped matters in l960 by telling audiences that he was *not* going to talk about his opponent's religion.

Let's take a sample then from recent presidential candidates, none of whom is Catholic. Recall George Bush's already legendary answer to what he thought about after being shot down in 1944: "Mother and Father…and God and faith, and the separation of church and state." [1] Now, one must presume that as the President mouthed the penultimate words, he saw his political life pass before him, and beheld a headstone engraved with the dread "G" word of big time politics, the "Gaffe." He forgot to privatize, and tacked on the necessary reassurances. (If Bush really *was* going to meet his Maker with the First Amendment as his final prayer, he deserves our prayers.) The Democratic rejoinder was supplied by Greek Orthodox officials. They were asked about Michael Dukakis' church standing after allegations of infrequent, indifferent participation surfaced. The Archdiocese "regret[ted]" recent attempts...to inject religion into the political life of this nation, in direct contradiction to the First Amendment. [2]

In 1984, Walter Mondale bared his faith commitments: "I believe in an America...where religion is a private matter between individuals and God, between families and their church and synagogues, with no room for politicians in between." [3] Mondale's opponent did cut a different figure. Ronald Reagan believed that religion and morality were necessarily linked, much as Washington and other Founders did. But it seems that, for Reagan as perhaps for some Founders, it was the moral teaching—not its sacred bedding, so to speak—that mattered to public life. Nevertheless this was too close for the comfort of *The Baltimore Sun*. "[E]ver since the president offered the dubious thesis that government needs the church as a guide and that politics and religion are necessarily related, the nation has been reverberating. Most Americans know instinctively when the wall separating church and state is under assault, and they don't like it." [4] Anyway, the more revealing episode concerns news reports that Reagan was curious about biblical apocalyptic, especially Armageddon. The response to such musings was negative. There *is* something unnerving about the man with his finger on the button thinking of divinely ordained violence. But the criticism overleapt reasonable bounds, and flowed into the ever-present jargon of privatization and parroting the incendiary mix of God and politics.

Against this background I pit Murray. With admirable clarity and great conviction, he said, "[a]ny interpretation of the First Amendment which reduces religion to a private matter—and the church to the status of a private, voluntary association—creates immediately in this country some 35,000,000 dissenters, the Catholic community."[5] Near the end of his career, in the *Theological Studies* piece published as *The Problem of Religious Freedom*, Murray reaffirmed that "all Catholics"—explicitly including adherents of his "Second View"—acknowledge "that an obligation to profess faith in God and to worship

Him is incumbent on Society." The Second View, according to Murray, rejects the sectarian Liberalist notion of religion as a purely private affair, citing Leo XIII's pronouncements on the subject. [6]

There you have "Murray and the Privatization of American Religion." He is against it. Privatization is profoundly incompatible with Roman Catholicism. All that remains for me is to convince you, if Bush, *et al.* have not already, that religion in America *is* privatized, especially as it is governed by our First Amendment. Then Murray can lead us into the countercultural posture that, as far as I can tell, is increasingly plausible for orthodox Roman Catholic Americans.

But I am not content to prove the critical point—the reality of privatization—with anecdotes. I propose to provide more reason to recognize its hegemony, *especially* in the constitutional law of the First Amendment Religion Clauses, right where Murray (in *We Hold These Truths*) detected a litmus test of the regime. I shall also suggest that Murray, despite the clarity of his opposition, is an unreliable defender against that nemesis. Murray's views on both the concept of religious freedom and the First Amendment provide insufficient resources to recognize the privatization in our midst and effectively to combat it.

First we need to get a handle on the phenomenon of "privatization." What anthropologist Mary Douglas calls "secularization" is a good provisional definition of privatization: the evacuation of religion from public life. Douglas warns against any inference of diminished religious devotion.[7] In other words, and in Richard Neuhaus' marvelous term, there is no necessary correlation between a "naked public square" and indifference to religion or widespread agnosticism. There certainly has been no such link in American history. Historians of American religion agree that the early national era was surprisingly indifferent to (at least organized) religion. Yet then existed our most "sacred" public square, including establishments of religion. Donald Lutz provides a good set of statistical measurements. Looking for what counted as "authority" in political discourse during the Founding (specifically 1760-1805), Lutz surveyed a large sample of public political literature. The most cited book was the Bible, and the biblical tradition accounted for about one-third of all citations. Saint Paul is cited as often as Montesquieu and Blackstone, the two most cited secular authors. Deuteronomy is cited almost twice as often as all Locke's writings put together. [8]

The great Christianization of society came after 1830 with the Protestant revivals and the influx of Catholic immigrants. There is, *unquestionably*, no way to understand either the electoral politics or the legal culture of that era without allowing for the vast influence of religion. Even so, the prevailing pietistic religion of the time, especially in the South, contained a profound privatizing component. The nineteenth century was a slow but a steady retreat from the sacralized politics of the eighteenth—even if it ended well short of twentieth century secularism—even though there was no corresponding diminution of belief. Now, I am quite certain that we have now all but stripped public life of religion, even as pollsters inform us that compared even to European countries with established churches—England, Italy— we are as avidly religious as they are religiously indifferent.

Neither the extent nor quantity of belief argues against privatization. We can all be religious yet, even in a democracy, divorce belief from public life. The crucial factor must then be the nature of belief, not quantity but quality. Let me explain, with reference initially to the architectonic principles of public discourse and religion, our constitutional law of the First Amendment.

The chief doctrinal weapons of privatization are the secular purpose and divisiveness parts of the *Lemon* establishment clause test. [9] The former excludes "religious" purposes from lawmaking, and is just reheated privatization. It has occasionally sufficed to overturn a law but where it has done so—creation science, [10] posting the Ten Commandments in a public schoolroom[11]—the conclusion was hardly compelled. Divisiveness is a general contributor to judicial analysis, not a particular test. Somehow the Religion Clauses are precisely designed to forestall public debate grounded in religious differences. We are supposed to believe that we might otherwise—that is, without judges depoliticizing issues—bring on another War of Religion. Never mind that the evidence is generally allusion to seventeenth century European history. Never mind the curious isolation of religion—not race, class, or ethnicity—as potential flashpoint. The *purpose* of the analysis is to discourage religious persons from participating in public life. So viewed, divisiveness is the most important, because controlling, First Amendment idea. Add to this picture the subordinate influence of a Free Exercise Clause which has been explicitly detached from any essential intersubjective base and from location within a recognized or coherent set of beliefs. That is, the untethered individual kook—so long as he is a sincere kook—is solicited by the Constitution as much as the fifty million strong Roman Catholic Church. [12]

Where does this leave us? Religion can only go public if (and this is a necessary but not sufficient condition) it makes objective claims about interpersonal relations—claims which are proposed as true for believers and unbelievers, whether they like it or not. Otherwise, there is no overlap between issues of justice—the concern of public life— and the realm of religion. Where a theory of justice like liberalism's seeks to operate, for various historical and philosophical reasons, independent of religion it will make "freedom of the individual conscience" its paradigm freedom. This is exactly what liberals like Rawls, Richards, and Rorty do. They include freedom of conscience within a subsuming individual right to privacy. That is and to take Richards' example, we start on solid ground with the traditional notion of free religious conscience, and proclaim it paradigmatic. The paradigm then swells to resemble an embracing right to pursue any conception of the good, so long as we do no harm to non-consenting third parties. This team forms the border between "public" and "private." I put the matter this starkly to flag one difficulty in Murray's thought: in the predominant mode of contemporary American political theorizing, "freedom of conscience" is the basis for the divorce of religion from public life. This notion (though *not* its terminology; Murray consistently uses "religious freedom" not "freedom of conscience") is a centerpiece of Murray's thought, and one is obliged to adjust one's appropriation of Murray to help him hold the line against privatization. Put differently, contemporaries use "freedom of conscience" and "freedom of religion" interchangeably and as linchpins of the privatizing projects in the interests of religious liberty. Murray is hard to distinguish away this company: he clearly contemplates a tight fit between a highly secularized constitutional order and religious freedom.

I do not unfairly slight the ostensible aim of much contemporary liberalism which is, more modestly, to deny public action upon religious belief. A good liberal democrat need not, it might be said, subscribe to individualized religion. He just publicly acts as if he does. For a host of reasons I do not believe such epistemic schizophrenia feasible. Nor do I think it possesses any historical explanatory power. I don't think liberalism can "take" in a culture unless the dominant mode of belief is politically impotent (i.e., privatized). I do not think our regime of religious liberty, to the extent that accurately describes our regime, is more than negligibly indebted to this dichotomy.

The Enlightenment helps us understand the genesis of such hospitable conditions. The "age of reason" marked the transition from traditional "cosmological" societies—characterized by a single value structure penetrating all subsystems—to "differentiated" society. In the latter, subsystems like culture, science, economics, family follow distinctive inner logics. In order: expression, "reality" as such, efficiency, intimacy. Jaroslav Pelikan, in the fifth volume of his master work *The History of the Development of Christian Doctrine,* located the corresponding religious transformation in the eighteenth century, when the doctrines of the faith were transposed into the category of affective dispositions.[13] William James put the upshot succinctly: religion is the experience of individuals in their solitude, related to whatever they may consider God.[14] Were it otherwise, I doubt our constitutional law would be what it is. It's not exactly that the Supreme Court, as Mr. Dooley said long ago, follows the election returns. Rather, constitutional law, like all law, has its feet deeply implanted in exogenous social developments even as it shapes their course.

Religion is emotional, affective aesthetic, non-cognitive. As if we were all Quakers. Religion is incapable of giving reasons because religion is non-rational. Since courts make sure laws all have a plausible rational basis—a basic requirement of all law, owing to the constitutional guarantee of due process—this makes for a thoroughgoing constitutional rule against religiously grounded political choices.

You may wonder at my indifferent use of privatization and liberalism. Privatization *is* liberalism in that both insist "religion" never legitimately provides a reason for acting in public.

Now that is the "liberal" view. What distinguishes contemporary "conservatives"? Consider this exchange from the *New York Times* transcript of oral argument in the *Webster* case:

> **Justice Scalia**: How can—can you derive [a right to abortion] without making a determination as to whether a fetus is a human life or not...
>
> **Mr. Susman** [representing the pro-choice parties]: I think the basic question,...is not something that is verifiable but by reliance upon faith.
>
> It is a question of labels. Neither side in this issue and debate would ever disagree on the physiological facts. Both sides would agree as to when a heartbeat can first

be detected. Both sides would agree as to when brain waves can be first detected. But when you come to try to place the emotional labels on what you call that collection of physiological facts, that is where people part company.

Justice Scalia: I agree with you entirely, but what conclusion does that lead you to? [15]

Another prominent judicial conservative is Robert Bork. In Bork's view, judges ought not overturn laws against sodomy, for instance, because courts deal in the rational review of legislation, and one can't rationally review moral judgments.

Perhaps the best example of judicial "conservatism" is the 1986 decision in *Bowers v. Hardwick*.[16] There, a bare 5-4 majority refuted a man's claim of fundamental right to commit sodomy with another man. (Just recently, one of the five—the retired Lewis Powell—recanted.) But the problem is that (and I speak as a defender of the result) the majority could not argue for its judgment. Against a fairly sophisticated and coherent liberal dissent, which was consistent with two decades of precedents, the "conservatives" limply responded, "law has always been based on moral judgments and that's that." Well, yes but that simply raises the question: to what extent is *that* tradition inconsistent with regnant liberal political morality as applied to "victimless" crimes. The majority never engaged the issue.[17]

I submit the following topography of extant cleavages on privatization of religion. Lots of liberals see religion (and religiously-grounded morality) as forbidden fruit, period. Some of these think little is lost, that the problems of constitutional, limited government do not implicate such convictions. We operate quite efficiently without the bad apples. Bruce Ackerman is the best example.[18] Others are not sure there is no loss. They are not sure that thinking through abortion (for instance) is possible without religion. This group bifurcates. Hardliners conclude, a bit nostalgically, that where non-religious reasons run out, autonomy or the private sphere begins. Diversity of views rooted in religious differences is a conclusive argument to privatize the issue. This is a popular view of how to deal with abortion, and is the conclusion Scalia's interlocutor would draw. Others, like Columbia legal philosopher Kent Greenwalt,[19] admit that even good liberal democrats may, because they need to, on occasion rely upon religious convictions. He cites abortion as an example but not, interestingly, sodomy. Greenwalt apparently believes that only religious convictions can supply the resources to condemn such sexual acts, and that secular reason affirms their morality. Where secular reason speaks clearly to an issue, believers must put aside contrary religious views.

"Conservatives" agree with Greenwalt that "faith" (or "emotion") is necessary to round out lawmaking, and they supplement that observation with others (probably true) rooted in social necessity. A functioning society needs some core of common moral commitments. This is a better course but it is still not very good. For one thing, when human life begins—the relevant question in the abortion debate is not a matter of faith but of fact and reason. And when did you last hear a prominent conservative (apart from clergy) flatly say that sodomy is immoral, that its immorality is a matter of truth, and that it is a legitimate purpose of lawmaking to inculcate in citizens the true morality. (Never mind that some conservatives may believe all that. The point is that one will not long remain prominent after *saying* it.) "Conservatives" settle for the Greenwalt "necessity" defense and the liberal characterization of religion as non-cognitive. They make no case for that which is essential to countering privatization: the political rationality of religion and the centrality of questions of truth to public life, even in our limited, constitutional government. I take it that "conservatives" have acquiesced in the privatization of truth. All this is why I think "conservatives" are mostly right-of-center liberals.

I have detailed privatization because I want to suggest that despite Murray's firm opposition, there are too many points of similarity to notions propelling privatization for him to qualify as our stalwart without a highly critical appropriation of his thought. For one thing, Murray's historicism rankles, and it props up privatization by undermining appeals to truth through its close affinity to relativism. Murray's highly contrastive "First" and "Second" views also disturb.[20] At one level I think Murray misunderstands—or caricatures—the freedom resident in each. Murray plays into the hands of privatizers by seeming to *oppose* the freedom available in our system to systems founded upon orthodoxy. But, as legal philosopher Joseph Raz observes, even an "establishment" works no measurable diminution of religious freedom.[21] That some privilege (say a monopoly upon benedictions at state occasions, or singularly generous support of its seminary) is accorded one church does not, by itself, coerce adherents to others. All this means is that there is, in a loose sense, commitment to a particular religious tradition in the body politic. Or there once was. And, as Eric Voegelin observes, "There was religious freedom aplenty during the Middle Ages, as is attested by the range of religious personalities from St. Francis to St. Thomas Aquinas, by the range of theological speculation from realism to nominalism" and by the range of religious orders founded and types of mysticism.[22]

We Americans see such privileges as a deep threat to freedom. That is why we rebel. We seem to have defined "freedom of religion" as "pluralism": absolutely *no* hint of formative religious tradition is allowable for fear of making religion relevant to one's standing in the public square. Finally, we simply need to now put to the test the claim that there is greater freedom. We may start by asking, what "freedom" is there when "truth" becomes an expression of the artistic self?

It seems to me that the Christian must avoid, even in polemics, opposing freedom to truth. The Christian believes that the truth sets us free. Nor can the Christian assert that the truth is freedom, for freedom is always tethered to the good of human persons as reason discovers it and bad reveals it. But freedom, even freedom of conscience, is not a terminus for political thinking either. "[B]eyond conscience lies the spiritual personality of the man who has it," says Voegelin.[23] One of the first liberals—Locke—did not believe in a right to "freedom of conscience." He always believed that "freedom of conscience" was anarchic because, taken seriously, it erected each man a law unto himself. So said, by the way, our Supreme Court in its first serious encounter with the Free Exercise Clause, the 1879 Morman polygamy case, *Reynolds v. U.S.*[24] For Locke, the reality of a plurality of conscience meant the spirit would roam where *it,* and not the sovereign, willed. That government need be indifferent to the truth about God expressed itself by limiting civil society to ends chosen by persons in a contracting original position—the prevention of force and fraud, and the security of property.

A greater difficulty is Murray's perplexing, almost inebriated, definition of "religious freedom" as "a human and civil right, personal and corporate...immune from restriction by any legal or extralegal force." [25] One can *articulate* such an ensemble of notions, but I don't think one can give it coherent meaning. Brought to the realm of concrete action the resident tension will likely break out into open warfare. Should the state protect the human right of individuals against the extralegal pressure exerted by the "institutional church"? What if we emphasize the "personal" right against "extra-legal pressure," and guarantee it by law? Would this provide the underpinnings for the disposition for those who wish to protect impressionable youngsters from the indoctrination of parents and parochial schools. The only way a right of freedom from all "extralegal pressure" might be approached, in the pluralistic society Murray accepts and may embrace, is at the very least as a completely privatized religion. That way, and only that way, can we stay the possible (and possible great) "pressure" of government seeming to approve of one option over another. In any event, so much for Murray's foundational distinction between "state" and "Society."

Another ground—likely *the* ground—of Murray's reflections upon the First Amendment is reconciliation: to read them as an armistice in a pluralist society. Now Murray insists that this view is to be contrasted to an Article of Faith. From a starting point similar to Murray's concern that no particular religious view be intimate with our political institutions (recall that Murray sharply identifies "limited government"—ours—with holding "truth" at bay) we can deduce privatization. That is because, in present conditions of "pluralism," any public religiosity may signal alien status to some, perhaps many, Americans. They will then dissent, because they consider others to have reneged on the treaty. Again, from premises like Murray's, more systematic thinkers have construed "justice" to privatize religion. One of the conditions of justice sounds very Murrayan: we want principles of "justice" which do *not* implicate persons' commitments on questions like the meaning and purpose of life. That is *why* we need articles of peace in the first place—our pluralism. To effectively do that, we have to operate publicly without implicating them. The only way to avoid implicating them is leave them *out* of public life. Since religion commonly carries answers to such questions, religion ought be kept out of public life too. Finally, at least some well intended persons have synthesized Murray's disjunctive into privatization. The *only* way to keep civil peace in our society is to finally eliminate all public religion. Accompanied by the slipperiest slope rhetoric in all constitutional law, to defuse the potentially deadly mix of religious belief and politics we need a "wall of separation" between religion and public life. The slightest breach might detonate the load.

These observations suggest the distinction is less useful than Murray thinks and might counsel soft-selling it. Instead, Murray hardens it into a dichotomy. "From the standpoint both of history and of contemporary social reality the only tenable position is that [they]...are not articles of faith but articles of peace."[26] The latter is the "only view that a citizen with both historical sense and common sense" can hold.[27]

Note well a move here whose importance seems to escape Murray. He has rejected "originalism" in constitutional law. That no doubt owes to Murray's perception that all one might recover, by way of original meaning, would be either a secular Enlightenment view of religious freedom or a Protestant evangelical account. Murray certainly conceives such accounts to be "articles of faith." As an aside, neither account at least in its historical origins is privatistic. Enlightenment thinkers like Jefferson, Madison and Franklin to be sure, thought revealed religion and most theology to be rather useless speculation, if not superstitious mumbo-jumbo. But they did distinguish the chaff from the wheat, and the wheat was the reasonable elements of religion, including in effect biblical morality. *They* were not historicists, and believed rightly or wrongly that reason could discover the truth about God contained in Christianity as well as universal principles of morality. Evangelicals, at least in those days, were at best proto-privatizers. But they too did not hesitate to link Christian morality and biblical injunctions to public life. Most critical is the question Murray suppresses. He says that he will abstain from any question of application.[28] But we must ask, what does the First Amendment *mean*? It states legal rules, but what are they? Murray does not answer that question in his "Two Articles" piece. In my view, that is because the question is in that context unanswerable. His argument can only succeed by holding definition at bay because, aside from the originalist account he eschews, *any* answer can and must rest upon presuppositions peculiar to some, but not all, faith commitments. But "Articles of Peace" are supposed to rest upon no such grounds. They are supposed to swing free of religion itself. That is what pluralism, limited government and freedom of religion seem to mean. Here Murray stakes his tent. He challenges as articles of faith any theological account of the Religion Clauses. The kerygma: "The questions could be multiplied, but they all reduce themselves to two. Is the no-establishment clause a piece of ecclesiology, and is the free-exercise clause a piece of religious philosophy?" [29] "In a word, does separation of church and state in the American sense assert or imply a particular sectarian concept of the church?"[30] If so, then the no-establishment clause established a religion.[31]

Murray adds for good measure that the suggestion is *prima facie* illegitimate and absurd.[32] Well, not only is it true, it is ever inescapable. Murray, therefore, does it too. Just start by thinking of it this way. "Separation of church and state" is a Christian discovery which is alien to many faiths in our pluralistic United States.

Law characteristically depends upon sources external to itself for its descriptions. Here, "establishment," "religion" and "free exercise" are the descriptors. Their broader heritage includes terms like "separation of church and state," "liberty of conscience," "spiritual liberty," "religious liberty." Any definition of them inevitably presupposes a set of descriptions. As the descriptions vary, so will the definitions. There are Protestant definitions, liberal secular definitions, Catholic definitions. There might as well be Jewish and Islamic accounts of some, but not all of them. In many systems of thought, the terms are unintelligible.

Protestants and Catholics have contended in America over the definition of two other critical terms: "liberty of conscience" and "spiritual" or "religious" liberty. To Protestants the former has always meant, positively, individual interpretation of Scripture and the direct unmediated encounter of the Soul with God through grace. It has also commonly, and negatively, been an anti-Catholic slogan which expressed hostility to the Church, especially the priesthood, and (relatedly) stood for Bible reading in the public schools.[33]

"Spiritual" or, less commonly, "religious" liberty has always meant to American Catholics about the same thing as "ecclesiastical" liberty. Not the Protestant individual liberty of conscience, but the immunity and freedom of the church, of an effectively organized religious body, in society. To Protestants, especially to Calvin, the "spiritual" in earthy manifestation was the person and his conscience.[34] The church was a more ephemeral teaching instrument, not the ark of salvation. Indeed, to most Protestant Americans the "ecclesiastical" has been the enemy of the "spiritual." To Catholics, they are not only harmonious but practically identical. The modern liberal mind, within and without the Church, defines "liberty of conscience" quite differently. To it "conscience" is bound to a relativist or subjectivist epistemology, and amounts to something like creation and mastery of one's own moral universe, and the "right" to act on its urges, so long as others are not "harmed." Respect for conscience means the sanctity of individual moral "autonomy," and its currency is "sincerity." It has, unlike both Protestant and Catholic accounts, no transcendent referent. It is a practical monism. It is no part of the Christian tradition.

The moral of this story may be that the problematic comprises competing conceptions of religious liberty, not a contest between fans of religious liberty and opponents of it. It helps to keep in mind that the Soviet Constitution has always protected religious freedom, and that the Koran explicitly rejects coercion in matters of religion. That neither system seems particularly free to us suggests that what is meant by "freedom of religion" in a particular tradition is the question worth asking. Interestingly, during the nineteenth century Roman Catholic and Mormon Americans remained steadfast believers in and defenders of the First Amendment, even as a bare Protestant majority, self-conscious guardians of our republican liberties, bore down on them. The issue then was competing conceptions of the First Amendment.

Murray has served the cause well by making clear that liberalism—at least what he calls secular or sectarian liberalism—is really just another competing conception. It is *not* a neutral toleration of all religions, showing preference for none. But does Murray think he proposes such an alternative? I believe he does. But I say that there is no generic religion, no "generic" notion of religious liberty. We are not thereby condemned to a pluralism without exit, a simple power struggle for hegemony. Rather, we need consider all the "sectarian" conceptions of religious liberty—including liberalism—to gauge their relative tolerance. And we must also consider finally, the truth of the implications each bears—their conceptions of man, freedom, truth, and, yes, God.

NOTES

1. For the full quotation, see G. Bradley, "Church Autonomy in the Constitutional Order: The End of Church and State?" 49 *La. L. Rev.* 1057 (1989).
2. See *Religion and Society Report* B5 (August 1988).
3. Quoted in Stephen Monsma, "A Pluralist Interpretation of Church and State" Chapter 2, p. 53 (unpublished manuscript in author's possession).
4. *Id.* at 58.
5. J. Murray, *We Hold These Truths*, 53 (1960) [hereafter *Truths*].
6. J. Murray, *The Problem of Religious Freedom,* 93 (1965) [hereafter *Freedom*].

7. M. Douglas, *How Institutions Think*, 94 (1986).
8. D. Lutz, *Origins of American Constitutionalism*, 140 (1988).
9. *Lemon v. Kurtzman*, 403 U.S. 602 (1971).
10. See *Edwards v. Aguillard*, 482 U.S. 578 (1987).
11. See *Stone v. Graham*, 449 U.S. 39 (1980).
12. This is the sum of a line of cases reviewed in, for example, G. Bradley, "Developments in Church-State Law: Analysis and Opinion," 77 *Illinois Bar Journal* 806 (1989).
13. J. Pelikan, *Christian Doctrine and Modern Culture*, 173 (1989).
14. See W. James, *Varieties of Religious Experience* (1902).
15. *New York Times*, April 27, 1989.
16. 478 U.S. 186 (1986).
17. For an extended discussion of *Bowers*, see G. Bradley, "Remaking the Constitution: A Critical Examination of the *Bowers v. Hardwick* Dissent," 25 *Wake Forest L. Rev. 501* (1990).
18. See his *Social Justice in the Liberal State* (1980).
19. See his *Religious Convictions and Political Choice* (1988).
20. See *Freedom*, supra note 6.
21. J. Raz, "Facing Diversity: The Case of Epistemic Abstinence," 17 *Philosophy and Public Affairs* 3, 34 (1988).
22. E. Voegelin, "The Oxford Political Philosophers," 3 *Philosophical Quarterly* 97, 104 (1953).
23. *Id.* at 106.
24. 98 U.S. 145 (1879).
25. *Freedom*, supra note 6, at 84.
26. *Truths*, supra note 5, at 56.
27. *Id.*
28. *Id.* at 48.
29. *Id.* at 51.
30. *Id.* at 50.
31. *Id.* at 54.
32. *Id.*
33. M. Holt, *The Political Crisis of the 1850's*, 178-79 (1978).
34. E. Smith, *Religious Liberty in the United States*, 167-70 (1972).

10

John Courtney Murray: A Reliable Interpreter of *Dignitatis Humanae*?

by Father Brian W. Harrison, O.S.

Introduction

A quarter-century after the promulgation of the Declaration on Religious Liberty, *Dignitatis Humanae*, at the end of Vatican Council II, Fr. John Courtney Murray's theses regarding what he called the "public care of religion" by the civil power[1] have assumed a new importance in the light of the painful rupture in the Catholic Church which took place at Econe, Switzerland, on June 30, 1988.[2] Archbishop Marcel Lefebvre made it clear during recent years that the teaching of *Dignitatis Humanae* (or what he took to be its teaching) was one of the principal obstacles to reconciliation with the Holy See. And Murray, as is well known, was one of the most important *periti* involved in drafting the conciliar Declaration. This essay, which will consider certain aspects of Murray's theology in relation to that of Vatican II and Catholic tradition, would be seen in light of the call issued by Pope John Paul II in the Motu Proprio *Ecclesia Dei* (July 2, 1988) immediately after the excommunication of Lefebvre and those whom he illicitly consecrated as bishops: the Pope asked for a deeper study of these controversial aspects of Vatican II's teaching, "so that the Council's continuity with Tradition may be made as clear as possible."[3]

So influential was Murray as an architect of *Dignitatis Humanae* that there has often been a tendency almost to identify his own theses on church and state with the teaching of the Council itself. In the English-speaking world during the first decade after Vatican II, this tendency was powerfully reinforced by Murray himself, through the medium of Walter M. Abbott's ubiquitous, best-selling edition of the Council documents. Murray was not only the principal translator of the Declaration on Religious Liberty for this edition; he also provided it with an introductory essay and very copious explanatory footnotes.[4] This and similar publications in other languages, often by Jesuit scholars, have contributed to the widespread impression that the conciliar Declaration represents a significant departure from traditional Catholic doctrine.

In the present essay no attempt will be made to enunciate a complete or general argument for the essential continuity of *Dignitatis Humanae* with the traditional doctrine.[5] There were basically two issues, closely related but distinct, in the controversy between Murray and his conservative critics before and during the Council: first, the question of special state recognition or 'establishment' of Catholicism; and secondly, the question of state repression of public religious manifestations on the part of non-Catholics. The first of these legal dispositions does not necessarily imply the second, but the second clearly presupposes the first. In any case, we shall not deal at all in this essay with the second issue—that of religious liberty as such. The present observations will be limited to some critical reflections on Murray's thought regarding the first and more general issue—the foundational principles of church-state relationships. It will be argued, first, that Murray's attempts to reconcile his theses on this issue with traditional Catholic doctrine were unsuccessful; and secondly, that while earlier drafts of the conciliar schema on religious liberty reflected these theses very closely, subsequent amendments which were incorporated into the final, definitive text (amendments which Murray seems to have overlooked in his explanatory footnotes in Abbott's edition of the documents) prevented the Council from endorsing these unorthodox aspects of Murray's thought. If these arguments are valid, then at least one major preoccupation of "traditionalist" Catholics in regard to Vatican II will be seen as unfounded. At the same time, one plank will be removed from the platform of many dissenters at the opposite end of the ideological spectrum: those who (like Fr. Charles Curran[6]) welcome *Dignitatis Humanae's* alleged contradiction of earlier Church doctrine, on the grounds that the Council thereby set a precedent for the kinds of doctrinal "reversals" which they advocate in other areas of Church teaching. One hears the argument, for instance, that since an

Ecumenical Council, no less, has now contradicted the doctrine of encyclicals by Popes Pius IX and Leo XIII, it is vain to appeal to the authority of the Encyclical *Humanae Vitae* in the attempt to sustain the immutability of the traditional teaching against contraception. The fact that this conclusion is clearly valid if the premise is correct should serve to underline the gravity of the question at hand. Nothing less than the credibility of the Roman Magisterium, and hence that of the Catholic Church herself, is at stake here.

I. Murray's Theses and Traditional Catholic Doctrine

John Courtney Murray's controversial views on this matter are conveniently set out in several succinct propositions in his comments on *Dignitatis Humanae* in Abbott's edition. By virtue of such a highly strategic location, they have now been assimilated by thousands of English-speaking seminarians, priests, religious, and educated Catholic laity as accurately representing the authentic teaching of the Catholic Church's Twenty-First Ecumenical Council. In commenting on article 13 of the Declaration, for instance, Murray says:

> The Church does not make, as a matter of right or of divine law, the claim that she should be established as the "religion of the state." Her claim is freedom, nothing more.[7]

The first sentence here is probably too ambiguous, as it stands, to be evaluated formally in terms of its orthodoxy. The expression "religion of the state," especially in view of the quotation marks used by Murray himself, might in itself be taken to mean nothing more than one particular historically-conditioned *form* of civic or state recognition of Catholicism's unique truth: that is to say, the kind of concordat which has been a feature of relations between the Holy See and various predominantly Catholic nations during the last two centuries. It is only relatively recently that the exact phrase "religion of the state" has been commonly used. And it would of course be correct to deny that divine law requires a particular type of legal document with certain set phraseology.[8] However, Murray's second sentence quoted above makes it clear that he is not making a relatively trivial observation of this sort. What he wants to deny is that divine law requires states or government to acknowledge *any kind* of special legal status for Catholicism by virtue of its own unique truth; all that the Church can demand from the state as a right given by God, according to Murray, is "freedom, nothing more."

This kind of affirmation about what *divine* law does or does not require is clearly 'doctrinal' in nature: if true at all, it is a universal and immutable truth. This is important, because at times, especially in his pre-conciliar writings, Murray was rather more tentative about such matters. In *We Hold these Truths*, for instance, the essay "Civil Unity and Religious Integrity" insists that the author, as an American Catholic, accepts the principles of "separation of church and state" as expressed in the First Amendment, "only as a law, not a dogma." It is "not invested with the sanctity that attaches to dogma, but only with the rationality that attaches to law."[9] In adopting this position, Murray has no difficulty in showing that it is in perfect harmony with what the Popes up to that time had consistently recognized: that in a religiously pluralist society such as the United States, this benign form of separation of church and state is a useful practical arrangement, conducive to freedom and peaceful coexistence between those of differing faiths.[10] Murray did not claim that this type of constitutional arrangement ought necessarily be adopted in all other countries, including predominantly Catholic ones. If he thought that, he did not say so. Rather, he confined himself to the observation that the experience of privilege in such countries, "especially in Latin lands," has often provoked enmity and persecution by way of reaction,[11] and that in America, "By and large ... it has been good for religion, for Catholicism, to have had simply the right of freedom"[12]—that is, the same freedom as the other religious denominations.

By the end of 1964, however, after two years of intense debate at Vatican Council II had still not produced the long-awaited Declaration on Religious Liberty, the climate had changed. Frustration and impatience were running at a high level in the ranks of the more liberal theologians and bishops, as a result of the Pope's decision *not* to overrule the Council's standard procedures so as to permit the latest draft of the religious liberty schema to be put to the vote (and in all probability promulgated) by the end of the 1964 session.[13] It was in this atmosphere of mounting tension that Murray's most polemical work on church and state, "The Problem of Religious Freedom," was published.[14] In this lengthy article the Jesuit theologian set out to provide a *tour de force*—a comprehensive rebuttal of his conservative

Catholic critics—so as to pave the way for a rapid victory in the Council's final session in 1965.

In this essay Murray does in effect maintain that the essential American formula—freedom for the Church, but no substantial legal or juridical privileges—should now be the norm everywhere, even in predominantly Catholic countries. His position is that even a merely nominal "privilege" in such countries is never morally obligatory (that is, required by God): mere freedom is always sufficient for the Catholic Church:
> The fact of the religious unity of a particular people in the Catholic faith does not make obligatory the legal institution of establishment, as if a situation of legal privilege were a Catholic constitutional ideal.[15]

Moreover, Murray now affirms that if, in a mainly Catholic culture, there *is* any constitutional privilege for the Catholic Church, it *must not be more* than merely nominal. It may not impact legally on the lives of citizens; and the state, in acknowledging such a purely titular "privilege," may not claim to be discerning or recognizing the religious truth of Catholicism, only the sociological fact of its local predominance. Thus, for all practical purposes, such a regime would be virtually indistinguishable from the American model. This is clear from the following passage:
> Furthermore, out of respect for historical custom, where it exists, it is not inappropriate or contrary to religious freedom that the people of a particular nation should declare their common allegiance to the Catholic Church in some sort of constitutional document. This declaration has no juridical consequences; it has the value of a statement of fact.[16]

This rejection of any kind of Catholic "establishment" which would have "juridical consequences" is an implication of another closely related thesis which Murray enunciates succinctly in his remarks on *Dignitatis Humanae* in the Abbott edition. Commenting on article 6 of the Declaration, Murray assures us that, according to Vatican II,
> government is forbidden to assume the care of religious truth as such...or the task of judging the truth or value of religious propaganda. Otherwise it would exceed its competence, which is confined to affairs of the temporal and terrestrial order.[17]

Once again, the first sentence here is perhaps too ambiguous in itself to be given any formal "theological note." It would be quite correct to deny civil authority the right to "judge" the truth of religious affirmations, or to assume the "care of religious truth," if by that we simply mean that lay officials or politicians may not usurp the magisterial role of the Pope and bishops by presuming to decide authoritatively what is or is not compatible with Catholic faith or morals. However, Murray wants to include here a denial of the age-old Catholic thesis that those who hold political authority (either the juridically sovereign citizen body in a democracy, or the juridically sovereign monarch in an autocracy) are in principle not only able (like all rational human beings) to discern the unique truth of Catholicism, but are obliged in principle, by virtue of man's social nature, to reflect this discernment in appropriate ways, in the exercise of their official functions.[18]

That Murray does in fact intend to deny this traditional Catholic thesis is clear not only from the next sentence in his commentary on *Dignitatis Humanae*, where it is said that the "competence" of government "is confined to affairs of the temporal and terrestrial order," but from more ample statements of his position in "The Problem of Religious Freedom." He asserts that in "the constitutional tradition" (the tradition with which he personally agrees),

> no public official is empowered, by virtue of his public office, to inquire into the theological credentials of any religious body, and to decide whether it exists *iure divino*, whether its doctrine and polity are in conformity with divine revelation.... The Erastian doctrine that the public powers are the arbiter of religious truth...is not only contrary to Christian doctrine but also contrary to political principle.[19]

This passage makes clear Murray's failure to make the distinction, explained above, between the kind of religious judgement which is the special competence of the Church's leaders and that which pertains in principle to the human race as such. The first sentence in the above quotation certainly excludes the idea that the Catholic Church as such can and should be recognized by public authorities as existing "*iure divino*." But the second sentence shows that Murray confuses this idea (which is straightforward traditional Catholic doctrine) with "Erastian doctrine" (which, as he says, is unorthodox, insofar as it usurps the rights of the Pope and bishops and sees government as a generalized "arbiter" of *all* religious truth). By rejecting as "Erastianism" *both* types of religious discernment on the part of public authority, Murray throws out the baby with the bathwater.

A little further on in the same essay Murray not only implies once again that civil authority is incompetent to recognize the truth of Catholicism, he also asserts that government may not put into effect any decisions *received from* the Church's Magisterium (a procedure which clearly would not usurp any function of the latter):

> The public powers are not competent to make theological judgments. Nor may their actions be instrumental in the public enforcement of theological judgments made by the Church.[20]

So far we have been concerned simply to expound two controversial theses of Fr. Murray, which are almost like two sides of the one coin: that the Catholic Church, by divine right, can demand only freedom, not recognition of her unique truth, from political authorities; and that these authorities in turn are not competent to recognize this unique truth, much less to allow any legal or juridical effects to flow from such recognition. In the course of our exposition we have stated that these theses are not in harmony with traditional Catholic doctrine. It will now be appropriate to justify this criticism by reference to pertinent pronouncements of the Church's Magisterium.

In fact, such pronouncements have always been well known to both sides in the dispute. In the Encyclical *Quanta Cura*, Pius IX condemned the view that "human society should be constituted and governed…without making any distinction between the true religion and false religions."[21] The Pope affirmed that this "evil opinion," along with others specified in the Encyclical, must be "absolutely held (*omnino haberi*) as reprobated, denounced and condemned by all the children of the Catholic Church."[22] The contradiction between *Quanta Cura* and Murray's view (that government recognition of the true religion is *not* a requirement of divine law) could scarcely be more emphatic or more explicit, given that Pius IX insists that the condemned error attacks

> that salutary influence which the Catholic Church, *by the institution and command of her Divine Author, ought to exercise even to the consummation of the world*, not only over individual men, but nations, peoples, and sovereigns.[23]

Leo XIII is scarcely less emphatic. He affirms in the Encyclical *Immortale Dei* that "it is not lawful for the State, any more than for the individual...to hold in equal favour different kinds of religion."[24] Indeed,

> it is a sin in the State...(to adopt) out of many forms of religion...that one which chimes in with the fancy; for we are bound absolutely to worship God in the way which He has shown to be His will.[25]

To make it crystal-clear that he is talking about *divine* law here, Pope Leo asserts at the beginning of *Immortale Dei* that the principles expounded therein represent,

> the *necessary growth of the teachings of the Gospel.* We deem it, therefore, of the highest moment, and *a strict duty of Our Apostolic office*, to contrast with *the lessons taught by Christ* the novel theories now advanced touching the State...so that one and all may see clearly *the imperious law of life which they are bound to follow and obey.*[26]

More recently Pope Pius XI, in instituting the Feast of Christ the King with the Encyclical *Quas Primas*, expressed his hope that, through his new enrichment of the Church's liturgy:

> Nations will be reminded by the annual celebration of this feast that not only private individuals but also rulers and princes are bound to give public honour and obedience to Christ. It will call to their minds the thought of the last judgment, wherein Christ, Who has been cast out of public life, despised, neglected, and ignored, will most severely avenge these insults; for His kingly dignity demands that the State should take account of the commandments of God and of Christian principles, both in making laws and in administering justice, and also in providing for the young a sound moral education.[27]

How did John Courtney Murray interpret these declarations of the Magisterium, which were often adduced against him by his critics prior to and during Vatican II? At the general hermeneutical level he called attention to profound philosophical differences between his school of thought and that of such critics—differences which he said made attempts at dialogue "abortive." The two contrasting views, he said,

> do not confront each other as affirmation confronts negation. Their differences are at a deeper level—indeed, at a level so deep that it would be difficult to go deeper. They represent the contemporary clash between classicism and historical consciousness.[28]

In evaluating the earlier pontifical declarations, says Murray, the scholar who possesses this "historical consciousness"

> asks the question...is not the historical context of the document and its doctrinal, polemic, and pastoral intentions to be considered, with the result that particular assertions may be regarded as historically conditioned and therefore subject to further development in what concerns their manner of conception and statement, under altered circumstances and with the rise of new questions which affect the perspectives in which the truth is viewed?[29]

In contrast to this "historical consciousness," the "classical" mentality which Murray rejects (he claims that both its "archaism" and its "anachronism" are "now forbidden" in the light of Pope John's "fuller acceptance" of this century's "altered historical context"[30]) is a misguided attempt (we are told) "to adhere or return to the synthesis or systematization of a prior age, which is judged to be simple and more pure."[31] This "classicism" admits that Leo XIII, for instance, "did indeed speak within a historical context"; however, it thinks "that his utterances transcended the context" and insists (mistakenly, it would seem in Murray's view) that:

> What matters is what he said—the propositions that he put down on paper. These propositions stand forever, true, certain, and immutable.[32]

One is tempted to reply to Murray's polemic—the various pejorative "isms" with which he labels his opponents—with other labels. The kind of "historical consciousness" which seems to cast doubt on whether some propositions can transcend their historical context seems perilously akin to historicism or relativism. And if the view that "What matters is what (Pope Leo) said—the propositions that he put down on paper" is to be stigmatized by Murray as a regrettable "classicism," this seems to suggest that the real object of his regret may in fact be none other than the perennial philosophy—the basic principles, insights and procedures of human reason itself. Pius IX, as we saw, "put down on paper" the absolute assertion that unique recognition of the Catholic Church by the political community is an obligation flowing from the "command of her Divine Author," valid "even to the consummation of the world." The perennial philosophy (along with ordinary common sense) would conclude from this that if Fr. Murray affirms (a hundred years later, but still well before "the consummation of the world") that in fact there is no such perpetual, divinely-imposed obligation, then the nineteenth-century Pope and the twentieth-century theologian cannot both be right. Their respective affirmations stand in clear and ineluctable contradiction, from which it follows that Murray should admit that his thesis really constitutes *dissent* from this and parallel affirmations of the nineteenth-century Magisterium, and is not just a "further development in what concerns their manner of conception and statement."[33]

Murray attempts to meet this kind of criticism as follows:
> The Second View [i.e. the view of Murray and his sympathizers] may urge the issue, citing the assertion of Pius XII that Boniface VIII's doctrine of the sun and the moon and the two swords was historically conditioned and is today archaistic. In reply, the First View [i.e. that of the "classicists"] changes the subject, raising the issue of the doctrinal authority of papal encyclicals, with appropriate citations. This issue is important, but it would seem to suppose an answer to the prior question. Again the parties fail to join in dialogue.[34]

Perhaps we can revive the dialogue on this point here and now. In the 1955 allocution to which Murray refers, Pius XII did not in fact say that Pope Boniface's statement was "today archaistic," but he did say that "[t]his medieval conception was conditioned by its era."[35] Pius XII was commenting on the affirmation of Boniface VIII in 1303 that:
> just as the moon has no light except that which it receives from the sun, so also no earthly power has anything which it does not receive from the ecclesiastical power....all powers...are from Christ, and from Us as the Vicar of Jesus Christ.[36]

Pope Boniface made this statement not as supreme pastor and teacher of all Christians, but only to the envoys of the German king, Albert of Habsburg; so even the most ultramontane Catholic should have little difficulty in granting that a papal utterance of that category might simply be erroneous.

But why does Murray fault his critics for "changing the subject" when they now raise the issue of the relative authority of different kinds of papal utterances? The "prior question" for which he says this issue "would seem to suppose an answer" is the question (just posed by Murray himself) as to whether "particular papal assertions may be regarded as historically conditioned and therefore subject to further development...under altered circumstances." His train of thought seems to be that his conservative critics, out of deference for Pius XII's authority if for no other reason, ought to admit an affirmative answer to this question; but that since this admission damages their case, they normally prefer to evade the point by "changing the subject."

But does it really damage their case? The expression "historically conditioned" (whether used by Pius XII or by other writers) is generally a kind of euphemism, and a rather vague one. We use it to intimate politely that although a certain respected belief or affirmation from the past is understandable in its historical context, it is now to be seen as erroneous, or at least inadequate. But the difference between "erroneous" and merely "inadequate" can be all-important. No Catholic who follows the perennial philosophy should have any difficulty in admitting that even *ex cathedra* definitions may be "historically conditioned," in the sense that they may prove to be *inadequate* for the needs of a subsequent age, because of the *way* their teaching was originally expressed. However, he will not admit that such definitions were *erroneous* in *what* they express, because he believes that they are infallibly true. But in the case of minor papal utterances such as the statement of Boniface VIII under consideration, our perennial philosopher will be prepared to admit the possibility of the kind of "historical conditioning" which includes downright error, not just inadequacy. It follows that since the *truth* or *error* of certain universal doctrinal propositions made by Pius IX and Leo XIII is really the point at issue here, the pertinent question to raise at this juncture is precisely that of their authority—that is, how "major" or "minor" they are in comparison with that of Boniface VIII, which Murray saw fit to introduce into the discussion. It is he, not his critics, who seems to be evading the central issue here—by focusing undue attention on the conveniently vague notion of "historical conditioning."

In any case, it is relevant to ask the further question as to what, in Murray's view, are the "altered circumstances" which he thinks justify such a different approach from that of the pre-conciliar Popes. Again and again, throughout the essay we are considering, we find recurring appeals to what Murray calls mankind's "growth in personal and political consciousness." According to Murray, the fundamental premise of the view he advocates is that

> the nature of man is a historical nature, whose rational exigences manifest themselves progressively, under the impact of the continually changing social-political con-

text, and in response to the growing personal and political consciousness.[37]

On the basis of this premise, and taking note of the "signs of the times," Murray tells us that the view of church-state relations accepted by himself and many other modern Catholics

> presents itself as the contemporary stage in the growing understanding of the tradition. This understanding cannot be found in ecclesiastical documents of the nineteenth century. It was brought into being by a dynamism proper to the twentieth century, the growth of the personal and political consciousness, first noted by Pius XII and more fully developed in its implications by John XXIII.[38]

The concept of "growth"—in this context a metaphor taken from biology—means, of course, change, and more specifically, change towards maturity or perfection—change *for the better*. But whether the widespread twentieth-century understanding of Church and State *really is* superior to that of the nineteenth-century Popes is precisely the point at issue. This superiority needs to be demonstrated, not merely asserted or insinuated. Of course, on the basis of a certain philosophy of history—belief in the *inevitable* progress of mankind—twentieth-century ideas are *by definition* superior to those of a century earlier, just as a fifteen-year-old boy is by definition, or by the exigencies of nature, more mature than a five-year-old. Murray's assertions often seem to presuppose some such philosophy of history; but at other times he admits that "history" can carry mankind downwards as well as upwards, in terms of the quality of political life. He maintains, for instance, that "the medieval conception of kingship" embodied a basically sound constitutional tradition of limited government, and laments the fact that by the nineteenth century, "the tradition had been obscured by history—by the decadence of the constitutional tradition after the *quattrocento*," leading to the rise of absolute monarchies.[39] But if that is true, then it cannot simply be *assumed* that the twentieth century's change in "consciousness" represents "growth," rather than "decadence," in relation to the teaching of the nineteenth-century Popes.

Moreover, Murray tends to talk of "the twentieth century" and "contemporary man" as though everyone, or practically everyone, now thinks as he does about church-state relations. But this is simply not true. Large numbers of traditionally-minded Catholics disagree emphatically, not to mention the great majority of the world's hundreds of millions of Muslims, large numbers of Hindus, Buddhists and Jews (in regard to the State of Israel) and many adherents of other religions and ideologies. That is, for a very considerable proportion of the contemporary human race—possibly even the majority—it is far from axiomatic that government, in our own time, is incompetent to recognize and favour some particular religion or world-view over others. Murray does indeed admit that the State's "incompetence" in religious matters is not "some sort of transcendental principle, derivative from some eternal law," but he immediately adds:

> The exact formula is that the state, under today's conditions of growth in the personal and political consciousness, is competent to do only one thing in respect of religion, that is, to recognize, guarantee, protect, and promote the religious freedom of people. This is the full extent of the competence of the contemporary constitutional state.[40]

However, shorn of its rhetorical appeal to "growth" (a word which carries question-begging overtones of inevitable progress or improvement) and of its implied statistical appeal to a non-existent consensus amongst "contemporary man,"[41] Murray's argument amounts to little more than the claim that the universal Church should endorse his view of the state's very limited religious role mainly because at present this also happens to be the view of a great many other people—especially in the liberal, secularized societies of Western Europe and North America. But that kind of claim, of course, does not sound nearly so imposing and irresistible[42] as a demand which is said to arise inexorably from something as august as a "growth in consciousness of contemporary man."

In his attempt to show that today's Church need not adhere to certain "propositions...put down on paper" by earlier Popes, notwithstanding their apparent gravity, Murray does not lean exclusively on general hermeneutical principles which appeal to man's "historical nature." He also presents a more specific argument, claiming that,

> after full assent has been given to the traditional papal condemnation of separation of Church and State as a matter of Catholic duty, there is still room for an unprejudiced examination of the American concept of separation, because this latter concept is different in point of

political principle from the concept condemned....the American "state" is not the Continental "state"; this is the root of the difference.[43]

The "Continental State," Murray explains, was a European product of the Renaissance and Reformation era, and was essentially paternalistic, deciding which world-view was most suitable for the illiterate masses who formed the great bulk of those whom it governed. We are told that, at heart, Leo XIII was (like Murray himself) basically only concerned to uphold the *freedom* of the Church from state interference. That was his "central notion."[44] However, given the prevailing "Continental" notion of what the State *is*—a notion he himself took for granted—the Pope felt bound to insist on "establishment," that is, *privilege*, for the Church as the norm, because that seemed to be the only practical means for assuring her freedom. The only alternative, under contemporary European conditions, was the kind of "separation" between Church and State which tried to impose some rival ideology, and thus amounted to harassment or even persecution of Catholics.[45] Murray then completes his case by arguing that the limited American "state" is so different from this authoritarian Continental model that it can safely be "separated" from the Church without endangering her freedom.[46] Therefore, he concludes, constitutions based on the American model of "separation" do not really conflict with Leo XIII's deepest intentions, only with the superficial reality of what he actually *said*.

This argument might seem plausible enough, until we begin to look for solid evidence that the *only* real end which Leo XIII had in view was in fact the freedom of the Church. Since Murray admits (at least tacitly) that the "paper propositions" of this Pontiff tell against his thesis, the onus of proof clearly rests with him to show that they are nonetheless no longer normative for the Church a hundred years later. It must be stressed that what Murray needs to prove is that this defence of the Church's freedom was the *only* end which Pope Leo had in mind when he insisted on state establishment of Catholicism as the correct or normative situation. But all that Murray actually does is present evidence that this freedom of the Church was Leo's "central concern," his *first priority*, in the contemporary struggle with Continental liberalism. He tells us:

> One could begin to appreciate its centrality by counting the number of times that the phrase, or an equivalent of it, appears in his writings (some eighty-one times in

sixty documents).... Freedom is the first property of the Church; and freedom is the first claim that the Church makes in the face of society and state: "This freedom is so much the property of the Church, as a perfect and divine work, that those who act against this freedom likewise act against God and against their duty."[47]

Murray then goes on to cite a number of Leonine texts which do indeed condemn very forcefully all forms of state interference with the Church's free activity,[48] telling us that "(the) decisive proof" of his own thesis "results from an understanding of the structure of Leo XIII's controversy with Continental sectarian Liberalism...."[49] But the most that these texts could possibly "prove decisively" is that attacks on the Church's freedom were the most immediate and most urgent problem that Leo had to face in his confrontation with hostile regimes. In none of them is there the slightest hint that state establishment of Catholicism is to be valued only, or even mainly, insofar as it is a safeguard against such attacks.[50] To argue that since the freedom of the Church from oppression was Pope Leo's "central concern," his insistence on state recognition of Catholicism's truth as the norm was only "historically conditioned," and not permanently binding, is quite simply a *non sequitur*. It is no more logical than arguing that since the defeat of Japan and Germany was the "central concern" of the American government in the early 1940's, its simultaneous efforts to promote (say) public health and improved agricultural methods were merely "historically conditioned" interests which arose as part of the war effort, and need not be pursued by subsequent governments—as if high standards of health and agriculture were valuable to a nation *only* to the extent of their (real or imagined) efficacy in helping to defeat armed foreign aggression.

Murray's thesis also depends, as we have seen, on the premise that Leo XIII did not appreciate the difference between the "Continental" state and the American state, and would not have found fault with the benign form of Church-State "separation" practiced in the latter if he had understood it better. But Pope Leo was surely not so politically ignorant as this theory supposes him to have been. Indeed, his Encyclical *Longinqua* (1895) on Catholicism in the United States, demonstrates both that he well understood the difference between the two types of constitution in question, and that he nevertheless rejected the idea (later revived by Murray and others within the Church) that the

American model of "separation"—full freedom but no privilege—is all that the Church can ever claim from the State as a matter of divine law. Leo XIII said to the U.S. Bishops:

> For the Church amongst you, unopposed by the Constitution and government of your nation...is free to live and act without hindrance. Yet, though all this be true, it would be very erroneous to draw the conclusion that in America is to be sought the type of the most desirable status of the Church, or that it would be *universally lawful* or expedient for State and Church to be, as in America, dissevered and divorced. The fact that Catholicity with you is in good condition...is by all means to be attributed to the fecundity with which God has endowed His Church...but she would bring forth more abundant fruits if, in addition to liberty, she enjoyed the favor of the laws and the patronage of the public authority.[51]

It is important to note here that Pope Leo mentions *lawfulness* as well as expediency as a criterion for evaluating different models of Church-state relationship. Too often it is assumed that the Church's traditional quest for unique recognition on the part of the state has been motivated exclusively by the real or imagined *benefits* for the Church and her members which are thought to flow from such recognition. On this assumption the case for "establishment," even in predominantly Catholic countries, would be convincingly refuted if it could be shown (and perhaps it *can* be shown) that judging by the practical experience of many centuries, the Church herself usually tends to enjoy better health, both spiritual and temporal, in constitutional situations like that of the U.S.A., where she is *not* established as the "state religion" and simply enjoys freedom of operation, unhampered by tiresome links to the temporal powers.

This assumption, however, is a serious misunderstanding of the traditional doctrine. As we have already seen, the great papal encyclicals on Church and State insist—contrary to Fr. Murray's thesis—that civic recognition of Catholicism *as the true religion* is an immutable precept of divine positive law. And God has imposed this obligation not primarily in the interests of the Church herself (her freedom, prosperity, security, or whatever), but because it arises inexorably from the social nature of man, the universal sovereignty of Christ, the rationally demonstrable truth of Catholicism,[52] and above all, the First Commandment. None of these truths, clearly, can be seen by Catholics as mere "historically conditioned" opinions. The best refutation of

Murray's thesis (i.e., that Catholic "establishment" was basically understood by Pope Leo XIII as a mere means for securing the Church's freedom) comes from Leo himself, in a passage from *Immortale Dei* wherein he not only asserts *that*, but also lucidly explains *why*, this civic recognition of the true religion is an obligation of divine law:

> The State, constituted as it is, is clearly bound to act up to the manifold and weighty duties linking it to God by the public profession of religion. Nature and reason, which command every individual devoutly to worship God in holiness...*bind also the civil community by a like law. For men living together in society are under the power of God no less than individuals are, and society, not less than individuals, owes gratitude to God*.... Since, then, no one is allowed to be remiss in the service due to God, and since the chief duty of all men is to cling to religion in both its teaching and practice—*not such religion as we may have a preference for, but the religion which God enjoins, and which certain and most clear marks show to be the only true religion*—it is a public crime to act as though there were no God. *So too it is a sin in the State...to adopt out of many forms of religion...that one which chimes in with the fancy; for we are bound absolutely to worship God in that way which He has shown to be His will.*[53]

It is clear from this and other key affirmations of the Church's Magisterium that, according to her *doctrine*—not just a historically conditioned policy—the civic community's recognition of Catholic truth is primarily a duty which it owes *to God*, not just to the Church: a duty which therefore obtains quite independently of whatever benefits *or burdens* for the latter might in practice result from its fulfillment.

Some further clarifications would seem appropriate at this point. Murray's denials that government is "competent" to "assume the care of religious truth," to "inquire into the theological credentials of any religious body," and so on, are obviously correct if we understand them in a certain sense. No one in his right mind has ever suggested that the attainment of political office automatically brings with it, *ex officio*, some kind of special infusion of heavenly or theological wisdom, so that, as a generally applicable practical rule, we ordinary citizens, and indeed, ministers of religion, in any country whatever, ought to submit questions of religious doctrine to the "magisterium" of princes, presidents or bureaucrats, and humbly allow our consciences to be formed by their sagacious decisions. However, Murray's way of stating the issue fails to make clear two important distinctions.

The first is the distinction in Catholic doctrine between one type of "theological judgement" which is the special competence of the Church's Magisterium, and another type which the responsibility for deciding whether Catholicism as such is true lies with all humans, as rational beings: one should not tell a *non-Catholic* that he ought to believe in the Immaculate Conception simply because the Pope, as "competent authority," has defined it to be true; one should present him with rational evidence—what are called the "motives of credibility"— for the truth of the Catholic religion as a whole, as a "package deal" which *includes* papal authority, the Immaculate Conception, and many other things.

The second distinction which Murray's treatment of governmental "competence" in the sphere of religion fails to make clear is that between being "competent" in the sense of being skilled and reliable ("Dr. X is a very competent physician"), and being "competent" in the sense of being legally or morally responsible for doing something. Being competent in the second sense (being the "competent authority" as regards this or that) is of course quite compatible with being totally *incompetent* in the first sense—totally unskilled and totally unreliable. Not every office-holder is worthy of his position.

If we keep in mind these two distinctions, the traditional Catholic doctrine regarding the religious duties of political authority does not sound nearly so preposterous as it might seem from Murray's presentation of it. It is not that government can be a "judge of religious truth" in the sense of usurping the role of the papal and episcopal Magisterium; only in the sense of *recognizing* that role as divinely-instituted, and thus conforming human law to the law of God under its guidance. Nor does ascribing "competence" to government authorities in this field imply that in reality politicians and rulers can in any way be *relied upon* to carry out consistently even this limited religious "judgment" (*recognition* of the true religion). It simply means they have the objective obligation to do so, regardless of how dismal their general level of performance may be in practice. Thus it is with our obligations at the individual level. God obliges, and with the help of grace enables, the human race to avoid mortal sin. Yet in general we show ourselves totally inconsistent and unreliable in fulfilling this primordial obligation.

II. Murray's Theses And Vatican Council II

If our argument so far has been correct, John Courtney Murray was not successful in attempting to harmonize the following two theses with Catholic doctrine by appealing to mankind's "growth in personal and political consciousness," and to the "historical conditioning" of earlier papal statements:

(1) The Catholic Church can demand from political authority, as a matter of right or divine law, only freedom and not recognition of her unique truth;

(2) Political authority is not competent to recognize the unique truth of Catholicism, much less to allow any juridical effects on the lives of citizens to flow from such recognition.

As we saw in Part I of this article, Murray claimed in his commentary on the conciliar Declaration *Dignitatis Humanae* that these theses have in effect been taught by Vatican II. It is now time to consider the truth of this claim.

In regard to thesis (1) above, Murray makes this claim in commenting on article 13 of *Dignitatis Humanae*, which, after citing Leo XIII to the effect that the Church's liberty is "pre-eminent" or "outstanding" (*praestantissima*) amongst those things which "concern the good of the Church" and are "always and everywhere" to be safeguarded, makes the following assertion:

> The principle of the liberty of the Church is fundamental in her relations with the public authorities and with the whole civil order.

This translation maintains the ambiguity, which, owing to the absence of definite and indefinite articles in Latin is found in the original text (*Libertas Ecclesiae est principium fundamentale*…). Murray, in the Abbott edition, translates this as "The freedom of the Church is *the* fundamental principle…,"[54] although official Vatican translations into Spanish and Italian maintain the same ambiguity.[55] Nevertheless, even if we were to concede to Murray that the Council means to say that this liberty is *the* fundamental principle in Church-state relations, not just *a* fundamental principle, this would by no means justify his footnote comment that "freedom, nothing more" is the *only* claim which the Church can make on the state as "a matter of right or of divine law." This inference is no more logical than arguing that if it is "the fundamental" duty of the public authorities (in purely temporal matters) to protect the lives, property, and freedom of citizens from violent attack, it follows that they are not bound by *any other* temporal duties. We can say that, in any kind of human enterprise, guarding against what is destructive or evil is more "fundamental" than the positive promotion of what is good, in the sense that warding off serious damage or destruction has a logical and temporal priority over proceeding with the further construction or perfection of what already exists.[56] If I am half-way through building my house and floods start to undermine the foundation, it will be foolish to neglect them in that moment in order to start putting on the roof. And if my little daughter is ill with hepatitis, sending her to the hospital takes priority over sending her to school. But this does not imply that the house needs no roof, or that my daughter needs no schooling. Nor does *Dignitatis Humanae* 13 in any way imply that there is no obligation in divine law for civic authorities to recognize the unique truth of Catholicism.

In the same footnote, Murray attempts to enlist the support of Pope Paul VI, quoting the conciliar Fathers' address to the world's political rulers at the end of Vatican II:

> And what is it that this Church asks of you, after nearly two thousand years of all sorts of vicissitudes in her relations with you, the powers of the earth? What does the Church ask of you today? In one of the major texts of the Council she has told you: she asks of you nothing but freedom—the freedom to believe and to preach her faith, the freedom to love God and to serve Him, the freedom to live and to bring to men her message of life.[57]

But once again, it is vain to look for any stated or implied conclusions about *divine* law in this passage. Indeed, the first two interrogatory sentences, emphasizing the constantly changing nature of the Church's *de facto* relationships with civil rulers throughout history, support a merely prudential and pastoral interpretation of this message, in keeping with the Council's overall goals. It simply answers the question as to what the Church deems appropriate *"today"* as a realistic request to modern political powers in general, not the question of what rights pertain to the Church in strict doctrinal principle. Given the fact that the populations of very few nations *today* are more or less united in the profession of Catholicism, it might only lead to harmful confusion to present the entire community of national governments with a direct request for the immediate fulfillment of divine law *in all its fullness*—that is, national, communal recognition of the unique truth of Catholicism. Such a request would be analogous in its imprudence to standing on a street corner in modern London or New York and handing out leaflets to all passers-by telling them that, as a matter of divine law, all men and women are required to receive valid Holy Communion, in the Catholic Church. This would of course be true: "Unless you eat the flesh of the Son of Man…you will not have life in you" (John 6:53). But the obligation to receive Holy Communion is an aspect of divine law the fulfillment of which presupposes the prior fulfillment of other more basic aspects—faith, Baptism, and if necessary, sacramental Confession. Likewise with the obligation of governments to recognize the truth of Catholicism. Civil rulers whose task is the *representative* government of largely or predominantly non-Catholic populations cannot reasonably be expected to enact laws recognizing Catholicism as the true religion *under those existing conditions.*

Looking at the same question from the viewpoint of the rights of the Church, as distinct from the duties of governments, the same basic point can be made by recalling that one does not *renounce* one's rights simply by not insisting on them in a determined situation. All that Vatican II's closing message to world rulers implies is that, *given today's conditions,* the Church deems it wisest to adopt a uniform global policy of *insisting* only on her right to freedom from State harassment or interference. No more than the text of *Dignitatis Humanae* does it imply, as Fr. Murray supposes, that the Church, by divine law, *possesses* only that right and "nothing more."

If the Declaration on Religious Liberty said no more than what we have already quoted, the above criticism of Murray's misleading commentary would be valid. But in fact it says significantly more. Not only does *Dignitatis Humanae* not teach the liberal thesis which Murray attributes to it in this footnote; it reaffirms the contrary traditional thesis.

This traditional thesis is implied in the very next paragraph of article 13, where the Church presents a twofold justification for that demand for liberty which she sees as "fundamental" in her relation to the state. One reason for this demand is simply the common humanity which her members share with all non-Catholics: she is a "society of men" who have the right to live in civil society according to their faith. Non-Catholic and secular powers and nations could reasonably be expected to sympathize with this claim, since it merely appeals to a natural human right.

But this is presented only as a secondary reason in article 13. The first reason why the Church demands freedom is at the supernatural level—that of revealed truth:

> In human society and before all civil authorities whatever (*coram quavis potestate publica*) the Church claims liberty for herself in her character as the spiritual authority (*utpote auctoritas spiritualis*), founded by Christ the Lord, which by divine mandate has received the task of going out to the whole world and preaching the Gospel to every creature.[58]

By stressing that this "divine mandate" is presented to "all civil authorities whatever" *as a reason* for the Church's title to liberty, the Council clearly implies that in principle all civil authorities ought to accept it as a *good* reason. Nobody makes an argued appeal to another person or authority unless he believes that this other person or authority, at least in principle, should be capable of perceiving the argument's validity. But for any government to recognize *this* argument's validity would be for it *ipso facto* to recognize the unique truth of Catholicism, since the Catholic church certainly does not claim—before civil governments or anyone else—to be merely one of a number of "spiritual authorities" bearing a divine mandate to evangelize the world.[59] Thus, both the doctrinal and the pastoral aspects of Vatican II's teaching on the Church's freedom become clear. For modern prudential and pastoral purposes the Church today has decided, in dealing with civil governments, to insist explicitly *only* on her right to freedom. But the very grounds given for that right to freedom implicitly assert the other right affirmed by traditional doctrine: the Church's divinely guaranteed right to be recognized by all human authorities and powers as the true religion.

Perhaps even more importantly, that same traditional doctrine, which Murray did not accept, was eventually reaffirmed more explicitly in the text of *Dignitatis Humanae* by late amendments which the Jesuit theologian simply ignored in his commentary in Abbott's edition of the documents. In the third-last draft (the *textus reemenda-*

tus) only a very brief statement was made (in the preamble) to safeguard the new declaration's continuity with traditional doctrine:
> Moreover this treatment of religious liberty leaves intact the Catholic doctrine concerning the one true religion and the one Church of Christ.[60]

Many Fathers complained that this was too cursory, so in the next draft (the *textus recognitus* of October 1965) this was expanded so as to affirm that the Council's teaching on religious liberty
> leaves intact the Catholic doctrine concerning the one true religion, the one Church of Christ, and the moral duty of men towards that Church.[61]

This draft still left a good many Fathers unsatisfied, and during the Council's final month conservative objections were taken more seriously than ever before by the drafting commission. In presenting the final text to the assembled Fathers, the commission's spokesman, Bishop Emil de Smedt, acknowledged that "some Fathers" had still expressed concern that previous drafts did "not sufficiently show how our doctrine is not opposed to ecclesiastical documents up till the time of the Supreme Pontiff Leo XIII."[62] In fact, an influential group of conservative Fathers had expressed their problems of conscience in regard to article 6, which spoke of "special recognition" being given by the state to one particular religion only "in the light of historical circumstances." That seemed to suggest that state neutrality towards the different religions was now to be seen as doctrinally normative, in contradiction of the nineteenth-century Encyclicals.[63] In his final *relatio* de Smedt explained the Commission's response:
> As regards the substance of the problem, the point should be made that while the papal documents up to Leo XIII insisted more on the moral duty of public authorities toward the true religion, the recent Supreme Pontiffs, while retaining this doctrine, complement it by highlighting another duty of the same authorities, namely, that of observing the exigencies of the dignity of the human person in religious matters, as a necessary element of the common good. The text presented to you today recalls more clearly (see nos. 1 and 3) the duties of the public authority towards the true religion (*officia potestatis publicae erga veram religionem*); from which it is manifest that this part of the doctrine has not been overlooked (*ex quo patet hanc doctrinae partem non praetermitti*).[64]

This explanation is of supreme importance, as it constitutes the only *official* commentary on the final and definitive version of the vital passage in the preamble whose textual evolution we have been considering. This final text (in which we have emphasized the words added) asserts that the Council's doctrine of religious liberty

leaves intact the *traditional* Catholic doctrine on the moral duty of men *and societies* towards the true religion and the one Church of Christ.

As we have just seen, the Council Fathers were officially informed that, in casting their votes for or against this final draft of the religious liberty schema they were to understand it as reaffirming the doctrine of earlier Popes such as Leo XIII on the duties of the "public authority" towards the true religion. And as we have seen, these duties of "society" as such, acting through its public authority, were always said by those Popes to include, as a matter of *divine* law, not only respect for the freedom of the Church but also theoretical and practical recognition of her unique authority as bearer of the true religion.

Strange to say, these vital amendments included in the definitive text of *Dignitatis Humanae*, together with the official explanation given for them, are passed over in complete silence by Fr. Murray, even though his footnotes on this section of the document, the preamble, are extremely copious—about three times as long as the text itself![65] Indeed, as we saw earlier, Murray attributes to the Declaration, in his notes on article 13, the very thesis which it rejects by these last-minute additions to article 1—the thesis that the Church, by divine law, can claim from the State "nothing more" than freedom.

The fact is that the amendments in article 1 are the Council's last word on this subject, so that the rather inadequate general formula of article 6 on special State recognition of one religion must be interpreted in the light of article 1, not *vice versa*.[66] In any case, article 6 itself was also changed in the final draft so as to avoid the apparent insinuation that such special recognition of one religion is more or less a relic from the past. The final text (which of course refers to the "establishment" of non-Catholic and non-Christian religions as well as that of the true religion) speaks of such special recognition as obtaining not "in the light of *historical* circumstances," but "in the light of *particular* circumstances" (*circumstantiis peculiaribus*).[67] As applied to Catholicism, that still seems to imply that the Church's "establishment" is some kind of exception to a norm. But in the light of the final amendments to article 1, this cannot be understood as a doctrinal or *de jure* norm, only as a *de facto* sociological or demographic norm. That is, article 6 must simply be understood as observing implicitly that most countries in today's world are composed of citizens of varying religions or no religion; but that in "particular circumstances" one specific religious group is in fact so numerous or influential that it is given special constitutional recognition of some sort. In this article the Council prescinds entirely from what Catholic doctrine (divine law) has to say about the civic community's recognition of the true religion. But the omission at this point is remedied by the restatement of that doctrine in the preamble.

If societies, acting as such through decisions of public authority, have the "moral duty" to recognize the truth of Catholicism, then obviously and *a fortiori* they have the *competence* to do so. In that sense the passages of *Dignitatis Humanae* which we have surveyed already constitute a sufficient reply to Murray's second controversial thesis, which he also attributes to the conciliar Declaration. Commenting on article 6, Murray tells us that "government is forbidden to assume...the task of judging the truth or value of religious propaganda. Otherwise it would exceed its competence, which is confined to affairs of the temporal and terrestrial order."[68]

Quite apart from the final insertions in article 1, which scarcely harmonize with this interpretation of the Declaration, it should be noted that in fact the Council deliberately decided *not* to teach what Murray says it does teach. The original draft of the schema on religious liberty (the *declaratio prior* of 1964) included the assertion that "the State, precisely because of the juridical quality of its authority, is not qualified (*ineptam esse*) to make judgments of truth in religious matters."[69] Murray does not tell the readers of Abbott's edition that this statement was dropped from all subsequent drafts, after many conservative Fathers complained that this first schema seems to call in question the very possibility of a confessional Catholic state.[70]

The next two drafts did nevertheless embody a statement equivalent to Murray's comment that the state's competence "is confined to affairs of the temporal and terrestrial order." The *textus reemendatus* presented to the Fathers at the beginning of the 1965 session said that civil authority should "restrict itself to the things of this world" (*sese ad res huius saeculi restringendo*), and should not "involve itself (*sese immisceat*) in those things which concern man's orientation to God."[71] But this passage too was deleted in response to sharp criticism, as it seemed to imply the ideal of a religiously "neutral" or secular State. It was replaced by a much more traditional statement (cf. end of article 3 of *Dignitatis Humanae* which, instead of saying that the care of terrestrial concerns [or "the things of this world"] is the *only* purpose of civil authority, affirms that this is its "characteristic" [or "distinctive"] purpose [*finis proprius*]). This is in harmony with the traditional doctrine that, while temporal matters are of course the State's special area of competence, it should also have an eye to man's eternal salvation, *recognize* the Catholic Church's divine mandate and special competence in that area, and thus give it full cooperation. And instead of rejecting any and every kind of State "involvement" in religious matters, the final text rejects only heavy-handed interference. It begins by observing that religious acts "transcend by their very nature the terrestrial and temporal order," and continues:

> Therefore the civil power, whose characteristic purpose is to care for the common temporal good, must recognize and favour the religious life of citizens; but it must be seen as exceeding its limits if it presumes either to take charge of or to hinder (*dirigere vel impedire*) religious activity.[72]

It is fair to conclude that, notwithstanding the very substantial contribution of John Courtney Murray's thought to the Declaration on Religious Liberty, the document finally promulgated by the Council, understood correctly in the light of its textual history and the official explanations given to the Fathers by the *relator*, did not adopt Murray's novel opinion—an opinion contrary to all Catholic tradition and to weighty pronouncements of the Church's Magisterium—that society's public authorities in principle need not, and indeed may not, recognize the unique truth of Catholicism, and express that recognition appropriately in their official acts. Unfortunately Murray and many other commentators in the twenty-five years since the Declaration was promulgated (especially his fellow Jesuits) have presented *Dignitatis Humanae* to the world as though it had endorsed this unapproved opinion, even though in fact the document ended up by reaffirming (albeit in muted tones) the traditional contrary thesis.

It might be objected that the post-conciliar revision of older Concordats between the Holy See and various traditionally "Catholic" countries (Spain, Italy, Argentina, for example) supports Murray's interpretation of *Dignitatis Humanae*, since in such cases the status of

Catholicism as the "religion of State" has been deliberately discarded. Unfortunately, there is no reason to doubt that this innovative, non-traditional understanding of Church and State has enjoyed widespread currency at very high levels in the Church: as we have seen, a large majority of the Council Fathers would have been quite happy to approve the schema on religious liberty even without the last-minute amendments which explicitly (though very briefly) reaffirmed the traditional doctrine.

Nevertheless, a majority opinion among bishops does not constitute an official position of the Church as such. Moreover, the "secularization" of these concordats by no means presupposes official Vatican acceptance of Murray's thesis that political authority as such is incompetent to recognize the truth of Catholicism; and as far as this writer knows, no official document of the Holy See has ever stated or implied that thesis. The concordat revisions are perfectly explicable simply in terms of a change in policy, not necessarily a change in doctrine. That is, in countries where secularization is now far advanced, and where considerable hostility exists *de facto* towards the enjoyment of any special recognition or privileges for the Church in civil society, the Church herself has decided not to *insist on* anything more than the freedom which other religious bodies enjoy. That in no way implies a renunciation of further rights which she possesses *in abstracto*, only a renunciation of their exercise in this situation.

In fact, we can go further than this. If the Church had in fact renounced the traditional *doctrine* regarding the political community's competence to recognize the true religion, she would in consistency have had to insist on the substantial revision of *all* existing concordats which expressed such recognition. But this has not happened.

It is true that the expressions "Catholic State" or "religion of the State" are no longer found in concordats approved by the Holy See; but this merely reflects the fact that in today's generally accepted democratic understanding of government, the "State," in the sense of the public authority within a nation, is not supposed to be the *sovereign* authority. It is juridically the instrument or servant of a sovereign citizen body, not the "master" of a mass of passive "subjects." The essence of the traditional doctrine is that the civic or political community as such—the *civitas*, to use the favoured word of Leo XIII—is in principle obliged to recognize the true religion, and to express this recognition in acts of the public power. Whether or not that public power is seen as *deciding for* the community (the older, paternalistic model) or merely *reflecting* a decision *already made* by the community (the contemporary democratic model) is not doctrinally relevant, since it does not pertain to divine law. The Church has always seen as legitimate alternatives the various forms of government—monarchy, oligarchy, and democracy—which have been recognized at least since the time of Aristotle.

It follows that under contemporary conditions the divine law is expressed more clearly by speaking of an obligation on the part of *nations* to recognize the true religion, rather than an obligation on the part of *states,* since the modern "state," insofar as it means "government,"[73] is not the ultimate *decision-making* authority. And this contemporary expression of the traditional doctrine is in fact found in several modern concordats between the Holy See and countries less secularized than those of the affluent West. Article 1 of the 1975 concordat with Colombia, for instance, affirms:

> The State, out of regard for the traditional Catholic sentiment of the Columbian nation, considers the Catholic, Apostolic and Roman religion as a fundamental element of the common good, and of the integral development of the national community.[74]

The current concordat between the Holy See and the Dominican Republic is more emphatic. It dates from a decade before the Council, but because it was already in harmony with the subsequent teaching of *Dignitatis Humanae* regarding the religious liberty of non-Catholics as well as Catholics, it has continued in force till the present day. The document begins "In the name of the Most Holy Trinity,"[75] thereby making the kind of "judgment of theological truth" which John Courtney Murray says political authority is incompetent to make. This judgment is repeated in the first article of the concordat:

> The Catholic, Apostolic, Roman religion continues to be the religion of the Dominican *Nation* and will enjoy the rights and prerogatives which pertain to it in conformity with Divine Law and Canon Law.[76]

This clearly goes much further than the kind of mere sociological "statement of fact" which is the most Murray will allow in the constitutional documents of a Catholic people.[77] And in the case of both Colombia and the Dominican Republic this *national* recognition of Catholicism further contravenes the norms advocated by Murray, in that it certainly has "juridical consequences": Catholicism is to enjoy a favoured legal status in regard to marriage legislation, public education, the designation of public holidays, the civil status of clergy, and other areas of the national life.[78] Perhaps more importantly, this recognition is a strong constitutional barrier against the legalization of neo-pagan barbarities which outrage natural law: abortion, homosexual "marriages," euthanasia, etc. An officially Catholic nation, one supposes, will accept the Catholic Church's role as authentic interpreter of the natural moral law, rather than entrust its interpretation to the fickle whims of majority opinion.

That concordats such as these continue in force a quarter-century after the promulgation of *Dignitatis Humanae* is perhaps the best evidence that, according to the authoritative interpretation of the See of Peter, the Declaration's disapproval of "discrimination amongst citizens" on religious grounds (article 6) does not mean that there can be no legal "discrimination" between religious bodies as such. In other words, such concordats are a practical testimony to the essential continuity between the nineteenth-century doctrine on Church and state and that of Vatican II. Murray in effect not only held, but also attributed to the Second Vatican Council, the view that the state, in principle, not only may, but must, do the very thing which according to Pius IX and Leo XIII (in the following quotes), the state has in principle *no right* to do: that is, it must "hold in equal favour different kinds of religion" and thus, govern society "without making any distinction between the true religion and false religions."[79] Those Pontiffs understood and promulgated their teaching on this point as a matter of definitive and unchangeable Catholic doctrine; and, in upholding that doctrine, Vatican II continues to uphold the honour of Christ the King, and His rights over human society.

NOTES

1. Murray, J. C., *The Problem of Religious Freedom (PRF)* (Westminster, Maryland: Newman Press, 1965), p. 94. (This essay was originally published in *Theological Studies*, vol. XXV, no. 4, December 1964, pp. 503-575.)
2. This happened to be the 25th anniversary of the coronation of Pope Paul VI.
3. Apostolic Letter Motu Proprio, *Ecclesia Dei* (2 July 1988), section 4b.
4. Cf. Walter M. Abbott (ed.), *The Documents of Vatican II* (New York: Angelus Books, 1966). Page xi of the Preface mentions that Murray translated the Declaration on Religious Liberty for this edition. His introductory essay, translation, and extensive footnotes are found on pp. 672-696. The note on

abbreviations (p. xiv) points out that in all documents in this edition the unofficial footnotes "are the work of the commentator (whose name is at the end of the essay introducing the document)."
5. The present writer's position in this regard is to be found in *Religious Liberty and Contraception* (John XXIII Fellowship Coop., Melbourne: Australia, 1988). In the U.S.A. this is available from Catholics United for the Faith, 50 Washington Ave., New Rochelle, N.Y. 10801 ($12 plus postage).
6. Cf. Fr. Curran's remarks to this effect in his press conference of March 11, 1986, published in *Origins* (N.C. Documentary Service) March 27, 1986, p. 666.
7. Abbott, *Documents*, op. cit., p. 693, n. 53.
8. Cf. Murray, *The Problem of Religious Freedom*, pp. 91-92.
9. Murray, J.C., *We Hold These Truths: Catholic Reflections on the American Proposition* (New York: Sheed and Ward, 1960), p. 49.
10. *Ibid.*, pp. 72-76.
11. *Ibid.*, p. 74.
12. *Ibid.*, p. 76.
13. Cf. Matias Garcia, S.J., "Analisis Historico," in *La Libertad Religiosa: Analisis de la Declaracion "Dignitatis Humanae"* (Universidad Pontificia de Comillas: Editorial Razon y Fe: Madrid, 1966), p. 68-69.
14. Cf. note 1 above for publication details.
15. Murray, *PRF*, p. 99. (This and all other references in this article to *The Problem of Religious Freedom* are to the Newman Press edition.)
16. *Ibid.*, p. 96.
17. Abbott, *Documents*, op. cit., p. 684, n. 14.
18. Cf., for example, Leo XIII, *Immortale Dei* (1885), nos. 6, 35; Pius IX, *Syllabus* (1864), no. 77; Pius XI, *Quas Primas* (1925), no. 32.
19. Murray, *PRF*, p. 39.
20. *Ibid.*, p. 42.
21. Pius IX, Encyclical Letter on Liberal Errors, *Quanta Cura*, 8 December 1864, no. 3.
22. *Ibid.*, no. 6.
23. *Ibid.*, no. 6 (emphasis added).
24. Leo XIII, Encyclical Letter on the Christian Constitution of States, *Immortale Dei*, 1 November 1885, no. 35.
25. *Ibid.*, no. 6.
26. *Ibid.*, (emphasis added).
27. Pius XI, Encyclical Letter on the Feast of Christ the King, *Quas Primas*, 11 December 1925, no. 32.
28. Murray, *The Problem of Religious Freedom*, p. 89.
29. *Ibid.*, p. 88.
30. *Ibid.*, p. 101.
31. *Ibid.*, p. 90.
32. *Ibid.*, p. 88.
33. *Ibid.*
34. *Ibid.*, pp. 88-89.
35. Pius XII, Allocution to the 10th International Congress on Historical Sciences, 7 September 1955: *AAS* 47 (1955), p. 678.

36. *Ibid.*
37. Murray, *The Problem of Religious Freedom,* pp. 87-88.
38. *Ibid.,* p. 100.
39. *Ibid.,* p. 101.
40. *Ibid.,* p. 41.
41. *Ibid.*
42. Cf. *ibid.,* pp. 103-104.
43. Murray, J.C., "Leo XIII: Separation of Church and State," in *Theological Studies,* vol. XIV, no. 2 (June 1953), p. 185.
44. Murray, *The Problem of Religious Freedom,* p. 61. Also cf. Murray, "Current Theology of Religious Freedom," in *Theological Studies,* vol. X, no. 3 (September 1949), p. 425.
45. Cf. the following passages in Murray's articles: "Leo XIII: Separation…" op cit., p. 168; "Current Theology…" op. cit., pp. 422-423; "Leo XIII on Church and State: The General Structure of the Controversy," in *Theological Studies,* vol. XIV, no. 1 (March 1953), pp. 12-13; and "Leo XIII: Two Concepts of Government," in *Theological Studies,* vol. XIV, no. 4 (December 1953), p. 561.
46. Cf. Murray, "Leo XIII on Church…" op. cit., pp. 20-21; also *We Hold These Truths,* op. cit., pp. 69-71.
47. Murray, *The Problem of Religious Freedom,* pp. 61-62.
48. *Ibid.,* pp. 62-63.
49. *Ibid.,* p. 62.
50. Cf. *ibid.,* p. 63.
51. Leo XIII, Encyclical Letter on Catholicism in the United State, *Longinqua,* 6 January 1895, no. 6 (emphasis added).
52. Vatican Council I, teaching against fideism, solemnly defined that externally accessible evidence, and not merely inward or private experience, rationally establishes the divine origin of Christian revelation. Cf. Denzinger-Schonmetzer 3009, 3033, 3034.
53. Leo XIII, *Immortale Dei,* no. 6 (emphasis added).
54. Abbott, *Documents,* op. cit., p. 693.
55. Cf. Accord between the Holy See and Spain, July 28, 1976 in which "*est principium fundamentale*" is translated "*e principio basilare*" in the Italian and "*es principio fundamental*" in Spanish. *AAS* 68 (1976), p. 509.
56. Cf. Psalm 11:3, "Foundations once destroyed, what can the just man do?"
57. Abbott, *Documents,* op. cit., p. 693, n. 53 (original text p. 730).
58. *Dignitatis Humanae,* no. 13 (present writer's translation). Murray's translation (Abbott, p. 693) weakens the sense by omitting any translation of the word *quavis* ("all/any…whatever").
59. Murray, however (loc. cit.), translates *auctoritas spiritualis* as "*a* spiritual authority."
60. *Acta Synodalia* (Rome, 1978), vol. IV, part V, p. 78.
61. *Ibid.*
62. *Acta Synodalia,* vol. IV, part VI, p. 719.
63. Cf. Ralph M. Wiltgen, *The Rhine Flows Into the Tiber* (British ed.: Augustine Publishing Co., Devon, 1978), p. 251.

64. *Acta Synodalia*, loc. cit. (cf. note 62 above).
65. Cf. Abbott, *Documents*, op. cit., pp. 675-678.
66. The official explanation given for the addition of *ac societatum* in no. 1 was "for greater clarity" ("*quia clarius*"). *Acta Synodalia*, vol. IV, part VI, p. 731, MM 28-29 and response.
67. Murray (Abbott, p. 685) translates *peculiaribus* as "peculiar," which in English has a pejorative connotation ("strange" or "odd"). *Peculiaris* in Latin has no such connotation.
68. Abbott, *Documents*, op. cit., p. 684, n. 14.
69. *Acta Synodalia*, vol. III, part VIII, p. 442.
70. Cf. Garcia, op. cit., (cf. note 13 above), p. 144.
71. *Acta Synodalia*, vol. IV, part V, p. 81.
72. *Dignitatis Humanae*, no. 3. The specifications of no. 7 are taken for granted at this point in the text; that is, government can indeed "hinder...religious activity" in the case of certain abuses.
73. In fact, it does *not* always mean "government," and this has added another element of confusion to the discussion. "State" sometimes means an entire nation, not just its government ("the State of Israel"); or it may mean a semi-autonomous region within a nation ("the State of Ohio").
74. *AAS* 67 (1975), p. 422 (present writer's translation, emphasis added).
75. *AAS* 46 (1954), p. 433.
76. *Ibid.*, p. 434 (present writer's translation, emphasis added).
77. Murray, *The Problem of Religious Freedom*, p. 96. An example of a constitutional document which Murray presumably *would* consider appropriate is that of the Republic of Ireland, which simply mentions Catholicism as the religion of the majority of its citizens.
78. Cf. *AAS* 67 (1975), pp. 423-434; *AAS* 46 (1954), pp. 435-457.
79. *Immortale Dei*, no. 35, and *Quanta Cura*, no. 3.

11

Religious Liberty and Political Morality

by Robert P. George

Practical Reasoning and Morality

*P*ractical reasoning not only applies but also identifies reasons for choice and action. These reasons include moral reasons. A full theory of practical reasoning includes a theory of morality. A theory of morality—a critical reflective account—seeks to identify the moral norms available to guide choice and action by distinguishing fully reasonable from practically unreasonable—albeit not simply irrational—choices.

Moral norms are themselves reasons for choice and action, albeit reasons of a particular sort. They guide choice and action in situations in which one has a reason (or, at least, and emotional motive) to do X, but at the same time a reason not to do X because, for example, one also has a reason to do or preserve Y, and the doing or preserving of Y is incompatible here and now with doing X. A moral norm forbids doing X when it provides a conclusive reason not to do X. Such a reason defeats, though it does not destroy,[1] whatever reason one has to do X. By the same token, if a moral norm requires one to do X, then it provides a conclusive reason for doing X. Such a reason defeats, but, again, does not destroy, one's reason to do or preserve Y. If, however, no moral norm dictates a choice one way or the other, then the choice is between morally acceptable, albeit incompatible, options. One may, for example, have an undefeated reason to do X and at the same time an undefeated reason to do Y. A choice for either of these possibilities is thus rationally grounded. Nevertheless, inasmuch as one lacks a conclusive reason for choosing one over the other (though one may have a conclusive reason to choose one or the other over some third alternative, e.g., the possibility of doing nothing), the choice between them is rationally underdetermined. [2]

Not all reasons for action are moral norms. [3] All moral norms are, however, reasons for action. Where a moral norm dictates a certain course of action, it is a conclusive reason for that action; it defeats any reasons one may have for doing what it forbids or not doing what it requires. Only by acting in accord with the moral norm does one act in a fully reasonable, i.e., morally responsible, manner.

Consider a case in which one has a reason for doing X, but one's reason is not itself a moral norm. If one has a non-moral reason to do X and is not forbidden by a moral norm from doing it, then one has an undefeated, albeit non-conclusive, reason to do X. One can reasonably opt to do X or not do it. If, in the circumstances, however, a moral norm forbids one's doing X, then that norm provides a conclusive reason not to do it that defeats one's reason to do it. Of course, in the opposite situation, where a moral norm requires one's doing X, then one has a conclusive reason to do it. Any reason one may have for not doing it is defeated by the moral norm requiring one to do it. The key point is that a choice is fully reasonable (as opposed to merely rationally grounded) when it is not only for a reason, but is also in conformity with all (i.e., when it is not forbidden by any) moral norms. Even actions that are motivated by one's regard for an end whose *intelligible* (and not merely emotional) appeal qualifies it as a *reason* (and not merely a subrational motive) for action can be practically unreasonable. It cannot be reasonable to do what one has a conclusive reason not to do. An action motivated by one's regard for a reason is nevertheless unreasonable precisely insofar as one is under a moral obligation not to do it.

In the case of immoral choices (at least insofar as they are not merely the products of conscientious but mistaken moral judgements), reason is fettered by emotion. Commonly, though not always, the emotion that motivates an immoral choice is allied with a (defeated and therefore morally inadequate) reason for that choice. In such circumstances, reason is typically instrumentalized and harnessed by emotion not merely in the cause of satisfying desires, but, also, for the purpose of producing rationalizations for immoral actions. My point can be illustrated by a hypothetical case. The acquisition of scientific knowledge is undeniably a reason for action. Knowledge of this sort is typically both intrinsically and instrumentally worthwhile; it is both an end-in-itself and a means to other valuable ends. Now, consider the case of a gifted research scientist who wishes to understand the etiology of AIDS. He desires to acquire this knowledge both for its own sake and in the hope of finding a cure. His preliminary research suggests a strategy for further research that, though promising, requires the performance of early experiments on a living human being. Lacking a volunteer, he considers the possibility of secretly performing the experiments on an unsuspecting patient who is in an advanced stage of AIDS. Of course, the proposal that he is considering violates various moral norms; but his desire to have the knowledge is strong. So he begins to rationalize his plan: "The life I will be destroying is, after all, a poor and unhappy one; and the experiments do promise to advance science significantly and may even lead to a cure that will save thousands of lives. Surely the great good to be achieved outweighs the little bit of evil I will have to do to achieve it."

Such a rationalization is possible because the advancement of science and the saving of lives really are reasons for action. They are reasons for the scientist to carry out his plan. They are not, however, the only relevant reasons in these circumstances. The scientist has reasons to abandon his scheme. The life that the scientist would destroy is a reason for action too, as is his own character which will be corrupted (or further corrupted) by his freely adopting a proposal to commit murder. Faced with reasons to perform the experiments and reasons not to perform them, what should he do?

If there were no (moral) norms to provide reasons to prefer one course of action to the other, the choice between them would be rationally underdetermined. It would be a choice as many choices—despite the existence of moral norms—are between morally acceptable options. Here, however, that is not the case. The moral norms enjoining us to treat every human being fairly and every human life as an end rather than as a mere means clearly exclude the option of carrying out the experiments. These norms provide conclusive reasons not to carry them out, despite the great goods that really may be achieved by doing so. Of course, the scientist may decide to carry them out anyway. He may fetter his own reason and subordinate it to his emotional desire to realize those goods: To act on one's emotional desire to realize goods that can only be realized here and now by doing what one has conclusive reasons not to do is, it is fair to say, the textbook case of practical unreasonableness.

Reasons for Political Action and Norms of Political Morality

A theory of political morality seeks to identify reasons for political choice and action. Among these reasons are norms of political morality that distinguish morally acceptable political choices and public policies from immoral choices and policies. Political action, for purposes of normative political theory, is action undertaken for the sake of the common good of such a society.

Are the basic reasons for political action some subset of the universe of basic reasons for action? Or are all the basic reasons for action reasons for political as well as for other sorts of action? To answer these questions it is necessary to clarify the notion of a basic reason for action.

A basic reason for action is a reason whose intelligibility does not depend on further or deeper reasons for action. Those ends or purposes that are intrinsically worthwhile provide basic reasons for action. While such ends or purposes may also be instrumentally desirable, i.e., desirable as means to other ends, they are distinguishable from purely instrumental goods inasmuch as they can be intelligently sought as ends-in-themselves. Instrumental goods do indeed provide reasons for action; they are reasons whose intelligibility depends, however, on further or deeper reasons. Thus, they are not basic reasons. The intelligibility of instrumental goods depends upon the intrinsic goods whose realization by choice and action they make possible. If there were no intrinsic goods, no basic reasons for action, practical reason would be what Hume, for example, thought it to be, namely, purely instrumental; and rationally motivated action would be impossible.[4] Intrinsically choiceworthy ends or purposes provide us with the basic reasons for action that make rationally motivated action possible.[5]

Qua basic reasons for action, the value of intrinsic goods cannot and need not be inferred from more fundamental reasons for action. Nor, as Germain Grisez has rightly insisted, can basic reasons for action be deduced from purely theoretical premises (i.e., premises that do not include reasons for action). As first principles of practical thinking, basic reasons for action are, as Aquinas held, self-evident *(per se nota)* and indemonstrable *(indemonstrabilia).*⁶ As fundamental aspects of human well-being and fulfillment, they belong to human beings as parts of their nature; they are not, however, derived (in any sense that the logician would recognize) from methodologically antecedent knowledge of human nature drawn from anthropology or any other theoretical discipline. Rather, they are grasped in acts of non-inferential understanding by the mind working inductively on the data of inclination and experience.⁷

What are the basic reasons for action? John Finnis has usefully classified them as follows: life (in a broad sense that includes health and general vitality); knowledge; play; aesthetic experience; sociability (i.e., friendship broadly conceived); practical reasonableness; and religion.⁸ Practically reasonable action in respect of the plurality of basic reasons for action is guided and structured by moral norms that are, as it were, methodological requirements of the good of practical reasonableness. That good, then, has a peculiar strategic or architectonic role in the moral life. To live in accordance with its requirements is to realize a fundamental aspect of the human good precisely by making one's self-constituting choices in pursuit of other goods intelligently and uprightly.

Let us now return to the question of whether the basic reasons for political action are some subset of the universe of basic reasons for action. According to one view, some intrinsic human goods are aspects of the common good while others are private goods and therefore not legitimate reasons for political action (or, at least, certain forms of political action). The extreme version of this view identifies some good, say, peace or justice, as the sole legitimate reason for political action. According to a familiar contemporary liberal position, for example, justice is the sole legitimate reason for any political action that limits legal liberty; legal prohibitions enacted for the sake of goods other than justice are themselves unjust.⁹

At one point Germain Grisez and Joseph M. Boyle, Jr. defended a political theory that bore some affinities to the liberal position. In *Life and Death With Liberty and Justice*, a book published in 1979, they argued that laws prohibiting voluntary euthanasia, while justifiable, could not legitimately be based on a putative public interest in preserving the lives of those who might wish to do away with themselves. Bodily life, they maintained, is a purely "private" good in the respects relevant to the question of whether people ought to be legally free to destroy their own lives. As such, it is not in itself a legitimate ground for limiting legal liberty.

Grisez and Boyle argued that "[t]he very notion of a *common* good or of a *public* interest suggests that there is a contrasting category of goods which are *individual* or *private*."[10] Their criterion for distinguishing the two categories was the effectiveness of political society in pursuing the goods in question: "the common good includes goods which the political society as such can *effectively* pursue."[11] Other goods, they maintained, provide reasons for action, but not for political action.

According to Grisez and Boyle, the primary purpose of public authority is to establish and maintain a just social order. To this end, those exercising public authority must forbid certain sorts of acts and require others. The requirements of justice frequently provide conclusive reasons for laws that restrict liberty. Thus, public authorities are ordinarily required, for the sake of the common good, to prohibit murder, rape, and theft, for example, and to require the payment of taxes. At the same time, the requirements of justice often provide public authorities with conclusive reasons not to enact laws that limit people's liberty. And, as Grisez and Boyle viewed the matter, these requirements provide conclusive reasons to not forbid acts (including immoral acts) that do not unjustly harm others: "[f]or the sake of justice and human dignity the liberty to act immorally must be respected and protected by law."[12]

Where, as in the case of legal prohibitions on self-administered suicide, for example, a law is motivated not by a concern to protect people from wrongs committed against them by others, but rather by a commitment to the "private" good of preserving bodily life, Grisez and Boyle argued that the law is unjust. "Although the law should not facilitate such acts, it should take care to avoid interfering with competent adults who freely choose to kill themselves."[13]

According to Grisez and Boyle, "liberty must be respected by political society, almost as an absolute, limited only by the demands of justice."[14] As we have seen, they did not hold liberty to be inviolable. Nor did they treat liberty as a basic good. They argued, rather, that liberty must be limited for the sake of justice; but, at the same time, liberty may not legitimately be limited except for the sake of justice. To limit liberty for the sake of other goods violates the good of justice.

Justice is the sole reason for political action that directly limits individual freedom.

Grisez and Boyle did not take the extreme libertarian view that justice is the sole reason for any form of political action. They held that other goods could rightly be understood as reasons for political action in a restricted sense. The good of knowledge, for example, could serve as a legitimate reason for a system of public education; similarly the goods of beauty and play could serve as valid reasons for public museums, parks, and recreation facilities; and indeed the goods of life and health could be sound reasons for public hospitals and publicly funded medical research. The restriction on treating these goods as reasons for political action, however, was that they could not serve as legitimate reasons for direct prohibitions on types of action deemed to be unwise, imprudent, or even immoral. Thus, the goods of knowledge, beauty, play, life, and health, together with the goods of personal integrity and authenticity (or what Finnis calls "practical reasonableness"), were, according to Grisez and Boyle, "private," goods in a way that the good of justice was not. *Qua* "private," these goods could not serve as valid reasons for public authorities to prohibit wrongful acts.

As I see it, there are two problems with Grisez and Boyle's position. First, to the extent that their argument relied on the claim that governments cannot promote or protect goods other than justice effectively except insofar as government action to promote or protect these goods is ultimately motivated by a concern for justice, it seems implausible. The fact is that governmental action—even coercive governmental action—can be effective in discouraging people from doing wicked things even when their immoral actions harm only themselves or those who collaborate with them. Laws designed to uphold public morality, for example, not only contribute to the moral education of the public, they may help to establish or maintain a milieu which encourages virtue and discourages at least the grosser forms of vice. But if political action to protect public morals with respect to putatively "victimless" immoralities such as pornography, prostitution, drug abuse, and suicide can have beneficial effects, then the goods of life, health, friendship, and practical reasonableness really are aspects of the common good and reasons for political action, even by the standard of effectiveness articulated by Grisez and Boyle.

My second reaction to the position once defended by Grisez and Boyle is that I see no warrant for the claim that direct limitations on liberty imposed otherwise than for the sake of justice are themselves unjust. I grant that in particular circumstances prudential considerations may very well tip the balance against the enactment or enforcement of laws to uphold public morality, for example. A legislator may reasonably judge that under the conditions prevailing in his society a particular morals law may be too costly, or doomed to failure, or even likely to do more harm than good. Even where morals laws are, for prudential reasons, however, inadvisable, they are not necessarily unjust.

One of the ways that a law can be unjust is by depriving people of goods that are rightfully theirs. And it is certainly true that laws can unjustly deprive people of liberties to which they are entitled. People are morally entitled to decide for themselves without arbitrary governmental restrictions whether or whom to marry, for example, or what profession to pursue, where to live, and how to spend their leisure time. For the government to deprive people of these or other honorable liberties is unjust. There is no warrant, however, for believing that people are entitled to the liberty to corrupt, pervert, or destroy themselves simply because the law cannot effectively prevent them from doing so. Whether or not they are effective, morals laws that do not imperil honorable liberties do not unjustly deprive people of goods to which they are entitled.

Another way in which laws can be unjust is by arbitrarily favoring the interests and well-being of some citizens over others. Are morals laws unjust in this way? Not if they are based on sound moral judgments and not on mere prejudices. To encourage virtue and discourage vice is not to favor the interests or welfare of the virtuous over the vicious. Laws that forbid the sale or possession of pornography, for example, do not favor the interests of people who happen to dislike pornography over those who happen to like it. If pornography is wicked, and thus destructive of one's character, then no one has a true interest in using it—not even pornography-lovers. On the contrary, everyone has an interest in not using it. In light of this common interest, reasonable efforts to curtail the availability of pornography are "for the common good." They are in the interests of everyone—especially those who are most vulnerable to the temptation to use pornography (and who therefore benefit most from the maintenance of a social milieu free of pornography's corrupting influences). To be sure, such efforts, to the extent they are successful, frustrate the *desires* of those who wish to use pornography; these efforts do not, however, fail to regard their interests and well-being as just as important as the interests and well-being of everybody else.[15]

Are there, then, no inherently private reasons for action? Are all the basic reasons for action aspects of the common good of civil society?

Religious Liberty and Political Morality

There is surely one item on Finnis' list of basic goods that will strike many Americans, even many devoutly religious Americans, as inherently private. Religion, they will say, is manifestly not a reason for political action. Getting right with God, if there is a God, is a matter for individuals and the religious societies they freely form. Religion therefore is in no way an aspect of the common good of civil society. Political action for the sake of religion is contrary to sound political morality.

Misguided constitutional interpreters will allege that the principle that government has no business concerning itself with the good of religion, if religion is a good, is laid down in the Constitution of the United States. The most that can be said for this claim is that it has impressed a fair number of modern Supreme Court justices. Under the most plausible interpretation of the Establishment Clause of the First Amendment, the federal government is forbidden to establish a national church or interfere with established churches in the states.[16] At most, the Establishment Clause requires what commentators sometimes call "non-preferentialism," i.e., the principle that government must be evenhanded in its treatment of competing religious sects. Despite its popularity in elite circles, there is surprisingly little textual or historical warrant for the so-called "strict-separationist" view that the Establishment Clause forbids the states or even the federal government from promoting religion generally or preferring religion to irreligion.[17]

Constitutional interpretation aside, what is the truth as a matter of political morality? Is religion a purely private good? Is it in no sense an aspect of the common good of civil society?

The correct answer, I think, is that the good of religion is a reason for political action and an aspect of the common good of civil society. To see why, however, it will be necessary first to get clear on the sense in which religion is a basic reason for action, and second to analyze more closely the concept of the common good. After that, I shall say a word about how the status of religion as a basic reason for political action grounds and harmonizes two norms of political morality identified in *Dignitatis Humanae*, Vatican II's document on religious liberty, one requiring governments to respect the immunity of persons from coercion in matters of religious belief and practice, and the other enjoining governments "to take account of the religious life of the people and show it favor, since the function of government is to make provision for the common welfare."[18]

Whether or not unaided reason can conclude on the basis of a valid argument that God exists—indeed, even if it turns out that God does not exist—there is an important sense in which religion is a basic human good. Agnostics and even atheists can easily grasp the intelligible point of considering whether or not there is some ultimate, more-than-human source of meaning and value, of inquiring as best one can into the truth of the matter, and of ordering one's life on the basis of a reasonable judgment. As Finnis explains, "if there is a transcendent origin of the universal order-of-things and of human freedom and reason, then one's life and actions are in fundamental disorder if they are not brought, as best one can, into some order of harmony with whatever can be known or surmised about that transcendent other and its lasting order."[19] Religion is a basic reason for action, then, inasmuch as one has reason, even without appeal to ulterior reasons, to ascertain the truth about ultimate or divine realities and, if possible, to establish "peace with God, or the gods, or some non-theistic but more-than-human source of meaning and value."[20]

Let us turn now to the concept of the common good. According to Finnis, the central sense of the common good is as "a set of conditions which enables the members of a community to attain for themselves reasonable objectives, or to realize reasonably for themselves the value(s), for the sake of which they have reason to collaborate with each other (positively and/or negatively) in a community."[21] As he observes, however, this sense of common good is related to two other senses: (l) there is a common good inasmuch as the basic goods are goods for every member of the community and, indeed, for all human beings; and (2) each of the basic goods can be participated in by innumerable persons in innumerable ways.

As a common good in both of these senses, religion, like all the other basic goods, is an aspect of the common good in Finnis' central sense. People have reason to cooperate with each other in their efforts to understand religious truth and order their lives in accordance with it. Obviously, religion is the central common good of religious communities. While religious communities enable their members to realize other goods, e.g., friendship, knowledge, aesthetic appreciation, and play, these communities are organized precisely for the sake of religion. Of course, these points establish nothing more than that religion is a reason for political action. Even if religion cannot be considered "private" in the extreme sense that would make nonsense of common worship and organized (or even disorganized) churches and religious orders, it may nevertheless be "private" precisely in the sense that it is not a reason for political action.

Do people ever have reason to make political judgments and support or enact public policies based on their grasp of the value of religion? Does concern for the good of religion give people reason to collaborate (positively and/or negatively) in the political community?

In positive collaboration, the collaborators work together on a common project. In negative collaboration, they collaborate precisely by taking care not to interfere with one another. I submit that the good of religion gives people reason to collaborate both positively and negatively in the political community. A concern for religion, that is to say, gives people reason to support and enact certain public policies that they would have less or no reason to support or enact were it not for the value of religion.

It is the value of religion, for example, that grounds the right to religious liberty and the corresponding duty of government not only to refrain from coercing people on the basis of theological objections to their religious beliefs and practices but also to protect individuals and religious communities from others who would coerce them on the basis of such objections. The point comes more sharply into focus when we consider that even where a proposal for governmental suppression of a religious practice is not grounded (at least not exclusively) in a theological objection to the practice—I have in mind here everything from a proposal to suppress the use of drugs even as part of a *bona fide* religious ritual to a proposal to suppress *bona fide* rituals involving human sacrifice—the good of religion provides a reason for government not to suppress the practice. I hasten to add that the reason may well be defeated. Clearly there are conclusive reasons to prevent human sacrifice, for example, and perhaps even to prohibit the smoking of peyote even at the cost of impeding people's devout religious practice. Where there are not conclusive reasons to suppress a practice, however, the good of religion provides a compelling reason to grant exceptions to general laws whose application forbids that practice in cases where the practice is important to the religious lives of some citizens.[22]

Political morality requires respect for religious liberty for reasons set forth eloquently in the first part of *Dignitatis Humanae*. The appropriation of religious truth and the general religious well-being of men and women is impeded rather than advanced by attempts to coerce religious belief and practice. Coercion is self-defeating, and usually counterproductive, even when it is exercised on behalf of the Church in which the fullness of religious truth subsists.[23]

> For, of its very nature, the exercise of religion consists before all else in those internal, voluntary, and free acts whereby man sets the course of his life directly toward God. No merely human power can either command or prohibit acts of this kind.[24]

It is precisely at this point, however, that the Declaration reminds its readers that religion is not a purely private matter, that religion indeed provides a reason for collaboration:

> However, the social nature of man itself requires that he should give external expression to his internal acts of religion; that he should participate with others in matters religious; that he should profess his religion in the community.[25]

And only an instant later the Declaration unambiguously affirms the status of religion as a reason for positive collaboration in the political community:

> There is a further consideration. The religious acts whereby men, in private and in public and out of a sense of personal conviction direct their lives to God transcend by their very nature the order of terrestrial and temporal affairs. Government, therefore, ought indeed to take account of the religious life of the people and show it favor, since the function of government is to make provision for the common welfare.[26]

Just as the common good of religion provides a reason for negative collaboration in the political community in the form of governmental respect for (and protection of) religious liberty, it provides a reason for positive governmental action to encourage religious reflection, faith, and practice. Of course, norms of political morality, especially the norm requiring respect and protection for religious liberty, limit the means by which government may legitimately act for the sake of the range of ends that constitute the basic reasons for political action.

Because prudential concerns of various sorts and other countervailing reasons will often militate against particular policies for promoting religion, the norm of political morality enjoining government to "show favor" to the religious life of the people is not an especially stringent one. By contrast, the norm requiring government to respect and protect religious freedom is quite stringent. Nevertheless, where there are undefeated reasons for government to support and encourage religion, such support and encouragement is for the common good.

There are many ways in which government can serve the common good by acting for the sake of religion. An obvious way is by collaborating (both positively and negatively) with religious schools. At the same time, government sponsored schools can help children to develop rich spiritual lives by, for example, cooperating with parents and religious leaders to provide opportunities for children to practice their religions and receive religious instruction as parts of the regular school week.

Outside the area of education, government can encourage and support religious broadcasting, especially the sort of broadcasting that fosters inter-faith understanding. It can, as our government does, grant tax exemptions to religious organizations and permit contributors to those organizations to deduct their contributions. Moreover, government can involve responsible religious leaders and their organizations in public policy deliberations and employ them in social services roles without requiring them to compromise their moral and religious scruples. And for the sake of people's spiritual lives, among other goods, it can carefully refrain from taking over social welfare functions that are better served in particular communities by religious institutions, inter-denominational and non-denominational charities, families, and other non-governmental providers.

Government can and should concern itself (acting again both positively and negatively) with the health and well-being of various communities of faith, just as it should concern itself with the well-being of families and other subsidiary communities, especially when these communities are threatened, as many religious people believe they are today, by a powerful secularist elite which would employ the principal institutions of cultural transmission to spread a pseudo-gospel of materialism and self-indulgence.

NOTES

1. If it *destroyed* one's reason to do X, then a decision to do X despite the moral norm against doing it would be not merely unreasonable but irrational and, therefore, in a certain sense, unintelligible.
2. For a careful explanation of how choices between rationally grounded possibilities can be rationally underdetermined see Joseph Raz, *The Morality of Freedom* (Oxford: Clarendon Press, 1986), pp. 388-389.
3. Even non-moral reasons for action are subject, however, to moral norms.
4. In Hume's famous statement, "reason is, and ought only to be, the slave of the passions, and can never pretend to any office, other than to serve and obey them." *A Treatise of Human Nature*, bk. 2, pt. 3 sec. III. Hume's thinking here is fully in line with his great predecessor, Thomas Hobbes, who said that "the Thoughts, are to the Desires as Scouts and Spies to range abroad, and find the way to the things desired." *Leviathan*, pt. 1, ch. 8.
5. I have explicated and defended the claim that the practical intellect can grasp such ends or purposes in "Recent Criticism of Natural Law Theory," 55 *University of Chicago Law Review* 1371-1429 (1988).
6. See *Summa Theologiae* I-II, q. 94, a. 2.
7. As the fruit of intellectual acts made possible by reflection on data, basic reasons for action are not mere intuitions or innate ideas. Nor does the truth of our knowledge of basic reasons for action consist in their "conformity to practical reason's own inner requirements, i.e., to itself or its directive structure." (Brian V. Johnstone among others, has mistakenly attributed this latter position to Germain Grisez. See Johnstone, "The Structures of Practical Reason: Traditional Theories and Contemporary Questions," 50 *Thomist* 417-466 (1986). For Grisez's reply rejecting this view and criticizing Johnstone's claim that it is implied by Grisez's theory of practical reasoning see "The Structures of Practical Reason: Some Comments and Clarifications," 52 *Thomist* 269-291 (1988).) Our knowledge of basic reasons for action has its truth, rather, in the adequation of those reasons to possible fulfillment that can be realized through human action. See my "Natural Law and Human Nature," in Robert P. George, ed., *Natural Law Theory* (Oxford: Clarendon Press, 1991). Of course, our knowledge of the possibilities of such fulfillment will depend, in any particular circumstances, on a measure of theoretical knowledge including a knowledge of empirical possibilities and environmental constraints. To hold that the basic reasons for action, as self-evident first principles of practical reasoning, are not inferred from prior theoretical principles is by no means to imply, then, that there is a "wall of separation" between practical and theoretical reasoning, *pace* Henry Veatch, "Natural Law and the Is-Ought Question," 26 *Catholic Lawyer* 251-265, 265 (1981), or that knowledge of the world is irrelevant to practical thinking, *pace*

Ralph McInerny, *Ethica Thomistica* (Washington, DC: The Catholic University of America Press, 1982), pp. 54-55.
8. John Finnis, *Natural Law and Natural Rights* (Oxford: Clarendon Press, 1980), pp. 86-90.
9. In Ronald Dworkin's equality-based liberal conception of justice, for example, "government must be neutral on what might be called the question of the good life." See *A Matter of Principle* (Cambridge, Massachusetts: Harvard University Press, 1985), p. 191. I have criticized Dworkin's liberalism in "Individual Rights, Collective Interests, Public Law, and American Politics," 8 *Law and Philosophy* 245-261 (1989), and in *Making Men Moral: Civil Liberties and Public Morality* (Oxford University Press, forthcoming).
10. Germain Grisez and Joseph M. Boyle, Jr., *Life and Death With Liberty and Justice* (Notre Dame, Indiana: University of Notre Dame Press, 1979), p. 36 (emphasis in the original). The authors no longer hold strictly to the theory of political morality that they defended in this book. See Germain Grisez, Joseph Boyle, and John Finnis, "Practical Principles, Moral Truth, and Ultimate Ends," 32 *The American Journal of Jurisprudence* 99-151, 150. Their revised position is closer to the view that has been defended in various places by John Finnis and myself, though differences probably remain.
11. Grisez and Boyle, *Life and Death*, p. 37 (emphasis in the original).
12. *Id*. at 58.
13. *Id*. at 450.
14. *Id*. at 456.
15. For a compelling argument that desire-satisfaction is not intrinsically valuable and therefore ought not to be confused with human goods that provide reasons for action, see Raz, *The Morality of Freedom*, pp. 140-145.
16. Established churches were still in existence in some states more than forty years after the ratification of the First Amendment. For an account of these establishments see generally Gerard V. Bradley, *Church-State Relationships in America* (New York: Greenwood Press, 1987). For the argument that a central purpose of the Establishment Clause was the protection of state establishments, see William C. Porth and Robert P. George, "Trimming the Ivy: A Bicentennial Re-Examination of the Establishment Clause," 90 *West Virginia Law Review* 109-170 (1987).
17. For a devastating critique of "strict separationism" see Bradley, *Church-State Relationships*, especially chapters 1 and 7.
18. *Dignitatis Humanae*, 3.
19. Finnis, *Natural Law*, pp. 89-90.
20. Grisez, Boyle, and Finnis, "Practical Principles," p. 108.
21. Finnis, *Natural Law*, p. 155.
22. I offer no opinion here as to whether judicially enforceable constitutional provisions ought to require such exceptions. Nor do I take a position on whether the "free exercise" clause of the First Amendment of the Constitution of the United States requires such exceptions absent a "compelling state interest" in enforcing general laws that happen to conflict with conscientious religious belief or practice. As to the latter question, the Supreme Court of the United States has recently held that such exceptions are not required. See

23. *Employment Division, Department of Human Resources of Oregon, et al. v. Smith et al.*, Slip Opinion No. 88-1213. Decided April 17, 1990.
23. *Dignitatis Humanae*, 1 makes it plain that the declaration on religious liberty in no way alters Catholic teaching that the "one true religion subsists in the catholic and apostolic Church, to which the Lord Jesus committed the duty of spreading it abroad among all men."
24. *Dignitatis Humanae*, 3.
25. *Id.*
26. *Id.*

ABOUT THE AUTHORS

WE HOLD THESE TRUTHS AND MORE

Murray's Thought in Light of Recent Developments

12

Murray and the Soviet Union

by John J. Carrigg

*T*his paper was written in August of 1990 following the collapse of the Soviet Union, the rejection of communism by its people and the breaking out of nationalistic uprisings in the Baltic states, in Central Asia, in Georgia, Azerbaijan, Armenia and even in Ukraine. These stunning developments caught the whole world by surprise and it hardly knew how to react to a result that none of us dared dream of. It was a possibility devoutly to be wished, but never would happen. But it did and there was much talk of a peace dividend. One scholar wrote a book about the end of history. Mankind was moving into a long era of peace, boring, but comfortable with no more overarching problems like nuclear confrontation between two superpowers...political conservatives suddenly had the rug pulled from under them. Their *raison d'etre*-anti-communism had lost its *raison,* so it was said. The liberal left, the hard core left and fellow travelers were disconsolate and reviled Gorbachev for undermining Marx and Lenin and leading the Soviet Union down the primrose path of free elections, free markets, and capitalism. There was much talk in the United States Congress of slashing the military budget by 25%; eliminating carriers, closing bases, cutting personnel, abandoning SDI and Stealth bombers and in general enjoying a return to normal relations among nations. Then came August 2, 1990 and the Iraqi invasion of Kuwait in a lightning strike that ended in a flash Kuwait independence, and added the immense oil reserves of that country to Iraq. The industrial world, faced by the threat of the loss of roughly 19% of the world oil reacted in unison, condemned the Iraqi invasion and began embargoing commerce with Iraq and placed a blockade on its ports. The United States sent large naval and military forces to the defense of Saudi Arabia and was joined symbolically by Syria, Egypt, Morocco, Great Britain, and France. The world teetered on the brink of war. Virulent Arabian nationalism was aroused and the ruler of Iraq, Saddam Hussein, called for a *Jihad,* a Holy War, (ironic since many Arabs opposed him as an secularist and agnostic) but it had much appeal in the streets of Jordan, Libya and other states.

What does this have to do with the Father John Courtney Murray? Father Murray devotes a large section of his book, *We Hold These Truths*, to American foreign policy during the period when the whole focus of that policy was relations with the Soviet Union. This single-minded concentration on the Soviet Union put every other foreign policy problem on the back burner and even off the stove. Chapters Ten, Eleven, and Twelve in his book are devoted to American relations with USSR and to the use of force and the Just War theory.

But earlier in his book, on page 88, he wrote a paragraph which would give him high grades among the modern prophets. He was writing about the widespread anti-Communist sentiment in the United States during the fifties and he said, "We reject the Communist idea of world order; we object to a Communist organization of the world." The trouble is that, after you have rejected the Communist order, you are still stuck with the sheer fact of the world's disorder. It is the fact of the century. Communism did not create the fact, though it exploits it. The disorder would persist, or be rendered even more chaotic, if Communist ideas and power vanished into thin air this very moment. Facing the massive fact of world disorder, the United States faces the question: What kind of order in the world do you want? What are its premises and principles? What is to be the form of its institutions, political, legal, and economic? How do you propose to help organize this disorganized world? Or do you propose not to help? Or do you think perhaps an order of peace, freedom, justice, and prosperity will come about in the world simply by accident, or by sheer undirected technological progress, or by the power of prayer, or by what? Order is, by definition, the work of the wise man: *sapientis est ordinare*.... It is the work of men and peoples who are able to say: There are Truths and we hold them. Hence the disordered state of the world itself puts to America the question: "What are your truths?" Now I am sure President Reagan would say freedom and democracy. Often the President referred to the march of democracy across the world and particularly in Latin America where a series of military dictators gave way to democratic regimes. But to Father Murray, the idolization of democracy was a threat to American society: "This proposition is that all the issues of human life—intellectual, religious, and moral issues, as well as formally political issues—are to be regarded as, or resolved into, political issues and are to be settled by the single omnicompetent political technique of majority vote." This, said Father Murray, is monism and the single realm of the secular without reference to the realm of the spiritual. He goes on to say: "On the surface, the monism is one of process: Madison's 'republican principle' affords the Final Grounds for the Last Say on All Human Questions. But the underlying idea is a monism of power: one there is whereby the world is ruled—the power in the people, expressing itself in the preference of a majority; and beyond or beside or above this power, there is no other." This is pure Rousseau.

What about a foreign policy based on anti-communism? It is not a public policy. "In fact," says Father Murray, "it has its dangers since it can furnish a pseudo-justification for misguided policies. It can distort the issues in public debate. It can distract attention from issues that are less visible, but no less urgent" (p. 89). What would Fr. Murray say about recent events in eastern Europe where the policy of the vast majority of people has been simply anti-communism? These people may disagree on religion—Vaclav Havel of Czechoslovakia and Lech Walesa of Poland are two examples that come to mind, the former is a secularist, the latter, a devout Catholic, but they both are in agreement on their anti-communism; communism must go. It has been a disaster for the people for the past forty to seventy years. Would Fr. Murray have been in agreement with his Jesuit successors in *America* magazine who never had a good word for the Contras in Nicaragua? After the election of February 1990, there was stunned silence in the editorial pages of *America*. Having lost there, they are now taking up the cudgels for the FMLN in El Salvador. All their articles concentrate on the alleged and real atrocities of the government forces, never of the FMLN. The murder of the six Jesuit priests by government forces has greatly influenced the Jesuit position, but they were on the other side well before that occurred. Recently, the President of Georgetown, in a letter to the alumni, urged that the legitimate government of El Salvador (duly elected in a free election) must sit down with the armed left-wing rebels and negotiate with them. *America* never urged the Sandinistas to negotiate with the Contras. Where would Fr. Murray have been? Since he was considered a leading liberal Jesuit in his day, one is tempted to place him with the Jesuits of *America*, but we will never know.

Fr. Murray analyzes our foreign aid and finds that it too is influenced by anti-communism. If a country lines up against the Communist bloc, we support it. Altruism as a basis of foreign aid is hard to sell to the people, but if the State Department wants to get an aid program through Congress, it has to be sold as good for America and it's good for America if it's bad for the Communists. Fr. Murray allows that national self-interest is the final controlling factor of economic policy. He admits that it is certainly popular and does not lack validity.

One wonders what Fr. Murray would be saying about the Persian Gulf crisis. President Bush did a remarkable job in lining up nearly the whole world against Iraq for its seizure of Kuwait. With the exception of Pat Buchanan, Charley Reese of the Orlando *Sentinel*, and a few others, he has overwhelming support in the American press, including the *New York Times* and the *Washington Post* for the dispatching of troops, ships and planes to the Gulf, but as of this writing, no shots have been fired and no American lives have been lost in combat, but I suspect that support would quickly melt away as soon as the casualty lists appear. Coexistence with the Communist Empire is the present fact, says Fr. Murray, and that has not changed in the years since his death in 1967. But know thy enemy or at least know "what kind of an empire we are coexisting with."

Much of Father Murray's analysis of the Soviet Union is out of date, but his description of the Soviet Union would easily rank him among the hard-liners and would make President Reagan's "evil empire" seem like an understatement.

Father Murray sees four unique aspects to the Soviet state. First it is a gigantic land mass occupied by 266,000,000 people, probably the biggest land power in the history of the human race. "It is a huge police state where there is no rule of law and no concern for justice and no sense of human rights. It is purely and simply despotism." (DeGaulle, observing Stalin up close, described him as an Asian despot and consciously so.) The Soviets seem to have missed the best in Western Civilization.

Moreover, he points out, this vast country has been centralized to a degree never before achieved. Ruled by the Communist party, it has socialized the economy and built a military power second to none on land, sea, and air. "Further it has produced an industrial and technological power second only to the United States." On this latter point Fr. Murray is far off the mark. The Soviet industrial plant is a disaster and the centralized state is being challenged by festering nationalist uprising in the Baltic states, Ukraine, Georgia, Armenia, and the Turkish Republics.

The second aspect of the Soviet state according to Fr. Murray is that it is guided by a revolutionary doctrine. "For the first time in history this doctrine has consciously erected atheistic materialism into a political and legal principle that furnishes the substance of the state and determines its procedures." It is inherently aggressive in its intent; and it considers itself destined to be the sole survival as an organizing force in the world of politics. Here again Fr. Murray, I feel quite sure, would be stunned to learn what has happened in the USSR recently or so with the opening of churches long closed, the restoration of seminaries, and the creation of bishoprics. Although the official anti-religious policy has not changed, the fact is that religion is returning at an almost breathtaking pace: more marriages in church, more baptisms, more people attending Mass. Could anyone in his wildest dreams imagine St. Basil's Cathedral in Red Square open for the first time since 1917 and celebrating Mass, and then unbelievably Mass being celebrated in the Assumption Cathedral inside the Kremlin with the faithful in the procession carrying a large photograph of the late Tsar Nicholas II!

The third aspect of the Soviet Union is that it is not a country, but a colonial empire; its republics are no more part of Russia than India was of Great Britain. Fr. Murray is completely right here and further quotes Edward Crankshaw with approval: "Even if Moscow retreated to the frontiers of the Soviet Union tomorrow, Russia would still be the greatest imperial power in the world." She already has made that retreat. I would add that if the Soviet Union retreated to the frontiers of Russia, it would still be a great power with 140,000,000 people, immense natural resources, a formidable military establishment and a going modern industrial plant in much need of major overhauling.

The empire, says Fr. Murray, excites a new type of patriotism which is not merely a thing of blood and soil, but of a higher order than feelings for *das Vaterland, la patrie,* my country. Although it contains some of this old-fashioned, traditional loyalty, it is elevated to another plain by devotion to the socialist revolution and to the homeland of the Revolution, Russia.

This so-called new Soviet patriotism we now know was pretty shallow stuff and it is widely acknowledged that nobody believes it any longer. Aleksandr Solzhenitsyn made that point many years ago and more recently in his Harvard address of 1978 he said, "In our Eastern countries, communism has suffered a complete ideological defeat; it is zero and less than zero." "Yet," he continues, "Western intellectuals still look at it with considerable interest and empathy, and this is precisely what makes it so immensely difficult for the West to withstand the East." Fr. Murray would agree with this latter point of Solzhenitsyn's statement—a sort of treason of the intellectuals which furnishes the Soviet state with a Fifth Column to penetrate and undermine the states not under her authority.

(If I may inject a personal note: during a rather extended tour of the Soviet Union in 1967, I observed much patriotism of the old-fashioned variety, "In my country we do this; in my country we do that" and "my country" was spoken with great respect and reverence.)

Significant, too, is that Stalin during the crisis of 1941 with the German legions thundering over the steppe called the church out of the catacombs and began emphasizing the old love of country and church to arouse his people against the invaders.

At Stalingrad I was struck by the fact that a huge statue was erected, not to Marx or Lenin, but to Mother Russia as a lasting memorial to the heroism of her soldiers who died for her.

De Gaulle was right when he described Marxism as a mantle that the Russians wore lightly. He thought they belonged to the European family of nations—a Europe that ran from the Atlantic to the Urals.

The final and fourth aspect of the Soviet state, according to Fr. Murray, was its role as inheritor both of Tsarist imperialism and mystical panslavist messianism. This is the myth of Holy Russia, the spiritual people whose destiny is to rescue humanity from the Promethean West. Moscow is seen as the Third Rome after which no more Romes shall there be. I am puzzled by Fr. Murray's statement that communism came out of the East as conscious apostasy from the West. Marx was a Westerner and his theory of class war and the victory of the proletariat and dialectical materialism, as far as I know, was not nurtured by any ideas out of the East. But all aside from that point, it is hotly debated among Russian historians whether the Communist victory in 1917 was a continuation of the Tsarist past or whether it was a total break with the past. Richard Pipes in his recently published book holds that it was a continuity. Alexander Solzhenitsyn vehemently disagrees.

One feels quite sure that Fr. Murray would have been as shocked as everyone else by the collapse of the Soviet Union. Solzhenitsyn, in his Harvard address, all but predicted the collapse of the U.S., so he too must be stunned at the wonderful turn in events.

I don't think Solzhenitsyn anticipated the collapse of the Soviet hold on the satellite states; Poland, Hungary, Czechoslovakia, Rumania, and Bulgaria are now on their own. He probably thought the West would collapse first even though Solzhenitsyn held that the Soviet states were rotten to the core, held together by lies and sheer terror. Now one wonders if even the leaders follow Communist dogma when Boris Yeltsin, the President of Russia, has formally disaffiliated from the Communist party. It is simply unbelievable.

Fr. Murray felt safe in asserting that there was little danger of all out nuclear war between the U.S. and USSR as long as America maintained its massive deterrent forces (barring some enormous stupidity), but limited war was possible and even limited war with nuclear weapons of low kiloton yield was possible and thinkable. America, said Fr. Murray, must avoid the false dilemma of either catastrophe or renunciation of all nuclear force.

After World War II, the ancient enemy of Russia, Germany, lay in ruins. If it was security that the Soviets sought, they had it in spades. They had built a huge cordon Sanitaire along their western front with friendly satellite states in the Baltics, Poland, Hungary, Romania, and Bulgaria. The United States was disarming at a breakneck speed and everywhere in the West there was goodwill toward the Soviet Union for all that it suffered in a terrible war.

So what did the Soviets do? They went on the offensive, refused Marshall aid, blockaded Berlin, and overthrew the Czech government. As a consequence, within three years the Soviets had dissipated the goodwill in the West which began to unite and arm itself against a threat now visible.

All this because of Soviet doctrine which decreed its happening. Fr. Murray thinks that this can happen again (the dictation of policy by doctrine). Soviet leaders change, but not the doctrine. Soviet leaders, he said, are not subject to change of heart. Could this apply to Gorbachev? We were told many times that he is a good Communist and his *perestroika* and *glasnost* were designed not to abolish the Communist system, but to save it. It is significant that his huge army and navy remained intact and his nuclear weaponry still pointed at us.

Fr. Murray allows that it is not impossible that some basic change may take place in Soviet doctrine. But any significant change would result in repercussions that would be felt all through the edifice of power erected on the doctrine; and if they were not checked, the edifice could not long survive. The basic Soviet structure is an indivisible and interlocking whole. It cannot permit itself to be tampered with at any point, save on peril of destruction. Even to speculate about making a basic change in the established doctrine would be to raise the specter of the disintegration of the empire. Fr. Murray concludes: "This specter, we may be sure, will be forbidden to rise." Have we reached that point, where tampering with the doctrine is causing the collapse of the Empire?

Father Murray considered the greatest Soviet threat to be spiritual: "the most demonic threat to human values that the world had ever known.... The future of the world would not be decided by the side which could muster the greatest military forces, but the side that could win the ideological battle." Is that battle over? Has the West won without firing a shot? Is the so-called Communist collapse for real? It seems to be. Yet Fr. Murray would say, I feel sure, that the West is still in crisis, that it doesn't know itself: If this be true, this failure of understanding, leading to a denial, more or less explicit, of the Western tradition by the West itself, would be the fateful "internal contradiction" that might lead to downfall. Ironically, he said, Marx never saw this form of "internal contradiction," although it is the greatest weakness in the camp that he opposed.

But the Communist threat seemed real enough in Fr. Murray's time and to counter it on the spiritual plane the United States had to go beyond mere anti-communism and formulate a foreign policy that was based on peace, justice, freedom, prosperity, and force.

> We have to project the notion of peace into a world that is divided and disordered and belligerent and unable to contain the pluralisms that exist within it and combine them into an order of peace. We have to project the notion of justice into a world of injustice and manifold inequalities. We have to project the notion of freedom into a world that is the scene of multiple enslavements. We have to project the notion of welfare into a world of misery. We have to project a notion of power into a world

that is all too prone toward the uses of force and violence in pursuit of political aid. Now I am suggesting that these five ends taken singly and in combination afford the basic criterion of all our foreign policy and action. They enable us to discern in general when policy erection is bad and since they are not arbitrary ends, but inherent in the existential ends of human society, they give us the norms of judgement of alien systems and tell us therefore what we must in principle oppose as well as what we must in principle support. (Quoted in Robert R. McElroy, *The Search for an American Public Theology: The Contribution of John Courtney Murray*, p. 133-134.)

This sounds so idealistic. Has any nation ever achieved such an ambitious program? And then Fr. Murray argues American interventions on the world stage would be determined by how they best observed the interests of the world community. Such a foreign policy based not on American interests, but on the interests of the world community, constituted the basic argument of those who urged President Bush to launch an attack on Iraq. The destruction of Iraq's war fighting capacity would benefit the world community. They argued it would give bully tyrants pause and teach them that aggressors get severely punished. As Norman Podhoretz put it in an issue of *Commentary*:

It [would be] a war to prevent control of a vital resource from falling into the hands of a ruthless aggressor. It [would be] a war to establish a more peaceful order in the post-cold-war world.

And if Bush had failed to act, Podhoretz warned "then he will fail to achieve even the more limited objectives he has set for himself, with incalculable damage to his presidency, to his country, and to the world."

But back to Fr. Murray. With war between the United States and the Soviet Union always a possibility in his time he applied the Just War theory to the situation. First he ruled out a war of aggression even to right a wrong. It cannot be justified. Pius XII clearly taught that "aggressive war is a sin, an offense and an outrage against the majesty of God." Here the essential fact is that there are no inherent limits to the measure of chaos that war might entail, whether by the use of nuclear arms or possibly by the methods of bacteriological and chemical warfare.

Having said this, "a defensive war to repress injustice is morally admissible both in principle and in fact." This has always been a part of Catholic doctrine. "By its assertion the Church finds a way between the false extremes of pacificism and bellicism." The reiteration of the right of defensive war derives directly from an understanding of the conflict and from a realization that nonviolent means of solution may fail. The Church is obliged to confront the dreadful alternative: "the absolute necessity of self-defense against a very grave injustice that touches the community, that cannot be impeded by other means that nevertheless must be impeded on pain of giving free field in international relations to brutal violence and lack of conscience."

In direct contradiction to the American Bishops' position condemning the use of nuclear weapons in war, Pius XII extended it explicitly to not only atomic warfare but even ABC warfare. But then there are certain conditions necessary before such a conflict can be waged:

> First "the war must be imposed by an obvious and extremely grave injustice. No minor infraction of rights will suffice, much less any question of national prestige."
>
> Second the war must be the last resort, all other means having been exhausted.
>
> Third is the principle of proportionality. The destruction of war must not exceed the damage done by the perpetuation of the grave injustice over which the war is being fought.
>
> Then there must be the probability of success in the forceful repression of the injustice.
>
> Finally, for the war to be just there is the principle of limitation in the use of force. Again, Fr. Murray quotes Pius XII. The force used must be confined to the strict exigencies of defense.

Murray expresses the latter point this way:

> In any case, when the employment of this means entails such an extension of the evil that it entirely escapes from the control of man, its use ought to be rejected as immoral. Here it is no longer a question of defense against injustice and of the necessary safeguard of legitimate possessions, but of the annihilation, pure and simple, of all human life within its radius of action. This is not permitted on any account.

Has any war ever satisfied all these conditions? Certainly World War II failed the test when the allies resorted to saturation bombing of German and Japanese cities.

But limiting the force used in conducting the war leads us to "limited war." And Fr. Murray argues that American policy must be based on the assumption that future conflicts will be limited.

Applying the Just War theory so emphasized by Murray to the Persian Gulf situation becomes extremely complicated. Will the war against Iraq be considered in retrospect to have been *aggressive* warfare waged to right a wrong (i.e., the invasion and conquest of Kuwait that occurred in August, 1990)? If so it would be forbidden even if justified on the grounds stated above of promoting the interests of the whole world community.

13

The Murray Thesis, Abortion, and the American Political Order

by Stephen M. Krason

The purpose of this paper is to inquire into what the legalization of abortion in America since the 1960's—i.e., the removal of legal protections for the lives of our unborn citizens—brought about most dramatically and sweepingly by the Supreme Court in 1973,[1] tells us about the past and present state of the "American Proposition" that John Courtney Murray wrote about.

I begin by summarizing the "Murray thesis" (i.e., what Murray had to say about the American Proposition and what he identified as its content). He said that America's "first principle of... organization," expressed in the Declaration of Independence, is "the sovereignty of God over nations as well as over individual men." This is "the conservative Christian tradition of America."[2] Next, he said that our nation was conceived in the tradition of natural law which embodied the two basic great principles of liberty under a government restrained by law and of the necessity of the consent of the governed to rule.[3] The American Proposition did not sanction moral license—"sheer libertarianism." Quite the contrary, its notion of freedom held that a government of liberty under law "can be realized only when the people as a whole are inwardly governed by the recognized imperatives of the universal moral law."[4] The rights that the American colonists "contended against the English Crown" for were not abstract, unrealistic concoctions like those of the French revolutionaries, but the rights of Englishmen, won over time by struggle but ultimately grounded in "age-old custom in which the nature of man expressed itself."[5] This, of course, is what we have called the common law.

Murray is hardly the first important thinker in this century or in the last who has spoken about the natural law basis of America's Founding principles. We can recall Alexis de Tocqueville writing the following in the 1830's about morality in religiously pluralistic America:
> There is an innumerable multitude of sects in the United States. They are all different in the worship they offer to the Creator, but all agree concerning the duties of men to one another…all preach the same morality in the name of God…all sects in the United States belong to the great unity of Christendom, and Christian morality is everywhere the same.[6]

The "Christian morality" he was talking about was, of course, identical with the natural law.

Another great nineteenth century Catholic thinker that had no doubt about the natural law background of the United States was Orestes A. Brownson who wrote that the "law of nature" or natural law was the foundation of "the codes of all nations" and that "every state acknowledges its authority," including, it follows, the United States.[7] In fact, Brownson believed that the unique, God-given mission of this country was, in essence, to bring about the fullest realization of the natural law that any nation previously had succeeded in doing. This was seen when he said: "The political destiny of the United States is to conform the state to the order of reality… to the Divine Idea in creation. Their religious destiny is… [*inter alia*] to realize the normal relations between… religion and politics as concreted in the life of the nation."[8] He says further that the latter mission involves recognizing that while church and state appropriately "mov[e] in different spheres, each one obeys one and the same Divine law."[9]

In the twentieth century, Edward S. Corwin, perhaps the greatest post-1900 American constitutional scholar, traced the roots of our constitutional principles to the philosophical understanding first arrived at by the ancient Greeks. He said the following: "The attribution of supremacy to the Constitution on the ground solely of its rootage in popular will [that is, a positivist idea] represents… a comparatively late outgrowth of American constitutional theory." Rather, he asserted, its "*legality*… its *supremacy*, and its claim to be worshipped, alike find common ground on the belief in a law superior to the will of human governors."[10]

The Murray Thesis, Abortion and America

In his monumental book, *The Roots of American Order*, Russell Kirk discusses the centrality of natural law in our Founding. He notes the appeals in the writing and rhetoric at the time of our break with England to the laws of nature or natural law and, while conceding that scholarship has been inconclusive as to whether our Founders could agree upon a "clear definition of the term," concludes—after tracing the origins of their ideas throughout the book—that "their general appeal to natural law runs back to the principles of Cicero... and the medieval Schoolmen."[11] This understanding of natural law represented "a blending of Hebraic, Christian, classical, and seventeenth and eighteenth-century theories."[12]

And as political scientist Paul Eidelberg, contrasting the Declaration of Independence and Marx's *Communist Manifesto*, asserts:

> What most distinguishes the Declaration...from the *Communist Manifesto* is that the former affirms, while the latter denies...the power of reason to apprehend transhistorical truths or the "laws of nature and of nature's God".... The appeal is from positive or statute law to the natural/divine law...the Declaration distinguishes between what is right by nature and what is right by convention, or between the just and legal.[13]

The point I make in giving these quotes is that Murray was correct in this aspect of his thesis: America emerged from and relied upon the natural law tradition. It is outside the scope of my specific topic to analyze how this was so; one can read the writing of the thinkers quoted and the remarks of other papers in this volume to understand this. While it is true that, contrary to what the term suggests, there have been differing and sometimes conflicting notions of natural law, I believe that the predominant tradition we speak of America as being grounded in—as made apparent by the above quotes—is what Thomas J. Higgins, S.J. refers to as the *Natural Law*, with first letters capitalized to distinguish it.[14] The "Natural Law" consists of the "necessary and obligatory rules of human conduct" established by God and discernible by man through human reason;[15] this is what the Catholic means by the term. It is clear that America did not fully embody the principles of the Natural Law for, as Kirk notes, the influence of eighteenth century rationalism and the Enlightenment with its radically new nation of natural law—i.e. the individualistic, secular, nonteleological version associated with Hobbes and Locke—was also there. I am inclined to agree with Kirk, however, that the effect of Locke on

American Founding ideas was not as sweeping and thoroughgoing as some would like to believe.[16] Indeed, when we consider Higgins' solidly Natural Law-based discussion of social ethics,[17] we can easily come to the conclusion that America, even with the views of popular government and consent embodied in our Founding, was, as Kirk contends, most basically reflective of "the 'Great Tradition,' drawn from Hebrew and classical and Christian teaching."[18]

When we consider abortion, there is no doubt—contrary to what the Supreme Court in *Roe v. Wade* and pro-abortion-inclined historical studies have contended[19]—that the Natural Law proscription of abortion was upheld earlier in American history through the vehicle of our common law tradition. The common law's treatment of abortion can best be observed by pointing to two of the greatest commentators on it, both of whom also substantially influenced its development: Sir Edward Coke and Sir William Blackstone. A famous passage in Coke's *Third Institute* (1644) is of note:

> If a woman be quick with childe, and by a Potion or otherwise killeth it in her wombe; or if a man beat her, whereby the childe dieth in her body, and she is delivered of a dead childe, this is a great misprision, and no murder: but if the childe be born alive, and dieth of the Potion, battery, or other cause, this is murder: for in the Law it is accounted a reasonable creature; *in rerum natura*, when it is born alive.[20]

This passage, especially the term "misprision," indicates that the common law viewed abortion as a grave matter. Contrary to the error of some contemporary commentators of translating this term to mean "misdemeanor"—a lesser offense in law—what it really meant in Coke's time and a century later in Blackstone's was "a high offense…under the degree of capital, but nearly bordering thereon";[21] in other words, it was almost the most serious kind of crime (i.e., a capital one). Coke indicated it was even more serious than the usual misprision—it was "a *great* misprision."

Blackstone discusses abortion in Book One of his great *Commentaries on the Laws of England*, which is entitled "On the Rights of Persons." He speaks about abortion as an offense against the rights of the unborn child—albeit, while punished treated less severely by the law than in Coke's time. Most importantly, he indicated that it violates the right to life which is part of a more basic right of personal security:

I. The right of personal security consists in a person's legal and uninterrupted enjoyment of his life, his limbs, his body, his health, and his reputation.

1. Life is the immediate gift of God, a right inherent by nature in every individual; and it begins in contemplation of law as soon as an infant is able to stir in the mother's womb. For if a woman is quick with child, and by a potion or otherwise, killeth it in her womb; or if anyone beat her, whereby the child dieth in her body, and she is delivered of a dead child; this, though not murder, was by ancient law homicide or manslaughter. But the modern law doth not look upon this offense in quite so atrocious a light, but merely as a heinous misdemesnor.[22]

The only reason Blackstone did not say the right to life is protected from the point of fertilization is because, following the biology of the time, he assumed life begins at quickening. It is clear from the quote, however, that he believed the right attaches *when life begins*. It seems fairly certain, then, that if he had had the biological knowledge that was to come only three quarters of a century later, he would have said this. We should note that Blackstone had a great influence on both legal and political ideas in eighteenth century America.[23] Indeed, as Kirk puts it, "[u]ntil the middle of the nineteenth century, or even later, there were not a few American judges whose chief source of legal knowledge was a copy of Blackstone" with its "natural-law foundation."[24] Actually, the common law's proscription of abortion antedated Coke and Blackstone. It was a crime even in the days before the Norman Conquest.[25] This is not surprising, of course, since until almost the twentieth century in England and America there was no question that the common law should be based on Christian principles, and thus embody the Natural Law.

After the discovery of the ovum in 1827, statutory law began to be enacted in both England and America making abortion a crime throughout pregnancy. By the time of the Civil War, thirty-one of the eventual fifty states had criminal statutes on the books against abortion. (This development perhaps reflected the urgency of changing the laws to reflect the new biological knowledge instead of waiting for judges to adapt them as cases came up, or else it just exemplified the growing trend to codify law in the Anglo-American world.) By the turn of the century, every state had anti-abortion statutes. These remained essentially in place—except for some states legalizing abortion to save the life of the mother—until the 1960's.

It is very clear, then, that abortion was proscribed by earlier American law and was, in fact, viewed as a moral abomination almost universally in our political society through the nineteenth century. I believe that this, indeed, was a definite reflection of both the natural law basis of our law and the pervasive, unquestioned Christian morality of which I earlier spoke. In fact, this morality was most rigorously adhered to in matters affecting sexuality, as Tocqueville, writing when the Republic was still in its formative years, attests.[26] I would thus argue that the reason abortion came to be universally legal, for any reason and at any stage of pregnancy, widely resorted to, and touted as a perfectly proper act in America was not primarily because of weaknesses in our Founding *principles*—in our "parchment regime," as Professor Joseph Cropsey has called it [27]—but because of developments since that time.

It could certainly be argued that the Hobbesian-Lockean perspective and Enlightenment thought—with their positivism, extreme notion of individualism, rejection of transcendent moral norms, and, to a degree, at least, moral relativism—which had at least some influence on the society of the Founders and on some of the Founders themselves, laid the groundwork for the later development of the pro-abortion perspective. Professor George W. Carey has argued, for example, that the Hobbesian-Lockean notion of the state of nature is pertinent here. It sees people as relating to each other only as autonomous individuals who are not subordinate to anything higher than themselves. The state exists only because of their consent and is the repositor of all rights and law. The state "build[s] itself on the lowest common denominator of the interests and values" of the individuals making it up and its chief purpose is to "provide for (their) material gratification," which represents what Carey calls a "crude utilitarianism." This latter is what he says is really at the core of the pro-abortion mentality, and he is right.[28]

My own thinking is that Carey has a point in seeing the roots, generally, of pro-abortionism in Hobbes and Locke (though momentarily I raise doubts about whether he is correct in the specifics he talks about). One must always be careful about tracing the source of a doctrine to another distant doctrine because often times qualitative changes will have occurred along the way in the latter which can result in its application in a way its originator could never have foreseen. Nevertheless, the liberalism of a Locke—restrained and prudent though it was compared with today's version—provided the germ because of the elements of its position—the Hobbesian-Lockean perspective—mentioned above. As Cropsey observed, liberalism of any time—and also conservatism, since much of what is called "conservatism" today is really a variant of liberalism—is conventional.[29] That is, it elevates convention over nature—even when it claims to be promoting "natural rights," it is really promoting a version of natural law which has been recrafted by men. In being conventional, liberalism of course rejects the true Natural Law and the Divine Law on which it is based.[30]

So, I do not doubt that there were ideas intermingled in the principles of our Founding which in some measure adulterated the tradition of the true Natural Law which I—with Murray—hold formed our foundation. These ideas do, in the basic way described, provide the ideological background of pro-abortionism. I have said, however, that these ideas were not the primary ones in our tradition. Perhaps the reason they were not is the pervasive influence of Christianity—or at least Christian morality—in America for so much of our early history, as noted by Tocqueville. Kirk gives us part of the explanation as to why America's Christian perspective—and the Natural Law embodied in it—was able to be sustained in the face of the assault of the Enlightenment in the crucial eighteenth century and thus become so essentially imprinted into our Founding. It was the Great Awakening, led by the renowned Jonathan Edwards. Kirk says that "[d]irectly or indirectly, most Americans were moved by...his powerful intellectual defense of revealed religion," and that his and his disciples' efforts brought America back from the threshold of an Enlightenment-inspired Deism to a "revived" biblical Christianity. Although there were Deists among our Founders, and the Great Awakening had its least impact among the upper classes who were the most politically active, Kirk tells us that our politics was still transformed by it because by the time of the 1787 Philadelphia Convention "[t]he American people came to expect their public men to be Christians, or at least give lip-service to Christianity." Later, it was said that Andrew Jackson had turned the Democratic party created by Jefferson into a party with "Jonathan Edwards' philosophy at its foundations."[31]

To bring this back to pro-abortionism, it is not so clear that we can even say that the early modern liberalism of Locke is truly what undergirds it except in the most general way. Fr. Francis Canavan, S.J., a political scientist, has written that what we see with pro-abortionism is a perspective which rejects the natural rights thinking of a Locke, which at least struggled to maintain a notion of rights as attaching because of man's unique character as a rational creature (even if it provided no solid basis for such a characterization of man). Rather, for pro-abortionism, "the rights of the individual are identified more and more with his desires." This new notion of rights implicit in the pro-abortion position, but characteristic generally of theories of rights today, sees the individual human will as the sole basis for right, limited only by the Millian harm principle.[32] Further, Canavan has asserted that by holding the right to abortion as something that a woman or girl can claim irrespective of whether her husband or parent(s) agree, the pro-abortionists implicitly have distorted the way the Hobbesian-Lockean notion of the social contract was meant to be understood. They have transformed it from a *political* notion—used to explain the origin and nature of political life—to one pertaining to the nature of marriage and family life. That is, they see marriage and the family as nothing more than a collection of individuals who relate to each other in the same way as the atomistic individuals in the state fashioned by the social contract, retaining all their prior rights and prerogatives. These institutions are thus merely seen as like a legal contract, with no given nature, and in no way taking the shape of a covenantal relationship which takes precedence over the whims and desires of the individuals making them up.[33] As Canavan puts it, however, the social contract theory "generally took marriage and the family for granted."[34] Locke, for example, spoke of the need for the parent or teacher of a young man to help him learn to control his appetites (no doubt realizing the sexual was one of the most intense of them),[35] condemned various offenses against marital fidelity and sound sexual morality[36] and stressed both the essentiality of the family for the procreation, rearing, and education of children and the authority of parents over their minor offspring.[37]

Moreover, political scientist Gary D. Glenn tells us that the abortion on demand claim of the pro-abortion movement—acceded to, for all practical purposes, by the Supreme Court in *Roe v. Wade* and *Doe v. Bolton*,[38]—is in outright opposition to the Lockean notion of inalienable rights—a Lockean idea which, *happily*, did find its way into our fundamental law. Glenn's argument, very briefly put, goes like this. The nature of inalienable rights means that they cannot be taken away and the individual cannot voluntarily surrender them. One, thus, does not have unlimited consent; that would be license, not true liberty. Any claimed right which is of the nature of license and thereby would have the effect of alienating liberty is unacceptable for Locke. Glenn says that abortion on demand is an example of such a right.[39]

As far as other sources of Enlightenment ideas affecting the Founders are concerned, we might look to Jefferson who was probably the preeminent child of the Enlightenment among them. Even he, however, did not simply reject, out and out, the tradition of the Natural Law. This is seen from what Eidelberg said about the Declaration of Independence, which was largely the product of Jefferson's pen. It is also seen in his stress on virtue as being indispensable for republicanism.[40] Moreover, as far as abortion is concerned, it is worth noting that Jefferson highly commended Edward Livingston's model penal code for Louisiana—Jefferson was a devotee of statutory law, as opposed to the common law—which included a provision against abortion (this was even before the discovery of the ovum). Jefferson, despite his rebellion against the Christian religion, did not repudiate the moral teaching of Christianity. He is perhaps a quintessential example of the nineteenth century intellectual, eager to push society to ever more civilized vistas, who lived off the moral capital of medieval Catholicism without realizing it.

In sum, even if the influence of Locke and the Enlightenment on the American Founding were greater than it really was, it is not so clear that it was the logical basis for the development of pro-abortion thinking.

As I said, it was later developments in thought in America which were most basically responsible for paving the way for the pro-abortion mentality. Obviously, many occurrences and actions in the practical and social realms led to its current triumph. I confine my following consideration, however, to the ideas and strains of thought behind it because we are trying to determine what it means for the Murray thesis which, after all, deals with *ideas*. Moreover, if one is really going to be able to understand changes in law, politics, or social mores, one has to look to the changes in ideas which preceded them.

As Richard M. Weaver said, "ideas have consequences."[41] I certainly believe this is the case with abortion.

Joseph Cropsey has pointed to certain intellectual trends, arising since the time of our parchment regime, which he says have helped to shape our current character as a nation and a people. I believe that the trends he mentions, along with probably two other ones, go a long way toward explaining why pro-abortionism took hold. He speaks about the influences of natural science, socialism, existentialism, and psychoanalysis. To be sure, he also mentions "scriptural religion" (i.e., revealed religion), but essentially in the context of the influence it has had in promoting these other trends. (Serious Christians know how much of these other trends contemporary religion has imbibed, at least in their vulgarized or popularized forms, "as they have sunk down into common understanding." [42]) Cropsey tells us that by means of public policy decisions, judicial actions, political developments, and through "unofficial" sources, these trends have become "mix[ed]…with the documents that embody the regime…and in so doing…perplex our understanding of the regime…what we stand for and what our goals are."[43] He is not suggesting that the American Proposition has changed—the Proposition, I believe, can only be identified with the Founding—but that these influences have made America something different from the vision projected by that Proposition. This is not essentially different from Murray's speaking of the "dissolution" of "the consensus" supporting the Proposition that he saw as underway even in his lifetime.[44]

Let us briefly look at each of the trends Cropsey delineates. I should note that he speaks of these only as sources of overall effects on American life; he does not show their connection to specific questions such as abortion. What he does say suggests, however, that this was a logical expression of these trends when he says that "[i]t goes without saying that modernity has generated radical reservations against property *and the family*, but th[is]…ar[ose] in the course of the development of modernity" (i.e., not at the time of Locke or the Founding, as I have explained).[45] The trend he categorizes as natural science—which might better be called scientism—is characterized by "the spirit of calculation" and "the promise" of "prolonging life and emending souls, if only the spiritual physics or mechanics can be elaborated" (in other words, the tools of physical science are seen as somehow being able to make us morally better if only we find the right "formula").[46] I have discussed at length in my previous writing how this manifests itself in the pro-abortion mentality.[47] The point about "calculation" is seen in the desire of the pro-abortion movement—reflected very well in its earlier writing before the feminists took center stage in it, but this is also a crucial continuing consideration on the practical level in the everyday decisions of women to have abortions—to insure that people have *control* over a critical aspect of life, reproduction. The "prolonging life and emending souls" point is seen in the facile inclusion of abortion in the grab-bag of things called "reproductive health," in the whole "quality of life" theme so frequently sounded (and used, *inter alia*, to justify the aborting of deformed unborn children), and in the optimism implicit in the "freedom to choose" mentality and the idea that abortion should be a decision between the woman and her physician. This is the old, nineteenth century-type optimism associated with a thinker such as John Stuart Mill which holds, in essence, that giving men complete freedom will necessarily, somehow, improve them. It is also the belief that relying on science—the "scientific expert" in abortion is the physician—will make things better. This linkage of freedom and science has been a powerful force affecting the American psyche since the time of Jefferson, and the optimism about these possibilities persists among Americans in spite of the disasters of the twentieth century.

As far as socialism, the next intellectual trend, is concerned, the United States obviously has not experienced it in its fiercest, most thoroughgoing expression—i.e., communism—or even in its milder, but still overwhelmingly statist, version associated with Western Europe. As Cropsey says, however, "[e]ach nation apparently modifies and vulgarizes available thought according to a principle of selection and mutation that is, or is best articulated in, its own parchment regime, its Constitution...."[48] The version of socialism that we have adopted was that initially elaborated in the Progressive Era and developed and expanded in the New Deal. What this featured was the same sort of attempt to substitute scientific solutions for traditional moral restraints, an increasing political and social egalitarianism, a heightening of social engineering which eventually spread to most areas of life, and an attempt to displace politics wherever possible with functional experts and a social science-fashioned "science of administration." The legacy of this is reflected in the pro-abortion phenomenon by the following: the new ethic of anti-natalism which holds it to be a virtue instead of vice not to procreate and sees no methods for doing this—even the brutal dismemberment of the infant in the womb—as morally wrong, since they are promotive of the scientifically determined good of reproductive health; the claim that abortion is needed to insure women's equality (it is worth noting that the contemporary feminist movement had its distant origins during the Progressive Era); the insistence that public funds be made possible so poor women can have abortions, since it is seen as an unacceptable discrimination for them not to be able to exercise this "right" (our new egalitarianism seems to include the equal right of rich and poor to do evil); the "quality of life" criterion mentioned above and the frequent claim made of the need for abortion to end the problem of "unwanted" children (these both smack of social engineering); and the pro-abortion movement's constant struggle to stop legislative regulation of abortion by turning to the courts and claiming it is simply an issue of individual privacy (this illustrates the attempt to displace politics).

We can easily see how the existentialism Cropsey speaks of manifests itself in pro-abortionism. He tells us that the form of existentialism currently prevalent among us is characterized, *inter alia*, by "moral latitudinarianism." Pro-abortionism is, of course, a necessary concomitant of the sexual revolution whose rallying cry has been "do what feels good"; it is the latest, and perhaps most vulgar, phase of the "modern project" of liberating the passions (the passion, in this case, is lust). Abortion is needed to eliminate the consequences of such liberation.

Finally, there is psychoanalysis, or what might best be characterized as the vulgarized, popularized notions of the principles and theories first set out by Freud. If our reigning existentialism gives way to a condition of moral latitudinarianism, this popularized version of psychoanalysis, Cropsey seems to indicate, provides one of our primary sources of putative moral justification for it. He says that "it points toward a license to violate the rules, especially the rules governing sexual behavior, that emanate from civilized society."[49] One cannot help but be struck by the place modern psychology has had in the abortion debate. I have written elsewhere about the overwhelming support the most significant practitioners of modern psychology, psychiatrists, gave for abortion legalization in the 1960's and how they provided a ready avenue for women to get abortions when, in those years, states legalized it for only such limited reasons as the woman's mental health.[50] I have also argued that the Supreme Court in *Roe v. Wade* and *Doe v. Bolton* was very clearly influenced by ideas coming from psychology and contemporary social theory. Major points of this were the Justices' identification of freedom with a kind of spontaneous expression of one's "personality" and the putative psychological effects—in a very broad sense of the term—of unwanted pregnancy on a woman.[51] More recently, in an implicit recognition of the importance of this subject in the issue, we have witnessed pro-abortionists and some medical professionals hurrying to downplay evidence of psychological aftereffects on women who have abortions.

What, then, has been the influence of religion in America—in its condition of having been transformed by the above intellectual currents—in stimulating the rise of pro-abortionism? First, there is no question of the crucial role religion has played in making our democratic republic what it is, as indicated by Cropsey above. Eminent figures such as George Washington, Tocqueville, and Lord Bryce all wrote about its indispensable necessity for us if our nation is to retain its republican character. [52] I have written elsewhere that I believe the secularization of religion in America was one of the main reasons why a pro-legalized abortion consensus emerged in the 1960's among the element of our society that is more affluent and has more formal education—and is thus more influential in shaping public policy.[53] The kinds of trends we have discussed are the very "stuff" of secularization. Indeed, can we imagine legalized abortion having came about in America if such a secularization of religious denominations had not already occurred?

Briefly, there are two other intellectual trends not mentioned by Cropsey which seem to me also to have helped reshape the character of our regime and ultimately helped lead to pro-abortionism. One is pointed to by Professor Glenn as a source of the latter: eighteenth and nineteenth century utilitarianism.[54] Most generally, utilitarianism means judging actions by their consequences, not their inherent rightness or wrongness, and the philosophical school of this name was distinguished by its "greatest happiness principle" (i.e., an action is right if it promotes "the greatest happiness of the greatest number")[55] and its "pleasure-pain calculus" (i.e., one should do an act which will maximizes pleasure and minimizes pain). Pro-abortionism, with its unwillingness to see abortion as an intrinsically wrong act and its blatant consequential (or situationist) appeal, its obvious attempt in its "quality-of-life" notion to assert the preferences of the majority over a helpless, unfortunate minority, and its concern about guarding temporal good and physical pleasure even at the expense of another's life, easily fits into this definition.

The other intellectual trend is pragmatism which is distinguished, *inter alia*, by its secularism, moral relativism, and rejection of any intrinsic, eternal value in things apart from their psychological, social, historical, or logical contexts.[56] This school of thought has been identified with such figures as John Dewey, William James, and Oliver Wendell Holmes, Jr. Again, we can easily see the ways that the pro-abortion perspective fits this: we see absolutely no basis for claiming abortion is morally right when we examine the (pre-secularized) Judeo-Christian tradition or the Natural Law[57]—i.e., pro-abortionism is strictly of secular origin; its moral relativism has been noted above; and it betrays an obvious unwillingness to see any intrinsic, permanent value in human life. It was probably through the expression of this pragmatism in law, through Holmes and others, that it most directly influenced the abortion issue—i.e., legal realism, sociological jurisprudence[58] and the like shaped the ambiance of the legal training of the justices in *Roe v. Wade* and *Doe v. Bolton*.

The above, then, are the intellectual trends and positions—probably not an exhaustive list—which have fashioned present-day America and, in turn, have spawned the pro-abortion perspective. They were *not* part of the American Proposition. Murray was right, I believe, in how he described the latter. He was substantially correct—except for the Hobbesian-Lockean liberalism which, in any event, was probably not a definite source of pro-abortionism—in seeing it as close to the Catholic tradition. The Supreme Court's pro-abortion decisions—which may wind up being sustained, for a time, by American legislative bodies, which may now become freer to act on this subject—are merely a few of many governmental actions which have helped reshape our regime (although they are among the most dramatic, significant, and tragic of such actions). They represent *one* very sharp departure from "the structure of...[our] fundamental law" and signal a further dissolution of the "original American consensus."[59] Murray indicated that while he could envision the substantial collapse of this consensus, he really did not expect it.[60]

The American Proposition was not *fully* in conformity with the Catholic moral tradition, as I have indicated. This is, again, because early modern liberalism (Hobbes and Locke) and Enlightenment rationalism generally were part of it, even if not the major part. If Murray thought otherwise, he was incorrect. I do not think he did, however. Moreover, he rightfully observed, as Kirk does,[61] that Locke's conclusions about politics and his groundwork for constitutionalism do not conflict with Christian tradition, even if his epistemology, metaphysics, and reasoning for his positions do.[62] Locke, like Jefferson, was living off the moral capital and ensuing political principles of the Catholic Middle Ages, although he was oblivious to this fact. So were our other Founding Fathers. If Murray was guilty of anything, it was of not being cognizant of the trends in his time—both in American society and in the Church—which, to the careful observer, would already have shown by the time he published *We Hold These Truths* that the dissolution of the American consensus was much further advanced than he thought and that American Catholics were not to remain united behind their Church's teaching and thus the Natural Law tradition for long.

Murray missed one other fundamental, intrinsic weakness in the *framework* of the American political order, one which—even if its Founding principles went back to the medieval Catholic synthesis—reflects most starkly the modern rebellion against the Church as a major influence in the public life of nations: it rejected any authoritative interpreter of the Natural Law. That is, it followed the medieval political philosopher Marsilius of Padua in rejecting that role for the papacy and, in effect, claiming it for the state. Eventually, of course, this role came to be exercised most preeminently by the Supreme Court and, as we know, unaided by the Holy Spirit, the Court has not done a very good job of it. Perhaps the reason Murray could not see this problem was because he was so taken with the American concept of church-state relations. Also, he was perhaps too sanguine that the American Proposition would be kept alive if only there were sound public philosophers, fully committed to it, constantly expounding about it (indeed, *We Hold These Truths* seems to have been his major effort toward helping reconstruct our public philosophy). We cannot fault Murray too much, however. It is remarkable how substantially our political order upheld the tradition of the Natural Law for our first one hundred twenty-five years or so, deviating only in one major area: economics. Perhaps this is what motivated a thinker like Brownson to believe that God destined America for a mission. The deviation from the Natural Law on economics involved our embracing of extreme individualism, our believing that our social good could automatically be promoted simply by each man pursuing his own self-interest, and our frequent eagerness to separate ethics from economic activity. This could be the subject of another whole essay by itself. In any event, this deviation on economics became more apparent and more pronounced as the nineteenth century wore on. It should have served as a warning not only that the liberal individualism present to a degree in our American Proposition could become an ever more corrupting force, but also that we indeed had been living off the moral capital of the earlier Catholic synthesis and our time was running out since we had no authoritative moral teacher to fall back on.

As we look back on the Murray thesis now, the question seems to be: "Is restoration of the American Proposition possible?" Indeed, the whole matter is problematical when one considers what great political thinkers such as Plato, Aristotle, St. Augustine, and the Founding Fathers themselves said about the essentially inevitable decline of political orders. In any event, it may be unlikely that public philosophers alone will be sufficient for the task. One wonders, as Charles E. Rice has suggested, if it is not necessary for our nation, Catholics and non-Catholics alike, to look to the Vicars of Christ to do what Our Lord commissioned them to do: provide the authoritative interpretation of His Law for men. If that sounds absurd, if Rice seems to stand alone in saying that "[i]n the nature of things, th[e] interpreter has to be the pope,"[63] we might consider some other quite surprising sources from which a similar nod to the leadership and even the uniqueness of the Petrine office has come: the rampantly secular American media who at the time of the election of two successive popes in 1978 called the papacy the "highest office in Christendom"; the Eastern Orthodox bishops and even some Protestant leaders who followed Pope John Paul II's leadership in making the Collegial Consecration of Russia to the Immaculate Heart of Mary in 1984; and Mikhail Gorbachev, who not only referred to the Pope as "Holy Father" during their December 1989 meeting, but told him he was the greatest religious leader in the world.[64]

NOTES

1. The cases were *Roe v. Wade*, 410 U.S. 113, and *Doe v. Bolton*, 410 U.S. 179.
2. Murray, John Courtney, S.J., *We Hold These Truths: Catholic Reflections on the American Proposition* (Kansas City, MO: Sheed and Ward, 1960), p. 28.
3. *Ibid.*, pp. 32-33.
4. *Ibid.*, p. 36.
5. *Ibid.*, p. 38.
6. De Tocqueville, Alexis, *Democracy in America* (Ed. J.P. Mayer; Garden City, NY: Doubleday [Anchor], 1966), Vol. One, pp. 290-291.
7. Brownson, Orestes A., *The American Republic* (Ed. Americo D. Lapati; New Haven, CT: College & University Press, 1972), p. 57.
8. *Ibid.*, p. 242.
9. *Ibid.*, p. 250.
10. Corwin, Edward S., *The "Higher Law" Background of American Constitutional Law* (Ithaca, NY: Cornell U. Press, 1928, 1955), pp. 45. (Emphasis in the original.)
11. Kirk, Russell, *The Roots of American Order* (Malibu, CA: Pepperdine U. Press, 1974), p. 403.
12. *Ibid.*, p. 409.
13. Eidelberg, Paul, "Karl Marx and the Declaration of Independence: The Meaning of Marxism," *The Intercollegiate Review*, Vol. 20, No. 1 (Spring/Summer 1984), p. 4.
14. See Higgins, Thomas J., S.J., *Man As Man: The Science and Art of Ethics* (Rev. ed.; Milwaukee: Bruce, 1958), e.g., pp. 90-99.
15. *Ibid.*, p. 90.
16. See Kirk, pp. 282-293.
17. See Higgins, Book Three.
18. Kirk, p. 292.
19. Among the latter, we could include Means, Cyril C., Jr., "The Law of New York Concerning Abortion and the Status of the Foetus, 1664-1968: A Case of Cessation of Constitutionality," *New York Law Forum*, Vol. 14 (1968) and "The Phoenix of Abortional Freedom: Is a Penumbral or Ninth-Amendment Right About to Arise From the Legislative Ashes of a Fourteenth-Century Common-Law Liberty?" *New York Law Forum*, Vol. 17 (1971)—these two articles were apparently very influential with the Supreme Court—and Mohr, James, *Abortion in America: Origins and Evolution of National Policy, 1800-1900* (NY: Oxford U. Press, 1978).
20. Coke, Edward, *Third Institute* (1644), p. 50.
21. *Oxford English Dictionary*, Vol. VI (Oxford, England: Clarendon Press, 1961), p. 523.
22. Blackstone, William, *Commentaries on the Laws of England* (Philadelphia: Childs & Peterson, 1859), Vol. I., Bk. I, pp. 129-130.
23. Corwin, pp. 84-85, 87; Kirk, pp. 191-192, 368-374.
24. Kirk, p. 373.

25. Krason, Stephen M., *Abortion: Politics, Morality, and the Constitution—A Critical Study of Roe v. Wade and Doe v. Bolton and a Basis for Change* (Lanham, MD: University Press of America, 1984), p. 140.
26. De Tocqueville, Vol. Two, pp. 595-596, 622. The other great nineteenth century foreign commentator on America, Lord Bryce, made a similar observation in the 1890's, even though he noticed increasing divorce especially among the lower classes. (See Bryce, James, *The American Commonwealth* [Third ed.; London: Macmillan, 1898], Vol. II, p. 724, n. 1.)
27. Cropsey, Joseph, "The United States as a Regime and the Sources of the American Way of Life," Horwitz, Robert H., *The Moral Foundations of the American Republic* (Charlottesville, VA: U. of Virginia Press, 1977, 1978), *passim.*
28. Carey, George W., "Abortion and the American Political Crisis," *The Human Life Review*, Vol. III, No. 1 (Winter 1977), pp. 45-46.
29. Cropsey, Joseph, "Conservatism and Liberalism," Goldwin, Robert A., ed., *Left, Right and Center* (Chicago: Rand McNally, 1965, 1967), p. 44.
30. Cf. Pope Leo XIII, Encyclical *Libertas Praestantissimum* (*Human Liberty*) (1888), Secs. 15-18.
31. Kirk, pp. 342-343.
32. Canavan, Francis, S.J., "Genetics, Politics and the Image of Man," *The Human Life Review*, Vol. IV, No. 2 (Spring 1978), p. 54. Actually, of course, with pro-abortionism even the harm principle is ignored, since abortion is a brutal, life-extinguishing assault upon a human person. In a lame way, it often tries to get around this reality by claiming, against all the evidence, that the unborn child is not human or not alive. When one considers, however, that pro-abortion groups often don't even try to claim this today, but merely say that the life in question has no value if the mother does not want it, he wonders if even the harm principle is not thrust aside by the thought undergirding pro-abortionism except in the most obvious, egregious cases of harm (e.g., killing or depriving a post-partum person of something).
33. See Canavan, Francis, S.J., "The Theory of the Danforth Case," *The Human Life Review*, Vol. II, No. 4 (Fall 1976), p. 5. The Supreme Court held that statutes requiring the consent of a married woman's husband for her to have an abortion and permitting a blanket parental veto of a minor girl's abortion decision were unconstitutional in *Planned Parenthood of Central Missouri v. Danforth*, 428 U.S. 52 (1976).
34. *Ibid.*, p. 13.
35. Locke, John, "Some Thoughts Concerning Education," in Gay, Peter, *John Locke on Education* (NY: Teachers College, Columbia U., 1964), p. 164.
36. Locke, John, "The First Treatise," *Two Treatises of Government* (Ed. Peter Laslett; NY: Cambridge U. Press, 1960, 1963), Sec. 59, p. 220.
37. Locke, John, "The Second Treatise," Laslett, Secs. 58, 78, p. 348, 362.
38. Citations *supra*, n. l.
39. Krason, pp. 402-403, citing Glenn, Gary D., "Abortion and Inalienable Rights in Classical Liberalism," *Amer. Jour. of Jurisprudence*, Vol. 20 (1975), pp. 68-69, 72.
40. See, e.g., Jefferson's letter to John Adams, Oct. 28, 1813.

41. Weaver, Richard M., *Ideas Have Consequences* (Chicago: University of Chicago Press, 1948, 1984).
42. Cropsey, "The United States as a Regime...," pp. 90-91.
43. *Ibid.*, p. 87.
44. Murray, pp. 42-43.
45. Cropsey, "The United States as a Regime...", p. 90. (Emphasis added.)
46. *Ibid.*, p. 94.
47. See Krason, pp. 408-428.
48. Cropsey, "The United States as a Regime...," p. 101.
49. *Ibid.*, p. 97.
50. See Krason, Chapter One.
51. *Ibid.*, Chapter Two.
52. See Washington, George, *Farewell Address* (booklet ed.; NY: General Society, Sons of the Revolution, 1963, 1982), p. 24; de Tocqueville, Vol. One, pp. 290-294; Vol. Two, pp. 442-449; Bryce, *op. cit.* (n. 26 *supra*), Vol. II, pp. 723-727.
53. Krason, p. 52.
54. Glenn, *op. cit.* (n. 39 *supra*), p. 79. He does not *specifically* say that "pro-abortionism" was an outgrowth of utilitarianism, but that the claimed right of abortion on demand perhaps is. Since the pro-abortion movement since the late 1960's has sought a public policy of, for all practical purposes, abortion on demand, I believe it is correct to say that he essentially holds that utilitarianism has led to "pro-abortionism."
55. Monro, D.H., "Utilitarianism," *Dictionary of the History of Ideas* (NY: Chas. Scribner's Sons, 1973), Vol. IV, p. 444.
56. Wiener, Philip P., "Pragmatism," *ibid.*, Vol. III, p. 553.
57. See, for example, Connery, John, S.J., Abortion: *The Development of the Roman Catholic Perspective* (Chicago: Loyola Univ. Press, 1977), and Grisez, Germain, *Abortion: The Myths, the Realities, and the Arguments* (NY: Corpus Bks., 1970), Chap. IV.
58. These are two of the leading schools of twentieth century jurisprudential thought which are based on the philosophy of pragmatism.
59. Murray, pp. 42-43.
60. *Ibid.* I infer this from Murray's saying the following: "Perhaps the dissolution, long since begun, *may one day* be consummated" and "The possibility that widespread dissent from these principles should develop *is not foreclosed. If that evil day should come....*" (Emphasis added.)
61. See Kirk, pp. 282-293.
62. Murray, pp. 302-314.
63. Rice, Charles E., *Beyond Abortion: The Theory and Practice of the Secular State* (Chicago: Franciscan Herald Press, 1979), pp. 134-135.
64. Fox, Robert J., Fr., *To Russia With Love: A Reporter's Account of Fatima and the Changing Face of Communism* (Alexandria, SD: Fatima Family Apostolate, 1990), pp. 65, 60-61.

WE HOLD THESE TRUTHS AND MORE

America, Catholics, and the Murray Thesis: The Future

14

The Catholic Interpretive Tradition, Deconstruction, and the Murray Project

By Dominic A. Aquila

The transformation Professor Lawler describes, and the thesis of his paper in this volume, is nothing less than Father Murray's accomplished transformation, if not the outright rescue, of the first principles of the American republic by his situating them in the larger context of the predominantly Catholic natural law tradition. "Genuine devotion to our Father's affirmation and intention," says Professor Lawler, indeed demands such "enlargement." And here Professor Lawler is particularly helpful in drawing out and embellishing Father Murray's most central insight: that the American Proposition stands or falls on the truth of its epistemology. Also helpful is Professor Lawler's use of Lincoln, which begins to sketch out, albeit thinly, a critical, interpretive tradition of the Founding principles.

What's unsatisfying in Professor Lawler's essay is the unfortunate characterization of Father Murray's reading as a choice. "Murray, again imitating Lincoln," says Professor Lawler, "chooses the interpretation which is most in accord with the truth about human liberty and dignity." It is not very assuring to have Father Murray's reading of the most fundamental question on the Republic, the basis of its principles, defended as merely a choice from among many possible readings. To be sure, this conclusion may seem unavoidable since it proceeds from Father Murray's own insistence on the deliberately sketchy and incoherent character of the Founding principles, which Professor Lawler sees as preferable to the closed and therefore irredeemably secular character of the French principles. But, as I will discuss later, I think there have been some developments in the academy that put us in a better position today to move *We Hold These Truths* beyond what may appear to be special pleading.

Before exploring Father Murray's transformation, Professor Lawler succinctly clears away the debris of misunderstanding surrounding Murray's project. As an historian, I would like to critically extend some of Professor Lawler's casual introductory remarks in order to place Father Murray's work more solidly in the main currents of American history and politics.

Rather than directly argue with Professor Lawler's provocative opening that "*We Hold These Truths* is the great work of political philosophy written by an American Catholic," let it be said more meaningfully that it stands in the tradition of timely philosophical explanations and reminders (a kind of Lincolnesque jeremiad) of the purpose, practice, and, most importantly, continuity, of the American republic, at a moment when the republic realized a fundamental, yet generally unacknowledged, change in regime. And in this tradition, Father Murray is preceded by another Catholic, Orestes Brownson. If, as Theodore Lowi has said, the United States followed the French practice of formally recognizing basic changes in its regime, then Father Murray's "reflections" written during the 1950's and compiled in 1960, came during the early ascendancy of the Fourth American Republic.[1]

The First American Republic would be that under the Articles of Confederation; the Constitution of 1787 the Second. And the first significant American contribution to Western political philosophy, *The Federalist Papers* of Madison, Hamilton, and Jay, attended this first fundamental shift in regimes. The end of Civil War delivered the first serious blow to federalism—the shared authority of the central and state governments sketched in the Constitution of 1787, would mark the next shift and the beginning of the Third American Republic. It was accompanied by Orestes Brownson's *The American Republic*, which, as Father Americo Lapati wrote in his "Introduction" to the modern edition, explained the re-formation of the American republic after the Civil War in much the same way that *The Federalist Papers* explained the republic of 1787.

The Fourth and present Republic was a near total victory of central over local authority, and, as Lowi has shown, nearly banished the rule of law in favor of executive discretion. It emerged hesitantly in 1937 when the U.S. Supreme Court changed the interpretive principles it had applied to the Constitution of 1787, but moved quickly to consolidate its power through the post-World War II era. The Fourth Republic also redefined the role, function, and purpose of the state and citizen. The state became tutelary, and, in the Hegelian mode of other Western states, the source of ethics. The chief ethic of the modern state is the formation of an indistinguishable egalitarian mass. Its high priests, the physicists, chemists, biologists, engineers, hospital administrators, advertising specialists, race relations managers, and scores of other experts, all found a living in the federal bureaucracy by the early 1950's. Its method of operation became that of a broker of interests. Such a scheme discourages open civil conversation, so fundamental to Father Murray's healthy pluralistic republic, in favor of bargaining behind the scenes.

The citizen of the Fourth Republic is a client who, in a reversal of the Aristotelian-Thomistic tradition, is unable to know the good. He must look to the state and its satellite agencies—health and human services, organizations and schools—for instruction on the good. With little chance for owning productive property, he is highly dependent on state entitlements—what Charles Reich called the "New Property" for economic security. Yet his only access to the state is through interest groups. And, where there are interests without groups, the state indirectly through incentives and directly through agencies like VISTA organizes them. Organizations must speak the language of indignation and outrage, trotting out documented histories of abuse. The citizen is no longer self-reliant with opinions of his own, but a victim of oppression. The new learning is consciousness raising, a term invented by the women's movement, which provides the common identity of the group and the basis of organization, and everything that separates it from the rest of society. The new citizenship does not link people but separates them. The reality of American pluralism is, in the Fourth Republic, not as Madison would have it, a necessary evil, but a positive good. Modern pluralist theory and practice have banished talk of the common good. Such common good as there is and need be emerges automatically from the tension of competing interest groups.

This rather lengthy digression into the character of the state and citizen of the Fourth American Republic is necessary because the two elements that are so central to Father Murray's work—pluralism and citizenship—have been wholly transformed. *E Pluribus Unum* no longer practically applies. But it is not my intention to portray Father

Murray as old-fashioned or as a naive idealist holding forth about citizenship and pluralism in a language nearly incomprehensible to modern ears. Rather, this fuller political context for Father Murray's writing is meant to highlight the prophetic role of his work, one that is akin to Publius and Brownson in their days.

But even more to the point, I find it telling that two of these significant American contributions to Western political theory were written by Catholics—Brownson and Father Murray. It underscores one of Father Murray's historical paradoxes: that should that "evil day" come whereby there is wide dissent from the American Founding principles, grounded as he understood them to be in the natural law tradition:

> The Catholic community would still be speaking in the ethical and political idiom familiar to them as it was familiar to their fathers, both the Fathers of the Church and the Fathers of the American Republic. The guardianship of the original American consensus, based on the Western heritage, would have passed to the Catholic community, within which the heritage was elaborated long before America was. And it would be for others, not Catholics, to ask themselves whether they still shared the consensus which first fashioned the American people into a body politic and undermined the structure of its fundamental law. [2]

Talk about a call to arms, a Church militant! These words are a powerful justification for Catholic action, coming as they did at a time when Catholics in America were historically coming of age, and when Father Murray's three other traditions—the Protestant, Jewish, and secular—were collapsing into the secular. Father Murray himself became something of a clearinghouse for such action. Before John F. Kennedy delivered his famous speech on the "religious question" to the Greater Houston Ministerial Association, for instance, his advisor Ted Sorensen read it over the telephone to Father Murray to make sure that there was nothing about it that would be offensive to the Catholic press.

Regrettably much of the Catholic action of the 1960's was wrongheaded and as Professor Lawler points out, mistakenly justified by Father Murray's work. Reading *We Hold These Truths* wrongly as a celebration of the Fourth Republic brand of pluralism, many Catholics enthusiastically embraced and financed America's premiere community organizer, Saul Alinsky, who did the most to institutionalize the interest group pluralism described above. Alinsky also had the ethical approval of Father Charles Curran. The Catholic Committee on Urban Ministry, which disbanded in the mid-1980's, the Catholic Campaign for Human Development, and the National Center for the Laity are direct descendants of Alinsky's organizing theories and methods.

Yet the implications of Father Murray's work, correctly read, remain largely unaddressed by Catholics in the academy. Let's return to what I said earlier about the unsatisfying tentativeness of Father Murray's interpretation of the Founding principles, mainly that it is just one among many competing interpretations. The problem of multiple interpretations has become more acute today with the growth and hegemony of the deconstructionists, a bunch Father Murray would no doubt include among his Brooks Brothers barbarians for their deliberate sabotage of meaningful public argument. But rather than view with alarm the barbarity of their project and recoil from their assaults, Catholic scholars should take the cue offered by non-Catholic and Catholic scholars, who have vindicated the Catholic interpretive tradition, reviled by Luther, and take a confident offensive position not just against the deconstructionists but by asserting authoritative interpretations of texts like the Declaration of Independence and the First Amendment.

The deconstuctionist position, as advanced by Jacques Derrida and Roland Barthes, denies that words convey fixed meanings. For them words or signifiers are not bound to the signified—the idea or object they signify. They argue that language is not a structured system which generates fixed meanings, rather it is an endless chain of signifiers in which meaning is always deferred and finally absent. There is no external point of reference no final point of rest where one can find meaning, no "transcendental signified" that guarantees meaning once and for all. Hence, since narrative, the medium and traditional object of the historian's study is built on words, it can no longer be trusted to render a final meaning. According to another deconstructionist, Jean-Francois Lyotard, the once coherent narrative with a discoverable meaning has been "dispersed into clouds of linguistic particles…each with its own pragmatic valence."[3]

Convinced that the historians, and especially intellectual historians, can no longer ignore the challenges of the deconstructionists, David Harlan surveyed various proposals advanced by intellectual historians to meet these challenges, dividing them into two categories: Protestant and the Rabbinical and Catholic interpretive traditions. He concluded that the Protestant tradition represented by the distinguished historians Quentin Skinner and J.G.A. Pocock, which tries to capture original meaning à la Martin Luther by peeling away the layers of history that contaminate meaning, cannot stand up to deconstructionist attacks. But the Rabbinical and Catholic interpretive traditions can, because they engage and make use of the interpretive traditions surrounding a text. The philosopher Hans Georg Gadamer, as Harlan and many others recognize, has led the way toward revitalizing the Catholic tradition of considering text and its interpretive tradition. Admittedly, the heterodox theologian, Father David Tracy, has used Gadamer to advance a centrifugal pluralism in the Church, analogous to the political pluralism of the Fourth Republic, but the post-liberal theologian Father Paul Giurlanda has used Gadamer more profitably for orthodoxy in his *Faith and Knowledge: A Critical Inquiry*.

In the field of politics and law, Sanford Levinson in *Constitutional Faith*, where the basic argument is that the Constitution is insufficient grounds upon which to build a meaningful and authoritative American consensus, used a more elaborate Protestant and Catholic typology to discuss constitutional interpretation. In his analytical schema Protestant interpreters of the Constitution look to recover its original meaning and deny the authority of the Supreme Court as its sole interpreter, just as they attempt to recover the original meaning of Scripture rejecting the role of the Church as interpreter. Catholic interpreters, on the other hand, are willing to interpret the text of the Constitution in the light of case precedents, Congressional debates and other related texts, but recognize only the Supreme Court as the final interpreter. The associations that emerge from Levinson's categories are sometimes quite engaging. Frederick Douglass and Edwin Meese, for example, are "both candidates for the category of 'protestant-protestant.'" Both insist on a highly textual Constitution, and neither one accords "ultimate authority" to Supreme Court decisions as being the "Law of the Land."[4]

While Levinson's is an engaging book, the usefulness of its categories is unclear. It is nonetheless an example of a non-Catholic scholar's appreciation for the distinction between Catholic and Protestant views of interpreting history.

Finally, as David Schindler has shown, orthodox Catholics are in a much better position to effectively rout the malevolent effects of the deconstructionists. In fact, Schindler appreciates Derrida for giving the final shove to topple the mechanized, desacralized culture of the liberal Enlightenment that Nietzsche had already fairly well undermined. Though no friend of logocentrism, Derrida acknowledges that the pre-modern mind recognized the fundamental connection between meaning, "as a present identifiable *logos*," and the Christian *Logos*. The relation between the signifier and the signified, indeed, the very idea of the sign, belong, in Derrida's words, "in a profound and implicit way to the totality of the great epoch covered by the history of metaphysics, and in a more explicit and more systematically articulated way to the narrower epoch of Christian creationism and infinitism when these appropriate the resources of Greek conceptuality."[5] In short, if God goes, if Christian creationism and infinitism go, so goes the foundation of meaning.

Though logocentrism persists through the liberal Enlightenment to the present, its links to the Christian *Logos* are cut. Hence the Deism and liberal strains of Christian theology that emerged from the Enlightenment are most vulnerable to the deconstuctionist subversion of meaning because there is in their systems no appreciation for God's immanence in creation. "A God who remains outside of the cosmos is a God whose being leaves off where the being of the cosmos begins." Such a God is infinite and is the same God who Nietzsche declared dead.

Schindler goes all the way to advocating a limited alliance with Derrida toward opening up meaning in order to convince liberals that, if there is no God or if God is not present in the created world, then there is no "transcendental signified," and indeed no meaning. But after this stage we must part company with Derrida, for his intent is to turn the death of God and meaning into a victory whereby "[t]he feeble—because merely implicit—nihilism of modernity must give way to the energetic nihilism of postmodernity."

Professor Schindler then commissions "anyone who accepts Christian creationism and infinitism to resacralize the world by restoring to it a God who is truly infinite affect[ing] all of our meanings all of the time," who "is the deepest center and principle of all created entities," who as a real creator, affects meaning by giving his creations a logos, that is "a form or logic." To illustrate these characteristics Schindler asks us to reconsider the following passages from St. Augustine's *Confessions*: "You have made us for yourself, and our heart is restless until it rests in you" and "You fill all things and you fill them with your entire self." As Professor Schindler points out, here "relation to God on the part of finite beings is not adventitious." That is, "that it is merely added on to an already formed identity." It is absolutely all that we are.[6]

So where have we gone with this discussion of deconstruction with respect to Father Murray? The point of departure, you will recall, was my dissatisfaction with Father Murray's transformation of the Founding principles as one among many plausible interpretations. The rise of deconstruction and the attempts to counter its corrosive power have led non-Catholic and Catholic scholars to rediscover and revalidate fundamentally Catholic methods and world views—the Catholic interpretive tradition and the pre-modern view of the world. With these we can extend and embellish Father Murray's project, by providing the needed cultural context without which his transformation of our Founding principles will remain less than compelling. In short, the rise of deconstruction affords orthodox Catholic scholars the opportunity to offer people a choice between a world of meaningless babble and special pleading, on the one hand, or one whose only possibility of meaning rests with a God immanent in all of creation as the "Transcendent signified" on the other. Then when Professor Lawler asserts that Father Murray's interpretation of the Founding principles "is most in accord with the truth about human liberty and dignity," it will have real meaning and force. We can then proceed to what Father Murray considered real argument.

NOTES

1. Lowi, Theodore, *The End of Liberalism: The Second American Republic of the United States* (2nd ed; New York: W.W. Norton & Co., 1979), p. 271. Lowi suggests the possibility of four American Republics, but, as his subtitle reflects, settles on calling the post-1937 era the "Second Republic," "only because previous changes were not given their due."
2. Murray, John Courtney, *We Hold These Truths: Catholic Reflections on the American Proposition* (New York/Kansas City, MO: Sheed & Ward, 1960), pp. 42-43.
3. Quoted in Harlan, David, "Intellectual History and the Return of Literature," *American Historical Review*, Vol. 94 (June 1989), p. 538.
4. Levinson, Sanford, *Constitutional Faith* (Princeton, NJ: Princeton University Press, 1988), pp. 3-51.

5. From Derrida, Jacques, *Of Grammatology* (Baltimore: Johns Hopkins Univ. Press, 1976), p. 13, quoted in Schindler, David L., "On the Meaning and the Death of God in the Academy," *Communio*, Vol. XVII (Summer 1990), p. 194.
6. Schindler, pp. 192-206.

15

The Confessional State and John Courtney Murray

by Regis Martin

*I*t is precisely because I agree with Professor Wilhelmsen's description in his paper of Murray as a man "quintessentially American and a child of his times," that I refuse to credit any enduring importance to his work (in civil theology, that is; on the other hand, the elegance and precision of his contribution to Trinitarian theology — see his *Problem of God* — is far likelier to endure). What I do attach enduring importance to, the conversation about civil theology, will become apparent from what follows. And the latter, I venture to predict, will crystallize along the lines laid out for us so luminously in the remarks written in L. Brent Bozell's paper. Nothing is more necessary, it seems to me, at this moment in history than the juxtaposition of politics and mysticism as understood by Brent Bozell.

I begin then with a proposition which I take to be axiomatic among committed Christians, specifically Roman Catholics; it functions, in other words, as a presumption fundamental to the discussion of a theology of the public life. That proposition is, to be sure, the absolute centrality of Christ to the life of the Church and, indeed, to the whole order of creation and cosmos. I say this because, in a Catholic economy of salvation, grace and nature need not be sundered one from the other; as, for instance, in Calvinist and Lutheran theology where the two realms are made to suffer permanent and unnatural separation. Thus, the entire weight of the truth concerning who Christ is and what He has done for the world bear enormously, intimately even, on the question of the shape and texture of the public life. Christ remains indisputably, therefore, *the* governing idea of Christianity, of Roman Catholicism; He is the Word who was with God from the beginning, without whom there could not be any beginning. In short, because Christ constitutes that which is finally and specifically Christian about Christianity, He necessarily subsists at the center of all that the Church distinctively is and does in the world.

If the Church is filled with Christ, she being after all His bride and body—mysteriously located along the line of horizon between earth and heaven—how then does she go about effectively bringing Christ to the world, maintaining, monstrating as it were, His presence among men? The answer, in a word, is by sacramentalizing the world, raising it to the very dignity and configuration of Christ Himself. And it is surely evident, is it not, how over the centuries the Church has elaborated basically two strategies pursuant to this end, neither of which is finally dispensable. The first is Evangelization, which consists in boldly proclaiming the Good News to every human being in the world, i.e., men and women for whose salvation Christ died on the Cross. Indeed, the very wood on which the Eternal Word consented to be bound bespeaks this universality: those crossbeams extended into the four winds are intended to evoke the most profound note of solidarity and kinship with other men. Thus we are to draw men to God through the Church, which Christ Himself fashioned as a sort of highway leading the world home to heaven. Yet, essential as that may be, it does not exhaust the possibilities of bringing Christ to the world. Indeed, the exoteric note struck with such deep evangelical resonance precisely enjoins still another strategy, the nature and necessity of which Fr. Murray seems not to have been greatly interested in. And that, of course, we call Culture, which has to do principally with the effort of men publicly to incarnate the Good News, pursuant not to this or that man's salvation but the world's. Culture, in other words, at least where it is Christian, bears fundamentally on the question of raising up a social order in which it is easier for men to be good.

Now both modes are necessary, the first personal and interior, dependent therefore upon the careful planting of an evangelical seed in another's soul; the other corporate, public and exterior, but equally mandated by the will of God, and in a profoundly organic way dependent upon the first, or evangelical imperative. However, it needs to be said, out of deference to this second approach, that simply to speak of the content of the Christian Faith as a thing to be communicated from one soul to another, is not nearly enough these days. One must engage as well the question of culture; in fact, Christ having come to consecrate all that has to do with man, we are solemnly enjoined to do so. The Good News we have been given is meant to give birth to both Christian men and Christian institutions which ratify the importance of that News; otherwise men are at liberty to think it not so Good. And this is surely of a piece with the understanding of a Church irreducibly *exoteric*, i.e., one whose hunger for souls is as wide as creation, as generous as salvation...evincing thereby an absolute, universal solidarity among men.

Joseph Ratzinger, in speaking of the most fundamental feature of Faith, namely its personal character, says that its central formula is not, "I believe in something," but "I believe in Thee." "It is the encounter with the human being Jesus, and in this encounter it experiences the meaning of the world as a person." (See his *Introduction to Christianity* where, with lucid and systematic attention, he discusses the articles of the Apostles' Creed, the political implications of which I am here considering.)

That being the case, *what* happens when this encounter with Jesus is raised to the level of human culture, so that more than just men in their interiority are captured by Christ, but the larger and more pervasive public texture of their lives as well?

In a word, what is Christian Culture, or Catholic Christendom? Is it not, at the deepest level, an answer to the question raised by the Hebrew Psalmist whose people languish in Babylonian captivity?

There by the waters of Babylon we sat down and wept,when we remembered Zion....How shall we sing the Lord's song in a strange land? (Ps. 136)

There is the question and, to be sure, in the context of Jewish captivity in the Old Testament, it is a song of lamentation, of sorrow. A people in bondage are very likely candidates for despair. But since the coming of Christ and His marriage of time and eternity, God and man, nature and grace, the world is no longer strange or menacing but rather redeemed. The world is a wedding, a sacrament, confected for the sanctification of men. Everything exists therefore under the Sign of our salvation, in the shadow of the Cross. What then is Christian Culture? Is it not what happens when men, wedded to Christ as spousal recipients of His love, undertake *publicly* to profess their common faith and devotion by soaking everything—all that they know and do, their institutions, civil arrangements, arts, education, family, work, play—immersing all of this in the grace of the Gospel, in the very

Blood of the Lamb? Not, how shall we sing the Lord's song in a strange land? Rather, how shall we render our experience of a land which ought not to be strange any longer and thus sing the Lord's song more easily, with felicitous grace and joy and delight?

Let us make a world, Dorothy Day used to say—sounding the great theme of Catholic solidarity amid a rampant and atomized individualism—where it is easier for men to be good. Let us, as Eric Gill liked to say, create a cell of good living amid the chaos of our world; a world modeled not on the ant hill but on the Mystical Body. And if, as Ratzinger reminds us, Christian faith absolutely depends upon our finding in the midst of this world the very presence of the eternal itself—and thus in God's unconditional devotion to men He gives us the very meaning which alone may bear us up—then isn't Christian Culture what happens when enough Christians conspire to shape everything in the world according to that truth, so that nothing human may be left out of account, thus free to shape itself without reference to God?

In other words, should not society in some way at least try and make the practice of virtue easier for men who desire to know and to love God? Surely this should be so in a society so many of whose members are already Christians! At the very least this could be done by not placing impediments in the way, i.e., by not actively deflecting such arrows as Christian men may care to aim in the direction of Beatitude.

This is what I mean by the question of culture and the possibility of ushering in one whose lineaments may be Christian. In such a configuration of forces, the first citizen would surely be the Church, the second the family. As the Mexican poet Octavio Paz once put it, "In the North American ethic, the center is the individual; in Hispanic morals (on the other hand) the true protagonist is the family" (whose ground, ultimately understood, is the Trinity, where membership is defined precisely by the relations which both distinguish and unite). This is why the idea and institution of the Confessional State—where the Triune God is first, followed by families configured to His own inner life—emerged *not* in the Protestant and Northern European countries, but in Catholic Spain.

Christopher Dawson, the eminent Catholic historian who wrote dozens of books on the subject of religion and culture—and argued with untiring scholarship that nothing could be more natural than that men should seek to integrate the two, faith and life—once defined

The Confessional State and Murray

Christendom as, "a political society or group of societies which find their principle of unity in the public profession of the Christian faith...." Or, putting it in pithy, epigrammatic form, as the Archduke Otto von Habsburg, heir to the Roman Catholic Empire of Europe, was wont to do: "The Cross does not need Europe; Europe needs the Cross." In other words, to recover her soul, the purpose of her existence as a people, Europe (and the Americas) need to rediscover their own roots in the Christian religion, which remains at the origin of all Western culture. Here, too, is the great and persisting theme of the Pontificate of John Paul II, of his many pastoral visits which attempt with tireless eloquence to recreate a Civilization of Love rooted in the Mystery of the Cross. "What have you done with your baptismal promises?" is the question raised by the Holy Father in his countless travels across Europe and the Americas. In order that, in looking outside one's windows, one not see only the TV antenna, but the cathedral spire, an entire order of existence must needs be renewed, repristinated. So much then for the definition.

Now the disclaimer: It is very difficult for native-born Americans to think like this (even urbane and educated Jesuit theologians). And not, for heaven's sake, because Americans happen to be less Christian in their witness to the moral life. Rather it is because Americans have had two hundred or more years in which the public and institutional life of the nation developed without any formal and explicit recourse to Christianity at all.

Ours is the first nation under God which makes no real provision for God in its public life. On the basis of a great wall of separation between religion and politics, church and state, the forms of Christendom could never have emerged organically in the American Experience. Look: What has been the central myth of America? The myth, the shattering of which would disturb the very order of the Republican soul, violating every shibboleth of secular virtue and piety? That in the public life men ought to be on their own, entirely at liberty, therefore, to go to Hell without the State either impeding or promoting the journey thereof. Corporate neutrality, in other words, concerning the great Questions of Faith and Salvation. And the result? A kind of soulessness ensues, in which there is a complete disappearance of the supernatural as an order of reality enjoying political significance. One thinks of Fellini's film, *La Dolce Vita*, in which a giant cross hangs suspended above the rooftops of a Modern Italian city; the sunbathers do not see it, so jaded have their Christian sensibilities become, but to Americans, nourished on the Great Myth of separation, it amounts to an act of war, of effrontery, in which the forces of medieval superstition have arrayed themselves in defiant mockery of the sheer reasonableness of the Myth. This at least is the convenient hobgoblin of, say, Norman Lear and other ACLU types. According to these fashionable taste makers, religion is simply what a man does with his privacy (benighted uses of individual privacy are equally subject to constitutional protection, they say). And thus the political illusion which grows out of such mythologized understanding, indeed giving shape to the whole dialectic between liberals and conservatives, is that all politics ought to proceed without any sort of reference to God at all. The evident result of such emptiness, it seems to me, is that America can sustain no large vision of the human spirit. (Where there is no vision, the proverb has it, a people will perish.) Nor is America able to impose much of a moral discipline, either. This is not live politics: this is dead politics: politics so profoundly sterile as to refuse at every turn to draw a political connection between the perception of what is—the indicative mood— with the purpose for which that which is, is, i.e., the imperative mood. Take, for example, the issue of the sanctity of life. What exactly is life for? Well, it is certainly not for the abortionist's knife, which exterminates nearly two million young children each year in the United States. What we are talking about here is a Christian consensus, at the core of which one sees and lays hold of a public philosophy whose wisdom is both true and worthy of realization.

God, then, is the Author of life, not doctors or hospitals or politicians; it makes all the difference in the world whether man is to be arbiter of life or its custodian, its shepherd. (Am I tenant of my own home, or is the rent being paid by Another?) Everything, therefore, touching life is of supreme interest to God. There are things we are not at liberty to do; there are things we are solemnly enjoined to do. And the Church is the guardian and guarantor of both; She alone is custodian and keeper of the moral tablets. "She is," to quote Vatican II, "a sign and safeguard of the transcendent dignity of the human person." It is the purpose, then, of Christian culture to enshrine and protect that exalted human status; not to permit, therefore, the emergence of that parody of pluralism which amounts to a grotesque caricature of the Christian religion, i.e., the situation in which there is a complete exclusion of Christian concerns and values from the formulations of public policy (what Richard Neuhaus calls "the Naked Public Square") and the growing acquiescence by Christians themselves to that exclusion. What, after all, holds a society together? What enables it to cohere? As the Venerable Newman reminds us, it is that "common reverence for a certain sacred possession," which alone may cement and sustain the civilized order. Thus, we either uphold and revere that possession—common and sacred to Christian men—and so shape the whole world according to its vision, or we submit ingloriously to the fallen spirit of the world which Christ came to judge and condemn. And if so, are we not effectively in despair, then, without hope in the Church's mission of sacramentalizing the world, of raising it to dignity of the Sons of God?

Let me now advance and defend a thesis which is at the heart of a wonderful little book by Jean Danielou, S.J. called *Prayer as a Political Problem*.[1] The book begins with a question, the answer to which, says Danielou, will "make the existence of a Christian people possible in the civilization of tomorrow." However, it is a most contentious question because it is rooted in a recognition not widely shared nowadays, which is that the "religious problem is a mass problem," and that there is something "incongruous" about the "juxtaposition of a private religion and an irreligious society." It is really the question central to the task of civil theology, to wit, the search for usable ways to graft the insights of the Gospel onto the institutions of men without doing violence to either. Indeed, it is the question he wrote the book to answer: "How are society and religion to be joined without either making religion a tool of the secular power or the secular power a tool of religion?" (Note please the planted axiom here: both ought somehow to be joined.) But whether they are or are not joined will decisively depend on one's conception of the Church, concerning which, Danielou says, there are two competing notions.

For some, the Church ideally should serve as a sign, "giving witness in the world to that which surpasses the world...keep it clear of civilization lest its purity be compromised." Such a notion of the Church will, as paradigm, be sublimely pure, but will likewise remain a sect, an arrangement, argues Danielou, unacceptable to the Mystical Body, whose thirst for souls is as wide as creation, as generous as salvation. To prefer that solution, Danielou is saying, is really to surrender the entire sacramental mission of the Church, to circumscribe even the redemptive reach of Christ Himself:

Christ has come to save all that has been made. Redemption is concerned with all creation, civilization is part of the order of creation…is sick and needs to be healed like all things that pertain to man in his wounded state…Christianity must take up and consecrate all that has to do with man.

The first solution, then, would effectively abandon both the poor and that civilization instituted to assist in their salvation. As Danielou puts it:

The Church has been given by God Himself the task of leading men to this heavenly city, and has therefore the right to ask of the earthly city that it put no obstacle in the way…a Christian people cannot exist without a milieu to sustain it.

A milieu, he is at some pains to insist, the maintenance of which will necessitate "creating an order in which personal fulfillment is possible," especially that highest fulfillment found in prayer. "If it cannot create the conditions in which man can completely fulfill himself," says Danielou, "it becomes an impediment to that fulfillment." Danielou identifies three levels of life, of ascending importance, each with its own appropriate fulfillment which it is part of the business of any humane social order to help secure. There is mastery of the material world, or technology; this is man in relation to things. Then there is the whole order of human relations which are to be rooted in justice and love; this is man in relation to other men. And, finally, there is the order of adoration, of man in relation to God. Again, each is of a piece with that total perfection and fulfillment of the human personality to which no society can remain indifferent.

Therefore, concludes Danielou, "it is unreal and dangerous to accept separation…to consider that the Church and the civil society ought to move in two separate worlds…it leaves that society to shape itself in an incomplete and inhuman manner." To countenance such separation, he is saying, is to indulge "that most detestable form of idealism which separates spiritual existence from its material and sociological substratum." And separates, as well, the poor from salvation.

Here we touch the theme most dear to Danielou's heart, the theme of the Religion of the Poor, which so exactly corresponds with the Pauline/Augustinian image of the Church as a vast net in which "all sorts of fish are caught, the task of separating the good from the bad is for the angels." The Church's task, in other words, is hardly so exacting: She exists evangelically. To enfold all of humankind into One Body, enabling thereby the weak and the wayward to endure. This is because they too have been invited to prayer, which is "an absolutely universal human vocation," and "what is offered to all must be within the reach of all."

What is prayer but a talking to God, a conversation with God; it is, in short, a relationship of dialogue destined to go on forever in which every human being has a right to enter. It is more: namely the effort, "the struggle." Danielou has called it, "to save man from asphyxiation." In fact, he says, "Destitution is the condition of man left to himself, deprived of the energies of God." Prayer is thus an absolutely vital and indispensable human experience; a means whereby men are given energy to survive spiritually. And, as Danielou will argue, because prayer is entirely necessary to man, both for his temporal well being and final, eternal felicity, it is a fundamental element in that *common good* which it is the chief business of politics to secure. Indeed, he insists, "no true polity can exist where there is no room for prayer." ("Man without grace," Eric Voegelin once said, "is demonic nothingness.") And "without prayer," and that access to God through adoration which yields the grace and repose of the soul, human society becomes a place where men literally are gasping for breath. Especially the poor, the average and mediocre, those whose strength of character cannot long survive a world impervious to prayer, to the whole "poetry of the transcendent," as my esteemed colleague and friend, Fritz Wilhelmsen, once put it. "If we accept a complete dissociation of the sacred and the profane worlds, we shall make access to prayer absolutely impossible to the mass of mankind. Only a few would be able to find God in a world organized without reference to Him."

Undeniably, therefore, religion remains a "mass problem." That is to say, "There cannot be a personal Christianity unless there is also a social Christianity." Or putting it in its most provocative form, "there can be no mass Christianity outside Christendom." It is the one medium most essential to the collective expression of the Catholic Thing. "Before the faith," says Danielou, "can be truly rooted in a country it must penetrate its civilization and bring into existence a Christendom." And for such a thing, *mirabile dictu*, to happen, what is above all necessary is to have the faith recognized, by Caesar, as right and good and true. Unless the temporal order, over which the Caesars of this world preside, makes suitable provision for God, for the truth of the Christian religion, the poor will remain necessarily bereft. "To cleave to Christianity," says Danielou, recalling the world before *res publica christiana*, "called then for a strength of character of which the majority of men are not capable." And so, argues Danielou, the conversion of Constantine, in removing these obstacles, the impediments to the public recognition of the reality of God and His Church, suddenly made the whole life of the Gospel accessible to the poor.

In other words, we must get Caesar to ground the state, its ultimate sanction for being and for doing business, in God, in the Church He founded to be His extension and prolongation in the world. In short, we must obtain as a political principle of unity the public profession of the Christian Creed. The alternative, it seems plain, is that blood and beastliness which marked the pagan Roman world without Christ; an instructive example of which being the savage spectacles of torture and death performed in the Colosseum to amuse the corrupt citizenry of the Empire. It is a setting which even now evokes those countless souls whose mortal agonies were staged to distract and divert the mob. Few acres on earth were ever drenched with so much human blood as this deadly oval. The ancient world, to be sure, was cruel and human life was cheap. But no ancient people seemed more systematic about its cruelties, its floggings, tortures, burnings, crucifixions, and massacres of prisoners, or as openly enjoyed watching them, as the Romans did.

Duels to the death between professional gladiators were fairly routine for the arena. What really filled the seats and produced full-throated delight in the mob was something especially bloody or grotesque, like Christians being torn to shreds by ravenous lions. Callousness was the darkest aspect of pagan Rome. It broods over the history of the city like the face of the Emperor Caracalla, who once received the leading citizens of Alexandria, inviting them to a sumptuous banquet and then having them all murdered. Only Romans would have let themselves be brutalized by habitual spectacles of sadism and still argue, as Cicero did, that they inspired manly disdain for suffering.

Charles Williams, in a marvelous work entitled *The Descent of the Dove: A History of the Holy Spirit in the Church*,[2] reveals something of the tremendous change wrought by Christ, which the conversion of Constantine ratified in the order of the public life, in the politics of prayer. Something momentous, he says, took place during the time between the missionary voyages of St. Paul and the arrival of St. Augustine in Carthage and Hippo as its Bishop. An entire world was transformed. "When St. Paul preached in Athens, the world was thronged with crosses, rooted outside cities, bearing all of them the bodies of slowly dying men. When Augustine preached in Carthage, the world was also thronged with crosses, but now in the very center of cities, lifted in processions and above altars, decorated and jewelled, and bearing all of them the image of the Identity of dying Man.... There was offered everywhere 'the clean sacrifice.' Men were no longer to die, for Man had died...."

Here, then, is the sublime, horizon shattering truth which even Fr. Murray's book, for all its elegant persuasiveness, cannot obscure. The problem, in other words, with the Murray thesis, can be stated very simply, and it turns on either an intellectual misconception about the nature of the confessional state, or an unwitting idolatry regarding this American state (but, then again, it may be both). It seems to me that Fr. Murray mistakenly saw the confessional state as merely a juridical theory whose usefulness had somehow been magically superseded by historical events, and thus the American state was canonically destined to become *the* paradigm around which men of reason and good will were to rally. How otherwise are we to account for his telling us (p. 34): "Religious pluralism is against the will of God. But it is the human condition; it is written into the script of history. It will not somehow marvelously cease to trouble the City." Or that (p. 19): "...the distinctive bond of the civil multitude is reason, or more exactly, that exercise of reason which is argument. Hence the climate of the City...is not feral or familial but forensic...." Is life then to be but one long conversation about different points of view? Are we in a seminar or something, a forensics tournament in which so many hardy little debaters aspiring after the swashbuckling style of John Stuart Mill, disport themselves in endless disputation? This may well be the American model, life as civics class in which we are all students, locked in perpetual argument about the uses of reason. But it is far from the confessional model on which a Catholic polity rests. Indeed, that model is not any sort of juridic theory at all, but rather an act or gesture of love anchored in the God whose Name is Love, and whose life is a Blessed Company, or Family, in whose very image and likeness we have all been graced to grow. *Christus totam novitatem attulit, semetip-*

sum afferns, announced the saintly Bishop Irenaeus, as long ago as the second century. Christ brought all things new by bringing Himself. Here is the real heart and center of the Christian religion; Who because He entered fully and irrevocably and forever into the human condition, religious pluralism is precisely *not* written into the script of history. Rather God's very Word is so written, He who wedded Himself perfectly to our world and thus urges men to anneal themselves, and their institutions, in the very fire of His life which is love.

NOTES

1. New York and London: Sheed and Ward, 1967.
2. New York: Meridian Books, 1956.

16

The Politics of Mysticism

by L. Brent Bozell

[*Editors' Note*: Mr. Bozell is a well-known writer and lay Catholic leader. He was the co-founder of the now-defunct Catholic magazine, *Triumph*. Although scheduled to speak at the conference upon which this book is based, his health prevented him from attending. This paper was read at a meeting of the "Catholic Rendezvous," a group which Bozell helped found to keep the spirit of *Triumph* alive and meets periodically to share fellowship and thoughts about the concerns which motivated the magazine.]

"*Mysticism has everything to do with reality—the reality of God and the reality of man.*" (*Ascent to Love, The Spiritual Teaching of St. John of the Cross*, by Ruth Burrows.) *Triumph* magazine was, above all, a political magazine. It was political in 1974 when, in its presence, Rendezvous was launched. It is political in 1990 when a spokesman for *Triumph* announces to a growing Rendezvous that the key to politics is mysticism.

Politics has been correctly understood by *Triumph* readers as the arrangement adopted at a given time and place for governing the affairs of the real world. Catholic politics has been understood as those arrangements that *should* govern the affairs of the real world.

Now there is a sense in which the real world exists only insofar as it contains a creature known as man, who is in some sense God; and insofar as it is presided over by a creator known as God, who is in some sense man.

What mysticism does is to bring into the grasp of the ordinary man, the poor man, the political man, the basic Catholic truths that while

God and man are distinct, there is a supernatural sense—mediated by love—in which one stands for, and thus *is*, the other.

There will be time, before this brief presentation is finished, to make clear how the world of politics is, or can be—for this is the point—influenced by the world of mysticism; but for the moment I would like to try to remove any possible doubts that the world of mysticism is true—that it is part of the Catholic faith.

Take Christ's account of the Last Judgement in St. Matthew's Gospel, which is probably the best-known instance of Christ mystically making men into God. Christ says in this account, to those who helped the hungry, the naked, the homeless, the prisoners, etc., that when you did this to the least of Mine, you did it to *Me*. Well, this makes all sufferers, at the very least, "other Christs"—mystic Christs, in some sense God: they are the ones specified in Christ's report of the way He will handle the Last Judgement.

But I don't think there is any reason to suppose that these mystic Christs are confined to suffering derelicts, or especially poor people. Everybody is a Christ in the sense apparently used here of a man in need.

These mystical Christs are the very ones signalled out by the Mother Teresa nuns as the beneficiaries of their work. Everybody whom they help is "Christ"—literally, they mean. I think we have every reason to think that these Christs are just as much a Christ as the Christ who died on Calvary—but in a deeply mystical sense. In any case, we are somehow called upon to rescue again and continually, in His multiple mystical forms, the crucified Christ.

What must be kept in mind here as a literal, mystical truth is that Christ identifies the people He wants to help as *Himself*. So that in this mystical sense in which He was speaking, Christ is identifying a man as God.

Similarly, Christ identified Himself as another man, or men, at the time of St. Paul's conversion before Damascus. When Paul (Saul) heard the words, "Why do you persecute Me?" and asked who was saying them, Christ answered: "It is I whom you persecute, Jesus Christ." And Saul could recall only, of course, that it was St. Stephen, and other human Christians, that he had persecuted. But Christ was saying now that *I* am the Church—or I am St. Stephen, which is really the point to be kept in mind when considering the Church as His mystical body. In His mystical body, Christ is St. Stephen as well as Himself.

Finally, every Catholic will recognize that the whole doctrine of the mystical body of Christ is an affirmation of the supernatural mixture of human and divine kind. What the doctrine of the mystical body says is that every baptized person—and baptism can be effected by other ways than water, e.g., by desire—is a member of the mystical body of Christ. This means that everyone of us, while he retains his human body and soul, is, at the same time, a part of the divine body of Christ.

I sit here writing this statement, a man with a human body and soul, and yet at the same time drawing on Christ's divine body and soul of which I am a member. (Indeed, we may be drawn on Christ's body, instead of simply "drawing on" it.) And here you are reading this, Christ's lovers, carrying your own bodies and souls, yet deeply linked with me in Christ's body. Together we should make good politics—because we are, in a sense, the same person: we are Christ.

But the Christ in us is usually not fully in charge of us: our human selves dominate. Therefore, the politics we make are faulted. When we deal with our neighbor, we are meant to do so in love. But it is hard to make love to our neighbor unless we remember that he is, in a mystical but fully true sense, God. So when we don't make love to our neighbor, we make, whether intentionally or not, war. The whole impact of the politics which we Americans participate in and embrace is war against Christ and His things.

At the present time, it is impossible to change American politics. What is possible is to adopt a Catholic politics that will take the place of American politics as the major attention of *our* lives.

This Catholic politics will help Christ do His work of carrying out the Redemption—just as American politics helps the American state carry out its secular work. Christ is the Redeemer of Humanity. By joining His work, we become co-redeemers of humanity. And since the work we are able to do will be a "substitute" for Christ's work, it will be a *mercy* to Christ for us to join Him; and our actions in this work should be called "redemptive mercies."

There are at least four categories of redemptive mercies that should be mentioned—even if just briefly. They are redemptive prayer, redemptive suffering, redemptive work, and redemptive play. In all of these redemptive mercies, our action takes the form of an assistance to Christ that, through Him, will reach some human in need.

A redemptive prayer is any prayer to God at all that is consistent with God's purpose of redeeming man for heaven, and His plan for their happiness on earth.

Redemptive suffering is any suffering by men which is offered to Christ as a substitute for His suffering, and thus as an alleviation of the suffering of other members of His mystical body. The co-redeemer, who is doing the actual suffering—the person—can initiate this role by an act of self-denial.

Redemptive work is any work done in imitation of Christ's creation; but the work that is the most conspicuously redemptive is works of mercy—where the co-redeemer does the work for God and neighbor that Christ Himself undertakes in His messianic mission.

Redemptive play is that relationship with Christ which the co-redeemer enters by abandoning himself to Christ. Abandonment and play are divine states; if the co-redeemer abandons himself to God, then he abandons himself to the play of God. Redemptive play is thus an enjoyment of creation which opens men to the promise of the Redemption.

Let me explain now how the world of politics is influenced by the world of mysticism. The answer is that the world of secular politics—American politics, if you like—is not; or, rather, it is a negation of the reality that is God. That is its main feature. To be sure, God has certain outposts, with apparent locations and activities, in the secular order. The Catholic Church is one of these. Rendezvous is another. But the answer to our question is that there is only one way for secular politics to be influenced by mysticism—and that is by conversion. And conversion is not a program, it is not a policy, it is not a campaign. It is exactly the opposite of all of these things.

It is the abandonment of self. Conversion means abandonment to Christ—in the total sense of giving up oneself to one's lover.

A redemptive mercy means making love to Christ with the total love of self-abandonment.

The carrying out of the Redemption, which Christ undertook after His death and resurrection, was given an enduring name by St. Paul. (Please remember the titanic work that was involved here: Christ had opened the doors of heaven to sinners by His death and resurrection, and now it remained to get us sinners through the doors!) The job of actually getting us into heaven Paul called the "Ministry of Reconciliation." As Paul saw it, no work was more important. Let us see it, as he saw it:

> The old order has passed away; now all is new! All this has been done by God, who has reconciled us to himself through Christ and has given us the ministry of reconciliation. I mean that God, in Christ, was reconciling the world to himself, not counting men's transgressions against them, and that he has entrusted the message of reconciliation to us. This makes us ambassadors for Christ, God, as it were, appealing through us.

Thus, by the ministry of reconciliation, God enlists us to help Christ. We say there was a time when Christ did the work by Himself, but now we, as other Christs, indispensably help in the work.

As His co-redeemers, we form an army, spiritual and corporeal, to win the world for Christ.

This is what the Second Vatican Council meant in calling for the renewal of the Church.

This is what Rendezvous has meant in giving surrogate Christs the experience of redeeming by prayer, of redeeming by suffering, of redeeming by work, of redeeming by play.

May God bless you mystical politicians.

Contributors

Dominic A. Aquila is a mentor at Empire State College. He previously taught at the State University of New York-College at Brockport, Monroe Community College, and Hobart and William Smith Colleges. His primary discipline is history, but he also has taught business, sociology, political science, economics, and labor relations. He has his bachelor's degree in music from the Julliard School, M.B.A. degree from New York University, and is a Ph.D. candidate in American history at the University of Rochester. He has served as Social Ministry Coordinator for the Diocese of Rochester and has held administrative positions in the entertainment industry. He has published in the *Journal of Business Ethics*.

L. Brent Bozell was born in Omaha, Nebraska in 1926. A graduate of Yale College, he took his law degree from the same institution in 1953. One of the founders of *National Review*, Bozell was senior editor of the leading conservative journal from 1955 to 1964. With Frederick D. Wilhelmsen, another contributor to this book, Bozell founded *Triumph* magazine and served as senior editor from 1966 to 1975. In 1986 he published his fifth book, *Mustard Seeds*, an anthology of essays about his pilgrimage from conservatism to Catholicism. Bozell's essay, "The Politics of Mysticism," appearing in the present collection, is excerpted from his forthcoming book, *Mission Guadalupe*, and reflects his lifelong search for true Catholic politics.

Gerard V. Bradley is Professor of Law at the University of Notre Dame. He was previously on the law faculty at the University of Illinois, was an Assistant District Attorney in New York City, and was a researcher for the Cornell University Institute on Organized Crime. He holds his B.A. and

Contributors

J.D. degrees from Cornell University. Among his books is *Church-State Relationships in America*. He has also published numerous articles in the *Saint Louis Law Journal*, the *Arizona Law Review*, *Social Justice Review*, and other journals.

John J. Carrigg is Professor of History at Franciscan University of Steubenville, where he has been on the faculty for over forty years. He previously taught history at Georgetown University where he received his Ph.D. He previously authored a chapter in *American Secretaries of the Navy*. He has also published a biographical essay on the life of Daniel Carroll. He has long been active in Republican party politics in Jefferson County, Ohio, and has served as President of the City Council in Steubenville, Ohio and Treasurer of Jefferson County.

Donald J. D'Elia is Professor of History at the State University of New York-College at New Paltz. He has also taught at Bloomsburg State College, Marist College, and New York University. He received his B.A. and M.A. degrees from Rutgers University and his Ph.D. from Penn State University. He has done post-doctoral work at the Angelicum. In 1976, the Institute of Early American History and Culture (Williamsburg) recognized his *Benjamin Rush: Philosopher of the American Revolution* as an outstanding contribution to Bicentennial scholarship. His book, *The Spirits of '76: A Catholic Inquiry*, is an appraisal of the Founding Fathers of the U.S. from the perspective of Catholic thought. His latest book, co-authored, is *Motion Toward Perfection: The Achievement of Joseph Priestley*. He was chairman of the International Francis Festival commemorating the birth of St. Francis of Assisi in 1981 and is a faculty associate and member of the Board of Advisors of The Marian Institute for Advanced Studies.

Robert P. George is an Assistant Professor in the Department of Politics at Princeton University. He has been a visiting Fellow in Law at New College, Oxford University and was the Justice Tom C. Clark Fellow at the U.S. Supreme Court in 1989-90. A member of the bars of Pennsylvania, New Jersey, and the U.S. Supreme Court, he holds the B.A. from Swarthmore College, the M.T.S. and J.D. degrees from Harvard University, and the D. Phil. degree from Oxford. A member of the editorial board of *The American Journal of Jurisprudence*, he has published numerous articles in legal and philosophical journals.

He is the editor of *Natural Law Theory* (Oxford: Clarendon Press, 1991), and is the author of *Making Men Moral: Civil Liberties and Public Morality* (forthcoming from the same press).

John A. Gueguen is Professor of Political Science at Illinois State University. He previously taught at the University of Notre Dame, San Francisco State University, and the University of Chicago. He received his B.A. and M.A. degrees from Notre Dame and his Ph.D. from the University of Chicago. He has authored many articles, book chapters, and book reviews. Since 1980, he has been U.S. coordinator of annual studies in connection with an international university congress in Rome. He was Teacher of the Year at Illinois State's College of Arts and Sciences in 1981.

Rev. Brian Harrison, O.S. is an Australian-born priest of the Society of the Oblates of Wisdom. He currently teaches theology at the Catholic University of Puerto Rico. He holds an M.A. in history from the University of Papua New Guinea and a Licentiate in Sacred Theology from the Angelicum. He is now a doctoral candidate in theology at the Pontifical Athenaeum of the Holy Cross in Rome. A convert from Presbyterianism, he has published the acclaimed *Religious Liberty and Contraception* and numerous articles and pamphlets.

James Hitchcock is Professor of History at St. Louis University. A well-known American Catholic scholar and layman, he previously taught at St. John's University (N.Y.), the New School for Social Research, and Long Island University. He received his A.B. degree from St. Louis University and holds his M.A. and Ph.D. degrees from Princeton University. He holds honorary degrees from Benedictine College and Franciscan University of Steubenville. A former Woodrow Wilson Fellow, he has served as Editor-in-Chief of *Communio* and President of the Fellowship of Catholic Scholars and received the Fellowship's John Cardinal Wright Award. He has published a substantial number of articles and among his many books are *The Decline and Fall of Radical Catholicism, Catholicism and Modernity,* and *What Is Secular Humanism?* He is on the Board of Advisors of The Marian Institute for Advanced Studies.

Contributors

Msgr. George A. Kelly is a research professor at St. John's University (N.Y.) and a well-known Catholic scholar and writer. One of the founders and a past president of the Fellowship of Catholic Scholars, he was also Director of the Institute for Advanced Studies in Catholic Doctrine at St. John's. For ten years, he was Director of the Family Life Bureau of the Archdiocese of New York and also headed the Archdiocese's Department of Education. He is also a member of the Board of Advisors of The Marian Institute for Advanced Studies. He received his M.A. and Ph.D. degrees from the Catholic University of America. He has published many articles and books on Catholic topics, including *The Battle for the American Church*, *The New Biblical Theorists*, and *Birth Control and Catholics*.

Stephen M. Krason is Associate Professor of Political Science at Franciscan University of Steubenville. He previously taught at the State University of New York at Buffalo. He received his B.A. from LaSalle College, M.A. and Ph.D. degrees in political science and J.D. from SUNY-Buffalo, and M.A. in theology/religious education from Gannon University. He is admitted to the bars of Massachusetts, Nebraska, the District of Columbia, and the U.S. Supreme Court. He has authored *Abortion: Politics, Morality, and the Constitution*, and *Liberalism, Conservatism, and Catholicism*, an evaluation of contemporary American political ideologies in light of Catholic social teachings. He co-edited *Parental Rights: The Contemporary Assault on Traditional Liberties*, edited *The Recovery of American Education*, and has published several articles and book reviews. He is President and a faculty associate of The Marian Institute for Advanced Studies and a founder of the Society of Catholic Social Scientists.

Peter Augustine Lawler is Professor of Political Science at Berry College. He is the editor of *American Political Rhetoric* (2nd ed.) and of a forthcoming volume on Alexis de Tocqueville and contemporary political analysis. His numerous articles on the relationship between religion, politics, and philosophy in the U.S. and other political science topics have appeared in such journals as *The Review of Politics*, *The Political Science Reviewer*, *Communio*, *Polity*, *Modern Age*, *Interpretation: A Journal of Political Philosophy*, and *Presidential Studies Quarterly*.

Regis Martin is Assistant Professor of Theology at Franciscan University of Steubenville. He previously taught at Gannon University, the University of Dallas Rome campus, and other Catholic faculties and institutes in Rome. He received his B.A. from Slippery Rock State College, M.A. from Gannon University, and S.T.B., S.T.L, and S.T.D. degrees from the Angelicum. He has published many articles in such journals as *Communio*, *Homiletic and Pastoral Review*, *Center Journal*, *Fidelity*, *Crisis*, *New Oxford Review*, *National Catholic Register*, and *National Review*. He is also a faculty associate of The Marian Institute for Advanced Studies.

John J. Mulloy is President of the Society for Christian Culture and Editor of *The Dawson Newsletter*. He holds his B.A. degree from St. Joseph's College and his M.A. from the University of Notre Dame. He also received an honorary doctoral degree from Franciscan University of Steubenville. He was a high school teacher in the Philadelphia Public School System for many years and an adjunct instructor in sociology at LaSalle College. He is a Contributing Editor of *The Wanderer*, and has published numerous articles and book chapters on Christopher Dawson's work, Catholic topics, and current issues. He edited Dawson's *Christianity in East and West*, and *Dynamics of World History*, and wrote an appendix about Christian Culture Studies for Dawson's *The Crisis of Western Education*. He is also a faculty associate and member of the Board of Advisors of The Marian Institute for Advanced Studies.

Robert R. Reilly has held a number of posts in the federal government. He is currently with the Voice of America. Previously, he served as Senior Advisor for Public Affairs at the U.S. Embassy in Switzerland, Special Assistant to the President in the Office of Public Liaison, and Director of the Office of Private Sector Programs at the U.S. Information Agency. He has served as President and National Director of the Intercollegiate Studies Institute. He has also worked in private business and as a professional Shakespearean actor. He holds his A.B. from Georgetown University and his M.A. from Claremont Graduate School. He has published numerous articles and book chapters. Among the journals his articles have appeared in are *Reader's Digest*, the *Wall Street Journal*, and the *St. Croix Review*.

Contributors

Frederick D. Wilhelmsen is Professor of Philosophy and Politics at the University of Dallas, has his degrees from the University of San Francisco, A.B., 1946; the University of Notre Dame, M.S., 1948; and the University of Madrid, Ph. et Litt.D., 1959. He is the author of fifteen books and some two-hundred-fifty articles; and has lectured and taught on three continents, including the University of Santa Clara, the Pontifical University of Navarre, Spain, and the University of Baghdad. The recipient of a John Guggenheim Fellowship among others, Wilhelmsen considers his collaboration with L. Brent Bozell in the launching of *Triumph* magazine to have been a significant point in his career. A Thomistic philosopher in the tradition of Etienne Gilson, he has also been a political philosopher and his articulation and defense of Spanish traditionalist thought has marked much of his more mature thought.

The Marian Institute for Advanced Studies

The Marian Institute for Advanced Studies was organized by a number of Catholic scholars to promote authentic Catholic scholarship in the humanities and social sciences. Although part of its work includes sponsoring scholarly conferences, such as the one this book is based on, and limited publishing activities, its main activity is its tutorial program. Geared primarily toward graduate students, but open to anyone with a bachelor's degree, it permits students to undertake *non-credit* tutorial studies with Catholic scholars around the United States. Tutorial programs are offered, in 7- or 14-week sessions during the academic year or summer, in the following disciplines: theology, philosophy, literature, classics, history, political science, and economics. Programs are graduate school level, with the student usually working one-on-one with the scholar in the latter's geographical locale. Such a program provides an opportunity for Catholic graduate students—the Catholic scholars of the future—whose own university degree studies are generally quite secularistic (even when undertaken at Catholic institutions), to learn about and understand the Catholic contribution to their chosen disciplines. It also helps them place their studies into a distinctively Catholic framework. The Institute believes that this will contribute to the restoration of Catholic intellectual life in America.

The Institute is a part of Christian Family Renewal, but is governed by its own Board of Overseers. It is, of course, under the patronage of Our Lady, who is the seat of all wisdom.

Inquiries are welcome from prospective students, and from scholars in the above disciplines who are devoted to the Church and who would like to direct students in tutorials. Inquiries are also welcome from scholars in any discipline whose interest extends only to the Institute's other programs. Write to: Dr. Stephen M. Krason, President, The Marian Institute for Advanced Studies, 1235 Maryland Avenue, Steubenville, Ohio 43952.

Index

A

Abbot, Walter M. (Vatican II transl.), 135, 136, 138, 152, 155, 158;
abortion:
    caused by privatized religion, 120, 125, 126, 230;
    philosophy behind, xiv, 195, 198-207;
    symptom of secularism, 25, 26, 46, 49, 56, 58;
    violates natural law, 27, 90, 162, 198
academic freedom, 115, 116
Ackerman, Bruce, 126
Acton, Lord, 24
Adams, Pres. John, 51, 87-89
Africa, 83
Age of Reason, 69
Age of Revolution, 69
agnosticism, 122, 175, 185
aid to religious schools, 4, 13
AIDS, 168
Albert of Habsburg, 143
Albornoz, A.E. Carrillo de, 13
Alexandria, Egypt, 234
Alinsky, Saul, 220
America House, 109
America, 3, 186, 187
American Civil Liberties Union (ACLU), 230
American Ecclesiastical Review, 6, 9, 10
American Museum, 70
American Political Science Association, 33
American Proposition, 67, 208, 210, 216
American Republic, The, 217
American Revolution, 63, 64, 67-71, 89, 183, 180n,
Americanism, 148ff
angels, 232, 233
Anglican Church, 68
anthropology, political, 69ff
Antinomianism, 67, 164
Apostles' Creed, 227
Aquinas, St. Thomas (Thomism), ix, xiv, 2, 13, 24, 27, 31, 39, 41, 50, 68, 101, 102, 105, 128, 170, 218
Argentina, 159
Aristotle, 41, 52, 68, 83, 101, 161, 210, 218
Armageddon, 121
Armenia, 184
Arminianism, 69
Articles of Conferderation, 217
Ascent to Love, 237
Asia, 184
Assyria, 82
atheism, 3, 69, 72, 87ff, 175, 188, 222
Athens, 79, 82, 85, 235
Augustine, St., 37, 68, 210, 223, 232, 235
authority:
    and the Church, 11, 26ff, 155;

and common good, 116;
definition, 27ff, 54;
and God, ix, 27-30, 58, 65, 155;
and state, 161, 217, 73n
Azerbaijan, 184
Aztecs, 91, 92

B

Babylonia, 82
bacteriological warfare, 192
Baltic States, 184, 190
Baltimore Sun, The, 121
Baptists, 11
Barthes, Roland, 220
beatific vision, 228
Bellah, Robert, 37
Bellarmine, Robert, 4, 5, 13
Belloc, Hillare, 21, 63
Bennett, John, 12
Berlin blockade, 190
Bible, The:
  in Declaration of Independence, 67ff;
  importance to Founders, xi, 64, 81, 87, 95, 122, 130 131;
  norm of majority in 18th cent, 68ff;
  private interpretation, 131;
  in public schools, 131, 204, 221, 226ff;
  in society, 231, 238
Biffi, Cardinal, 92
Bill of Rights, 49, 105
Bishirjian, Richard, 38, 44
Blackstone, Sir William, 122, 198, 199
Blanshard, Paul, 11, 13
Bodin, Jean, 29ff
Boniface VIII, Pope, 143
Bork, Robert, 126
Boudinot, Elias, 69
Bower, V. Hardwick, 126
Bowers v. Hardwick, 126
Boyle, Jr., Joseph M., 120 121, 123, 170ff
Boyne, Battle of, 24
Bozell, L. Brent, 225
Bradford, M.E., 66

Brownson, Orestes, vii, 71, 196, 209, 217, 219
Bryce, Lord, 76n, 207, 212n
Buchanan, Patrick, 187
Buddhism, 146
Bulgaria, 190
Burrows, Ruth, 237
Bush, Pres. George, 120-122, 186, 192

C

Calvin, John (Calvinism), x, 13, 68-71, 131, 225
Cambodia, 90
Canavan, S.J., Fr. Francis, 202, 212n
canon law, 7, 26, 161
capitalism, 184
Caracalla, Emperor, 234
Carberry, John J., 11
Carey, George W., 200
Carlyle, Thomas, 62, 63
Carthage, 235
Casti Connubii, 113
Catholic Action, 220ff
Catholic Campaign for Human Development, 220
Catholic Committee on Urban Ministry, 220
Catholic Rendezvous, 237ff
Catholic University of America, 2, 5, 6, 9, 10
Catholicism (the Church), vii, 3ff, 21ff, 30, 33, 35;
  abortion, 120ff;
  American way of life, 57, 59, 60, 64ff, 71ff, 219;
  Calvinism, 71, 94ff;
  defense of, 41ff, 48, 56;
  evangelization, 226ff;
  magisterial theology, 114-116, 135-137, 147;
  moral teacher, 210, 219;
  mysticism, 237;;
  number in 18th cent, 67
  opposed by academia, 116, 220ff;
  secularism, 104;
  sexuality, 45n;
  and state relations, 104, 135ff, 149ff,

Index

155ff, 231—236
worldview, 57-59, 67ff, 78ff
Catholicism and the Renewal of Democracy, 33
Catholics United for the Faith, 163n
censorship, 10, 13
chemical warfare, 192
Chesterton, G.K., 20, 21, 37, 79
China, 90
chosen people, Americans as, 68ff
Christian culture:
  as confessional state, 226-236;
  based on natural law, 195-201;
  influence on Founding Fathers, 65-67, 70, 105;
  influence on U.S. culture, 123;
  and Protestantism, 104;
  opposed to secularism, 57-60
Christianity:
  anti-Catholicism, 131;
  biblical, 201;
  centrality of Christ, 225-236;
  downplayed by Murray, 60;
  early, 59, 234;
  influence on Founding Fathers, 52ff, 66-68, 70-72, 78, 79, 86, 88, 89, 100, 105, 106, 130, 203;
  influence on Western culture, 84-86;
  mysticism, 225, 237-241;
  and natural law, xi, 52;
  opposed to abortion, 200, 225ff, 231, 232;
  opposed to secularism, 125, 131, 204;
  truth over freedom, 128
Church of England, 68
Church of the Latter-Day Saints, 132
church-state relations:
  and American Proposition, 48ff;
  Church teaching on, 6ff, 134ff, 149ff, 160ff;
  Danielou on, 232, 233 ;
  George Bush on, 120 130;
  in positive law, 149ff;
  in natural law, 27ff, 71ff;
  "new state", 59;
  Orestes Brownson on, 196, 209ff, 229ff;
  Protestant theory on, 27ff, 71;
  separation of, 9, 104, 120, 129-131, 137, 148, 150, 158, 159, 174, 229, 231, 232;
  treaty of Westphalia, 73n
Cicero, 51, 87, 197, 234
City University of New York, 116
Civil Unity and Religious Integrity, 137
Civil War, 36, 51, 199, 217
civil religion, 36ff, 41, 48ff,
Civilta Cattolica, 10, 12
classics, 20
clericalism 103, 104
Cogley, John, 12
Coke, Sir Edmund, 198
Coleman, John A., 64
Columbia, 161
Colosseum, 234
Commentaries on the Laws of England, 198
Commentary, 191
Common Sense, 47
common good, 169ff, 218, 233ff
common law, 23, 26, 87, 195, 198, 199, 203
Commonweal, 12
communism, xiv, 21, 101, 184-187, 190, 191, 205
Communist Manifesto, 197
Concord, Massachusetts, 63
Condcorcet, Marquis de, 87-89
confessional state, 20, 31, 158, 228-236
Confessions of St. Augustine, 223
Congress, U.S., 184, 187
Connell, Fr. Francis, 2, 6-8, 110
conscience, 3-5, 7, 59, 105, 111, 112, 124, 128, 131, 132
consensus, 22, 24, 31, 32, 35, 39, 48ff, 53, 64ff
conservatism, viii, 6, 10, 13, 125-127, 135, 195, 201, 230
Constantine the Great, 234
Constitution, U.S.:
  allows religious freedom, 48, 174;
  Catholic interpretation, 221ff;
  Dawson on, 51-54, 70, 71;

embraces natural law, xi, 27, 51, 78, 79, 92;
federalist, 217, 218;
First Amendment, 3-5, 123, 124;
influence of Declaration, 99;
limited spiritual vision, 7, 86, 87, 90, 106;
product of Christian culture, xi, 65, 66, 78, 79;
recognised evil and flawed nature, 86, 88;
rooted in popular will, 196;
Supreme Court interprets, 125, 221;
tradition of civility, 21, 27, 35ff
Constitutional Convention, 65, 201
Constitutional Faith, 221
constitutionalism, 64, 67
Continental Congress, 68, 69
"Continental State," 147 148
contraception, 25, 112, 113, 136
Contras, 186
Coolidge, Calvin, 91
Corwin, Edward S., 196
covenental theology, 67, 68
Crankshaw, Edward, 188
creation science, 123
creation, 79ff, 82, 106, 237
Cromwell, Oliver, 24, 70
Cropsey, Joseph, 200ff
Crosby, Bing, 21
culture, modern, 57, 59, 60, 67, 228ff
Curran, Charles, 135, 220
cynicism, epistemological, 25
Czechoslovakia, 190

D

D'Ors, Alvaro, 27ff
Danielou, S.J., Jean, 231-234
Dante, 84
Darwin, Charles, 100
Dawson, Christopher, 46-48, 50-52, 56, 67, 70, 71, 228, 229, 232, 233
Day of Public Humiliation, Fasting and Prayer, 68, 69
Day, Dorothy, 228
De Potestate Regia et Papali, 4

Declaration of Independence:
affirms Christian principles, x, 65-67, 69, 71, 86, 87, 105, 106, 195, 203;
affirms Western constitutionalism, 64;
affirms natural law, 91, 99, 197, 203;
affirms sovereignty of God, 50, 52, 65, 69, 81, 86, 99, 195;
Catholic interpretive tradition, 223, 73n,
compared to Lenin and Hitler, 91;
compared to Marxism, 91, 197;
deconstructionist analysis, 220;
mixture of Christianity and secularism, 106;
quoted by Lincoln, 95
deconstructionism, xv, 50ff, 220-223
DeGaulle, Charles, 187, 189
deism, 66, 106, 201, 222
democracy:
first principles, 216ff;
Jean Bodin on, 29ff, 33, 37ff;
modern, ix, 13, 14, 207;
Murray on, xii, 22ff, 26, 41, 53, 55ff;
Tocqueville on, x
Derrida, Jacques, 220, 222
Descent of the Dove, The, 234
development of doctrine, 114
Devil, The, 21, 24, 56, 231, 233
Dewey, John, 41, 208ff
Dignitatis Humanae (*Declaration on Religious Freedom*), 10, 93, 111, 112, 134-162, 175, 177, 106n, 181n
divine law, 136, 137, 149, 150, 152-154, 157, 158, 161, 196, 201
Doe vs. Bolton, 202, 207, 208
Dominican Republic, 161
Dougherty, Jude, 35, 41, 43, 45n
Douglas, Mary, 122
Douglass, Fredrick, 221
drug abuse, 25, 172, 176, 177
Dukakis, Gov. Michael, 121

E

Eastern Orthodox Church, 210

Index

Ecclesia Dei, 2, 3, 24, 109, 136
Econe, Switzerland, 134
economics, and ethics, 210
ecumenism, 2, 3, 17, 24, 136
education, 40, 52, 57, 60, 161-162, 172, 178
Edwards, Jonathan, 69, 70, 201
egalitarianism, 101, 205ff, 218ff
Egypt, 79, 80, 185
Eidelberg, Paul, 197, 203
El Salvador, 186
Elias the prophet, 60
Ellis, Msgr. John Tracy, 12
Emerson, Ralph Waldo, 62ff
England, 49, 62, 122, 185, 188
English Traits, 62
Enlightenment:
  influence on French Revolution, 52, 89, 90;
  influence on Founding Fathers, x, xi, 78, 87-89, 200-203;
  minimized natural law, 41, 197, 200-203, 209;
  opposed to Christian principles, 65, 68-71, 200-203, 209;
  opposed worship of God, 65;
  privatized religion, 125, 130;
  source of abortion mentality, 200-203
epistemology (Lockean), 209
equality, 49-50, 52, 66, 88, 89, 91
erastianism, 139
essentialism, 2
ethnicity, 123
eugenics, 83
euthanasia, 25, 162, 170ff
evangelization, 70, 226ff
evil, 88, 111, 206
existentialism, 204, 206

F

Faith and Knowledge: A Critical Inquiry, 221
family, 25, 39:
  divorce, 212n;
  grounded in Trinity, 228ff;
  cultural attack upon, 60. 83, 90, 178, 204ff, 212n;
  social contract, 202
Farrell, James T., 13
FBI, 21
federalism, 217
Federalist Papers, 65, 217, 219
Federalist party, 70
Federalist, The, 35
Fellini, Frederico, 229
feminism, 205, 206, 218
Fenton, Msgr. Joseph Clifford, 6-8, 10, 110
fideism, 164n
Fifth Monarchy Party, 70
Finnis, John, 170, 172, 174, 175, 180n
First Amendment, xii, xv, 3, 4, 35, 103-106, 121-123, 129, 130, 132, 137, 174, 180n, 220, 108n
First Things, 37
Ford, Fr. John M., 113
Fortescue, Sir John, 23
Fortune, 20
Founding Fathers:
  belief in natural law, 23, 35, 64, 99, 197;
  compared to Church Fathers, 216;
  concern for personal rights, 98-100, 104;
  distrust of civil theology, 108n;
  influenced by Christianity, 78, 79, 85-89, 92, 104-106, 121, 122, 130, 209, 73n;
  influenced by constitutionalism, 49, 51, 64, 65;
  influenced by Enlightenment, 71, 78, 87-89, 200, 203;
  and modern Americans, 39;
  originators of American Proposition, 95-100, 210;
  and pluralism, 103
"Fourth American Republic," 217-219
Fragments of a Century, 115
France, 48, 49, 51, 62 85, 89, 90, 185
Francis, St., 128
Franco, General Francisco, 26
Franklin, Benjamin, 46, 66, 130
free elections, 184

255

free exercise clause, 123
free markets, 184
free will, doctrine of, 69, 82, 85ff
freedom, 86, 100-102, 104, 111, 112,
    115, 116, 122, 152-154, 175, 185,
    191, 195, 205, 207;
    and democracy, 50, 52, 69;
    Calvinism, 69;
    Dignitatus Humanae, xiii, 3, 4, 162;
    magisterial teaching, xiii, 3, 4, 162,
    185;
    religious, xii, 8ff,, 69, 124ff, 128ff,
    137;
    scientific view of, 205;
    secular view of, 130ff, 205
French Revolution, 9, 48, 65, 69, 88, 99,
    100, 106, 195
Freud, Sigmund, 160, 206
Furfey, Paul Hanley, 2

G

Gadamer, Hans Georg, 221
Gelasius I, Pope, 7, 143
general will, 50
Georgetown University, 21, 33, 186
Georgia, Republic Nation of, 184
Germany, 10, 148, 190. 193
Gettysburg Address, 85
Gill, Eric, 228
Gilson, Etienne, 21
Giurlanda, Fr. Paul, 221
glasnost, 190
Glenn, Gary D., 202, 203, 207
gnosticism, 23, 41, 231ff
Goerner, E.A., 14, 106
Gorbachev, Mikhail, 184ff, 190, 210
Gould, William, 33, 34, 39, 42, 44
grace, 151, 225ff, 233ff
Great Awakening, 68, 69, 70, 201, 75n
Great Britain, 50ff, 62, 67, 123, 154,
    185, 197
Greater Houston Ministerial Association, 219
Greek Orthodox Church, 121
Greek philosophy, 69, 79, 82, 83,
    85, 222
Greenwalt, Kent, 126, 127
Gregory the Great, Pope, 117

Grisez, Germain, 169-172
Guardini, Romano, 69, 73n

H

Habsburg, Archduke Otto von, 229
Hamilton, Alexander, 217, 73n, 74n
happiness, pursuit of, 66, 69, 86
Harlan, David, 220, 221
Harrington, Michael, 115
Hartley, David, 75n
Havel, Vaclav, 186
Hecker, Isaac, 69
Hegel, Georg (Hegelianism), 62, 218
Heimert, Alan, xi, 70
Herberg, Will, 12, 21, 23, 62
Higgins, Thomas J., S.J., 197, 198
Hinduism, 146
Hippo, 235
historical consciousness, 141-146, 148,
    149, 151
historicism, ix, xii, 2, 4, 5, 63, 110, 127,
    141ff
historico-critical method, 113
historiography, liberal, x, 67ff
*History of the Development of Christian
    Doctrine*, 125
history, 13, 24, 25, 34, 43, 46ff:
    ancient concept of, 80, 81, 86;
    Christian interpretation of, 221,
    107n;
    Dawson on, 59, 67;
    deconstructionist view of, 220ff;
    distortion of, 63, 67;
    "new history", 48ff, 51;
    salvation, 82ff, 110, 236
Hitler, Adolph, 91
Hobbes, Thomas, xiv, 87, 197, 200-202,
    208, 209
Hoffman, Ross, 69
Holmes, Oliver Wendell, Jr., 62, 208ff
homeschooling, 60
homosexuality, 25, 46, 56, 58, 125, 126,
    127, 162
Houston, City of, 14, 219
human nature, 23, 26ff, 30, 41ff, 79, 82,
    83, 89, 90, 102, 113, 114, 170,
    73n

Index

human sacrifice, 176
Humanae Vitae, 136
Hume, David, 88, 89, 169, 179n
Hussein, Saddam, 185
Hutchinson, Anne, 67

I

idealism, 232
Immaculate Conception, 151
immanentism, 222
Immortale Dei, 140, 141, 150
Incarnation, 84ff, 233ff
Index (of Forbidden Books), 22
India, 92, 188
indifferentism, 2
individual, rights of, 50
individualism, xi, xv, 35ff, 64, 65, 85, 96-99, 101, 102, 104, 105, 200, 209, 210, 228
Inquisition, 24, 48
instrumentalism, 41
integralism, 6
Introduction to Christianity, 227
Iraq, 184, 187, 191, 194
Ireland, Archbishop John, 36, 165n
Irenaeus of Antioch, 236
irrationalism, x
Islam, 131, 132, 146, 185
Israel, State of, 146
Italy, 62, 123, 159

J

Jackson, Pres. Andrew, 201
Jacobinism, 49, 51, 62,
Jaki, Fr. Stanley, 84
James, William, 125, 208ff
Japan, 148, 193
Jaspers, Karl, 26
Jay, John, 217
Jefferson, Pres. Thomas, x, 47, 51, 65-69, 89, 130, 201, 203, 205, 209, 73n, 75n, 108n
Jeremiad, The, 68ff, 217
Jerusalem, 79, 85
Jesuitism (Society of Jesus), ix, x, 3, 9, 10, 11, 13, 20, 42, 47, 110, 113, 135ff, 159, 186, 187, 229

Jesus Christ, 68-71, 84-86, 114, 149, 162, 225-236, 238-241
John LaFarge Institute, 109
John of Paris, 4
John of the Cross, St., xvi, 237
John Paul II, Pope, 134, 210, 229
John the Apostle, St., 84
John XXIII, Pope, 10, 142, 145
Johnson, Pres. Lyndon B., 115
Johnson, Samuel, 24
Journal of Church and State, 11
Judaism (Jews), 12, 20, 23, 34, 56, 57, 68ff, 71, 79, 81, 85, 109, 120, 131, 146, 193, 197, 219, 221, 227
Judeo-Christianity, x, xi, 21, 56, 69, 82, 83, 198, 208, 75n
just war theory, 185, 192-194
justice, 24, 79, 83, 84, 129, 171-173, 180n

K

Kant, Immanuel, 66, 104
Kendall, Dr. Willmoore, 20, 21
Kennedy, Pres. John F., 14, 43, 63, 120, 214, 219
King, Jr., Martin Luther, Jr., 115
Kirk, Russell, 197-199, 201, 209
Koran, 132
Kuwait, 184, 186, 187, 194

L

La Dolce Vita, 229
Lapati, Fr. Americo, 217
last judgement, 238
Latin America, 185
law, as reason, 86, 151ff
Lawler, Fr. Ronald, 216, 217, 219
Lear, Norman, 230
Lefebvre, Archbishop Marcel, 134
Legion of Decency, 10
legislature, bicameral, 49
Leiber, Robert, 10
Lemon test, 123
Lenin, Nikolai, 91, 184, 189
Leo XIII, Pope:
    analyzed by Murray, 10;
    freedom of Church, 147-150, 152,

156;
   not culturally conditioned, 142, 144;
   product of 19th century, 6, 9, 37;
   rejects privatized religion, 122, 140, 141, 160, 162;
   supports *Humanae Vitae*, 136
Levinson, Sanford, 221
liberalism:
   and abortion, 202, 208;
   competes with Christianity, 132;
   and democracy, 30, 94;
   Hobbesian-Lockean, 201, 202, 208, 209, 222, 230;
   influence on Catholic Church, 6, 34, 42, 93, 170;
   influence on American Founding, 64, 67;
   opposed by Leo XIII, 122;
   promotes freedom of conscience, 124, 131;
   promotes privatized religion, 122, 125, 126, 132;
   Protestant, 12, 13, 37, 39;
   and Scholasticism, 39;
   secularized, 67, 132, 146, 201;
   and Supreme Court, 126;
   view on justice, 170;
   view on natural law, 201
libertarianism, 172, 195
liberty:
   according to Founding Fathers, 69, 105, 195, 216;
   anti-Catholic, 203, 216;
   and common good, 169, 171-178;
   of conscience, 131, 166ff;
   in Constitution, 79;
   Dawson on, 50;
   in Declaration, 66, 195;
   and Leo XII, 152;
   and Lincoln, xi, 13, 20;
   Locke's idea of, 100-104, 203;
   modern crisis of, 97;
   religious, 22, 104, 124, 125, 131, 134-162, 174-178;
   and Vatican II, 152, 153, 156, 174-178
Libya, 185

Life and Death with Liberty and Justice, 170
Life, 217
Lincoln, Pres. Abraham, xi, 39, 51, 94-99, 101, 105, 216, 217
Lindbeck, George A., 12, 13
Lippman, Walter, 22
Livingston, Edward, 203
Livy, 87
Locke, John:
   criticized by Adams, 88;
   freedom of conscience, 128;
   ideas support abortion, 200, 204, 208;
   individualism, 101, 102, 104, 105;
   influence on Christianity, 36, 68;
   influence on Founding, xiv, 35ff, 65, 67ff, 87;
   influence on Enlightenment, 35, 87, 98, 197, 200, 203, 208, 209;
   law of nature, 99, 100, 102;
   quoted by Fathers, 122;
   view on marriage, 202
logocentrism, 222
Longinqua Oceani, 148ff
Lord of Hosts, 25
love, 69, 70, 82, 236
Lowi, Theodore, xiv, 217ff
Luce, Clare Booth, 21
Luther, Martin (Lutheranism), xv, 21, 71, 220, 221, 225
Lutz, Donald, 122
Lyotard, Jean-Francois, 220

M

Madison, Pres. James, 105, 130, 186, 217, 218, 107n
Magisterium, 42, 60, 115-117, 136, 139-142, 150, 151, 159
Manhattanville College, 105, 116
Manicheism, 82
Marian Institute of Advanced Studies, The, 248, 249
Maritain, Jacques, 2, 3
marriage, 113, 173
Marshall Plan, 190
Marsilius of Padua, 209

Index

Marx, Karl (Marxism), 68, 91, 100, 184, 191, 197
Mary, Blessed Virgin, 26, 151
materialism, 179, 188ff
Matthew, St., 238
McElroy, Robert W., viii, 192
McNichols, Archbishop John T., 11
Media, The, 24, 25, 46, 60, 61, 210
medical industry, 59
Meese, Edwin, 221
Mein Kampf, 91
Melville, Herman, 48
Mesopotamia, 79
messianism, in Murray's thought, x, 46ff, 67ff, 70ff
metaphysics (pre-Kantian), 66, 99, 209, 222
Meyer, Albert G. Cardinal, 11, 112, 113
Middle Ages, vii, xi, 5, 36, 51, 128, 197, 209, 108n
Mill, John Stuart, 202, 205, 235
millennialism, 70, 76n
Miller, Perry, xi, 68, 74n
Missouri Compromise, 51
modernism, x, xii, 6, 38, 41, 46ff, 69ff, 94ff, 101, 102, 131, 204, 222
monarchy, 161
Mondale, Walter, 121
monotheism, 79, 82ff
Montesquieu, Charles de Secondat, 87, 122
Mooney, Cardinal Edward A., 11
moral law, 28, 31, 62, 71, 98, 111, 195
morality, 24ff, 43, 45-56, 58, 59, 62, 67, 88, 113, 116, 121ff, 126, 130, 131, 139, 195, 203, 204ff, 208, 226ff, 45n
Mormonism, 128, 132
Morocco, 185
Moscow, 189
Mother Theresa of Calcutta, 238
Murray, Fr. John Courtney:
 abortion, xiv, 25ff;
 American Proposition, 62ff, 71, 72, 105ff, 208ff;
 Church-state relations, xii, 5ff, 14, 22ff, 37ff, 94ff, 104, 105, 110, 138ff, 144-147, 159ff, influenced by concept of, 209, 235, 236, American wall of separation, 129, 136ff;
 civil religion, 37ff, 46ff, 105, 225ff;
 communism, 101, 132, 186-192;
 conscience, 111;
 conservative Christianity, 98ff, 105, 223;
 criticized Catholic traditionalism, 5, 7ff, 22ff, 30ff, 48ff, 93, 139ff, 158ff;
 Dignitatis Humanae, xii, 10ff, 20, 22, 93ff, 134, 135, 146, 152-160ff;
 failure of Protestantism, 104ff;
 First Amendment, 3, 4, 7ff, 35, 103-106, 121, 130ff;
 Founding Fathers, 95ff, 106n, 99, 100ff, 105, 219, 220;
 Hegelianism, 48, 142ff, 145ff;
 John Kennedy, 14, 63;
 liberty, xi, xii, 13ff, 38, 52, 94ff, 101ff, 105;
 pluralism, xii, xv, 12, 13, 22ff, 40, 54ff, 94ff, 103ff, 131, 132, 191, 235;
 power and authority, 22ff, 46ff;
 religious toleration, 4, 7ff, 13, 40, 48ff, 93ff 104, 139ff;
 secular humanism, 132, 186, 108n;
 sexuality; 112, 113;
 at Vatican Council, ix, 22ff, 42ff, 93ff, 109ff, 113ff, 134ff;
 warfare, 193, 194
Mystical Body of Christ, xvi, 228ff, 233, 239
mysticism, Christian, xv, 128, 225, 237-241

N

National Center for the Laity, 220
nationalism, 70ff, 184, 185, 189
natural law:
 and abortion, 26, 208;
 applicability to politics, 27, 28, 30;
 basis of American unity, 3, 13, 14, 24, 39, 106;

259

believed by Founding Fathers, 78, 79, 97, 99, 197, 203, 219;
Calvin's view of, 71, 96ff;
Church interpreter of, ix, x, 29, 31, 162;
Church tradition of, 35, 94, 103, 104, 197, 209, 216;
and common law, 23;
divisive, 45n, 73n;
freedom of conscience, 3;
and French Revolution, 36;
harmony with American principles, 51, 52, 94, 195-201, 203, 216, 219;
Murray's view of, xi, xii, 7ff, 12, 13, 22, 23, 27, 29, 30, 35, 36, 42, 49, 64, 94;
neo-pagan resistance to, 162;
opposed to American principles, 42, 98, 210;
opposed to liberalism, 201, 208;
promotes worship of God, 7, 8;
rooted in Christianity, 52, 103, 104, 198, 201;
state bound by, 6, 8;
and Thomas Aquinas, 31, 102, 103;
universal, 62
naturalism, 69, 70
Navarre, University of, 27
neo-paganism, 162
Neuhaus, Richard John, vii, xii, xiii, 33, 44, 122, 231, 107n, 108n,
New Deal, 205
New Israel, The, 63
New Jerusalem (in America), 68ff
New York Times, The, 125, 187
New York University Club, 86, 110
New York, City of, 25
Newman, John Henry, 67, 231
Nicaragua, 186
Nicholas II, Tsar, 188
Niebuhr, Reinhold, 21
Nietzsche, Friedrich, 222
nihilism, 222
Nixon, Pres. Richard M., 120
nominalism, 35, 128
Notre Dame, University of, 14, 26

Novak, Michael, 24

O

O'Boyle, Archbishop Patrick A., 11
O'Connell, Marvin, 36
O'Neill, James M., 11
Old Testament, 81
oligarchy, 161
optimism, 205
oral Constitution, 65ff
original sin, 82, 85, 88
originalism, x, 47ff, 68ff, 85, 88ff, 130
Orlando Sentinel, The, 181, 187
Orthodox Church, Eastern, 121, 310
Other America, The, 115
Ottaviani, Cardinal Alfredo, ix, 9-11

P

Paine, Thomas, 47, 48, 66, 69
pantheism, 84, 85
papacy, 6-8, 111, 114, 134, 137, 139, 145, 151, 209, 210
Passion, The, 56, 179n
Paul the Apostle, St., 84, 116, 232, 233, 235, 238, 240
Paul VI, Pope 9, 153
Pavlischek, Keith, 37, 38
Paz, Octavio, 228
peace, 65
Pelikan, Jaroslav, 125
Pennsylvania Packet, 70
perestroika, 190
Persian Gulf War, 184, 185, 187, 191, 194
pietism, 58, 68, 123, 130
Pilgrims, 63, 67
Pipes, Richard, 189, 190
Pius IX, Pope, 136, 140, 142, 144, 162
Pius XI, Pope 141
Pius XII, Pope 4, 9, 10, 143-145, 192, 193
Plato, 34, 38, 40, 84, 87, 106, 210
pluralism:
cultural, 12, 13, 54-56, 103-105, 218-221, 230, 231;
religious, 13, 23, 24, 39, 40, 56, 94,

Index

103-105, 128-130, 132, 137, 196, 230, 231, 235, 236
Plutarch, 87
Pocock, J.G.A., 221
Podhoretz, Norman, 192
Poland, 186, 190
political action, reasons for, 170, 172, 174-176, 178
Politics of Heaven and Hell, The, 85
popular sovereignty, 36
pornography, 46, 49, 56, 60, 172, 173
positive law, 26, 27, 65, 196
positivism, 41, 114, 206
Powell, Justice Lewis, 126
power (and authority), 27, 28, 54
pragmatism, 41, 43, 62, 208ff
Prayer as a Political Problem, 231
prayer, 232-236, 239ff
Pribilla, Max, 3
Primeau, Bishop Earnest J., 11
privatization of religion, 120, 125, 133, 176ff
Problem of God, 225
Problem of Religious Freedom, The, 121, 137, 139
Progress of the Human Mind, The, 87
property, 128, 204ff, 218
prostitution, 172
Protestant, Catholic, Jew, 12, 21
Protestantism:
  of Benjamin Rush, 65, 66;
  confessional state, 228;
  developed state church, 8;
  discovery of Murray, 11, 13;
  ecumenism, 24, 40, 56, 103, 104, 109;
  evangelism, 123, 130;
  Immaculate Heart of Mary, 210, 219, 221ff, 228, 167n;
  influence on Founding Fathers, 71;
  Kennedy campaign, 14;
  liberal, 12, 13, 31, 37;
  resistance to Catholic schools, 4;
  resistance to natural law theory, 23;
  scripture scholarship, 221;
  secularized, 219;
  suspicion of Catholicism, 103, 104;
  view of religious liberty, 131, 132
psychoanalysis, 204, 206
Public Philosophy Reader, 38
Publius, 35, 219
Puritans, 13, 47, 70, 71

Q

Quakers, 125
Quanta Cura, 140
Quas Primas, 141

R

racism, 91, 123
rationalism, x, 3, 23ff, 35ff, 52-54, 65, 68, 70, 95, 98, 100, 106, 197, 209
Ratzinger, Joseph Cardinal, 227, 228
Raz, Joseph, 127
Reagan, Pres. Ronald, 121, 185, 187
realism, x, 13, 23, 41ff, 54ff, 58, 66, 128, 131, 132, 216
redemptive suffering, 240
reductionism, 64
Reese, Charles, 187
Reformation, 64, 147, 73n
Reich, Charles, 218
relativism, 6, 63, 91, 92, 94, 113, 114, 127, 131, 142, 200, 208
Religion and the American Mind, 70
religious liberty (see liberty)
religious schools, 178
religious toleration (see toleration)
Renaissance philosophy, 69, 145, 147
Republic, The, 24
Republican party, 70, 132, 207ff, 229
Reynolds vs. U.S., 128, 159ff
Rice, Charles E., 210
right to privacy, 124
Rights of Man, 71
Roe v. Wade, 26, 29, 58, 64, 90, 198, 202, 207, 208
Roman Empire, 38, 60, 61, 85
Rome, 9, 22ff, 42, 72, 79, 134ff;
  imperial, 60, 85, 234
Rommen, Heinrich, 11
Roots of American Order, The, 197

Rousseau, Jean Jacques, xiii, 23, 29ff, 34, 50, 100, 186
Rumania, 190
Rush, Dr. Benjamin, 65-70
Ryan, Msgr. John A., 5

S

sacraments, 154, 226ff, 231ff
Sacred Congregation of the Holy Office, 9
Sadinistas, 186
sadism, 234
Saudi Arabia, 185
Scalia, Justice Antonin, 125, 126
Schall, Fr. James, 85
Schindler, David, xv, 222, 223
Schlesinger, Jr., Arthur, 14
Scholasticism, 2, 30, 37, 39, 197
scientism, 204, 205
Scully, Bishop William A., 10
sectarianism, 67, 122, 130ff, 196
secular humanism, 41, 132, 45n
secularism:
    and American Proposition, vii;
    caused by pluralism, 40;
    caused by Protestantism, 37, 39;
    caused by technology, 53;;
    competes with religion, 231
    condition of pluralistic America, 34, 38, 40, 56, 123, 146, 160;
    Dawson's view of, 53;
    elites, 178, 185, 207ff, 210, 216, 219, 229, 239ff;
    and First Amendment, 103, 104;
    and Founding Fathers, 95, 100;
    and French Revolution, 216;
    and mysticism, xvi, 6, 9, 24ff, 34ff, 37, 39ff, 43, 53, 56, 57, 59;
    privatizes religion, 122;
    pro-abortion, 207, 208;
    rejects spiritual values, 186, 45n, 107n;
    and religious liberty, 131, 160;
    social results of, 25;
    and "soul" of America, x, xii, xiii, xv;
    substitute for religion, 102, 114, 132, 178, 179, 219;
    threat to Catholicism, 41, 43, 57-59, 70, 102, 114, 122, 178, 179, 219;
    utilitarian, 67
separation of church-state (see church-state relations)
sexual issues, 56, 58, 113, 142, 202, 206, 208, 45n
Shea, George W., 7, 8
Sheen, Bishop Fulton J., 20, 45, 65, 66, 69, 75n
Shehan, Lawrence J. Cardinal, 11
situationism, 207
skepticism, 53, 113, 114
Skinner, Quentin, 221
slavery, 49, 51, 82
Smedt, Bishop Emil de, 156
Social Justice Review, 33
social contract doctrine, 39, 100, 202ff
social engineering, 205, 206
socialism, 204
sociology, 232
Socrates, 80, 83, 84
Solzhenitsyn, Aleksandr, 41, 189, 190
Song of Bernadette, 20
Sorenson, Theodore, 14, 219
soul, 58, 79, 82-84, 131
South America, 22, 83
Soviet Union, 20, 90, 184-190, 205
Spain, 13, 26ff, 159, 228, 164n
Spanish Armada, 24
Spellman, Cardinal Francis J., viii, 9-11, 116
Spirit of the Laws, 87
St. Bartholomew's Day, 24
St. Patrick's Cathedral (NY), 25
Stalin, Josef, 187, 189
Stalingrad (St. Petersburg), 189
Stanford University, 21
state church, 8, 111, 136, 137, 149, 150, 157, 160, 161
statism, 29, 50, 59, 205, 218
Stephen, St., 238, 239
stoicism, 23
Stritch, Samuel A. Cardinal, 11
subjectivism, 111, 131
suffering, 238, 239

Index

suicide, 170-172
Summa Contra Gentiles, 31
supernatural, 57, 58, 71, 72, 229, 238ff
Supreme Court: xi, 4, 46, 58, 90, 125, 128, 174, 195, 198, 202, 207-209, 217, 218, 221
Syria, 185

T

technology, 232
Ten Commandments, 112, 113, 123
Tenelly, Joseph, 12
Teresa, Mother, 238
Theological Studies, 3, 121
Third Institute, 198
Third World, 49
Thomism (see Aquinas, St. Thomas)
Three Lectures Upon Animal Life, 69
Time, 13, 14, 20, 21
Tinnelly, Joseph, Rev., 12
Tocqueville, Alexis de, x, 50, 67, 70, 101, 196, 200, 201, 207, 108n
toleration, religious, 3, 4, 7, 39
Torquemada, 48
totalitarianism, 83
Tracy, Fr. David, 221
traditionalism, 98, 99
tribalism, 83
Trinity, The, 84, 228ff
Triumph, xv, 237

U

Ukraine, 184
ultramontanism, 143
United States Catholic Conference, 113
universal law, 62
Universalism (Unitarianism), 69
utilitarianism, 67, 200ff, 207, 213n
utopianism, 48, 52

V

Vagnozzi, Archbishop Egidio, 10
Varro, 38
Vatican Council I, 164n
Vatican Council II:
    attacked by dissenters, 113;
    on Church renewal, 241;

Dignitatus Humanae and Murray, 134-162, 175;
ecumenism, 2;
human dignity, 230;
and mysticism, 241, 106n;
participation by Murray, ix, 10, 13, 14, 22, 109, 111-113;
and state, 158ff, 230;
viewed by liberals, 42, 43;
view on abortion, 26, 49;
vindication of Murray's ideas, 6, 111
Vaughn, Bishop Austin, 113
Virgin Mary, (see Mary, Blessed Virgin)
VISTA, 218
Voegelin, Eric, 128, 133n, 233
voluntarism, 23, 202ff

W

Wanderer, The, 58
War on Poverty, 115
Washington Post, The, 187
Washington, Pres. George, 47, 73n, 121, 207
Weaver, Richard M., 204
Webster vs. Reproductive Health Services, 125
Weigel, George, vii, 24, 33, 39, 41
Weigel, Gustav, SJ, 11
Welesa, Lech, 186
Western civilization, 91, 92
Wilde, Oscar, 63
Wilhelmsen, Frederick, 225, 233
William III, 24
Williams, Charles, 234
Wolfe, David, SJ, 11
women's movement, 205, 206, 218
Woodstock School of Theology, 11, 110
World Council of Churches, 13
World War II, 2, 20, 36, 48, 190, 193, 194
Wright, Bishop John J., viii, 4, 11

Y

Yale University, 21
Yanitelli, Victor, xvii, 11
Yeltsin, Boris, 190
Young, Loretta, 21